W9-DAR-391

CHILDREN *of* ISRAEL, CHILDREN *of* PALESTINE

Also by Laurel Holliday

THE CHILDREN OF CONFLICT series:

Children of the Holocaust and World War II: Their Secret Diaries

Children of "The Troubles": Our Lives in the Crossfire of Northern Ireland

Coming Soon:
Children of the Dream: Growing Up Black in America

Published by POCKET BOOKS

CHILDREN *of* ISRAEL, CHILDREN *of* PALESTINE

∞

Our Own True Stories

∞

LAUREL HOLLIDAY

POCKET BOOKS

New York   London   Toronto   Sydney   Tokyo   Singapore

The jacket photo is of a Palestinian girl in the Arab quarter of East Jerusalem. Israeli security forces sometimes paint a number inscribed in the Star of David, such as the one on the building behind the girl, as an indication of the danger they feel is posed by Palestinian inhabitants.

POCKET BOOKS, a division of Simon & Schuster Inc.
1230 Avenue of the Americas, New York, NY 10020

Copyright © 1998 by Laurel Holliday

All rights reserved, including the right to reproduce
this book or portions thereof in any form whatsoever.
For information address Pocket Books, 1230 Avenue
of the Americas, New York, NY 10020

Library of Congress Cataloging-in-Publication Data

Children of Israel, children of Palestine : our own true stories /
    [edited by] Laurel Holliday.
        p.   cm.
    Includes bibliographical references.
    ISBN 0-671-00802-1
    1. Arab-Israeli conflict—Biography.   2. Children—Israel—
Biography.   3. Children, Palestinian Arab—Biography.   4. Israelis—
Biography.   5. Palestinian Arabs—Biography.   I. Holliday, Laurel,
1946–   .
DS119.7.C468   1998
920.05694—dc21
[B]   97-42545
                                                              CIP

First Pocket Books hardcover printing May 1998

10   9   8   7   6   5   4   3   2   1

POCKET and colophon are registered trademarks of
Simon & Schuster Inc.

Printed in the U.S.A.

Friday morning, a week and a half ago, it happened again in a cafe in Tel Aviv. I was there all over again. Skeletons of busses in the streets, the mourning songs on the radio, the dark cloud hanging over everything. All I could think was, "Not again! Not again! They can't steal Purim away again!"

—Jeffrey Klein, "Not Again!"

Late at night when everything is quiet I think about how I will ever forgive the Israelis for what they did to me. I don't mean stealing my homeland, killing my people, turning me into a refugee, or depriving me from having a Palestinian state. I'm talking about myself—what they did to my personality. I wish I had a normal life: no tension, no rage, no hatred, no hard feelings towards anybody. Even if they leave my country and give me back my rights, how will I overcome these feelings inside me?

—Nihaya Qawasmi, "Children of a Tenth-Class God?"

"How can you talk about murder as if you were talking of . . . cockroaches? Haven't you any sympathy for the Arabs' condition? They are like us in the Holocaust. Germany and Poland had been our homeland. And we didn't have any place to go. We expected to be left as we were, but they hated us just as you hate the Arabs now. . . . And they talked about killing us just as you are talking now. They are no different from what we were back then."

—Redrose (pseud.), "Face of Peace"

Contents

ACKNOWLEDGMENTS xiii

INTRODUCTION xv

NO OTHER STORM
by Moshe Shamir 1

THUMBPRINT
by Ehud Ben-Ezer 11

MARKED BY THE TEETH
by Moshe Dor 21

THE ARAK OF ABU-ANTON
by Yehudit Hendel 29

THE DARK VILLAGES
by Reuven Miran 37

EARLY LESSONS OF SEPARATION
by Anan Ameri 45

I SURVIVED THE WAR
by Musa Jamil Jaffer (pseudonym) 51

Contents

GOING TO JERUSALEM
by Gunter David   59

A CHRISTIAN PALESTINIAN'S STORY
by Wadad Saba   73

YEHEZKEL
by Yitzhak Bar-Yossef   83

PARADISE ON THE BORDER
by Yael Medini   97

TEN CENTIMETERS OF DUST
by Shammai Golan   125

TRACINGS
by Basim Abdoraad (pseudonym)   135

HOPES ARE HOPES
by Leah Ayalon   147

TZIPORI
by Reuven Miran   151

MARKED FOR DESTRUCTION
by Ibtisam S. Barakat   165

A CHILD IN RAFAH CAMP
by Ahmed Younis   177

Contents

IN THE COURTYARD OF THE CHILDREN'S
HOUSE OF THE KIBBUTZ
by Shuli Dichter   185

A CHILD'S MISGIVINGS ABOUT THE WAR
by Mohammad Zahaykeh   189

SHARDS
by Tanya Gardiner-Scott   199

BORDERLAND
by Mohammad Masad   205

BORN IN BETHLEHEM
by Marina N. Riadi   217

CHILDHOOD/MANHOOD
by Omar Mahdawi   227

CHILDREN OF A TENTH-CLASS GOD?
by Nihaya Qawasmi   241

ALTI ZACHEN
by Victoria Kay-Feinerman   245

CAUGHT IN CONFLICT
by Rivka Rosen (pseudonym)   251

Contents

ONE MORE RIVER TO CROSS
by Nahla Mary Beier   261

MY MOTHER PALESTINE
by Ramzy Baroud   279

A LOOK INTO MEMORY
by Ghareeb (pseudonym)   293

HEALING THE WOUNDS OF CHILDHOOD
by Ammar Abu Zayyad   297

FACE OF PEACE
by Redrose (pseudonym)   303

MY LIFE ON THE FIRING LINE
by Racheli Tal   311

THE POWER OF LIFE
by Racheli Tal   321

TWO AWFUL WEEKS IN MARCH
by Liran Zvibel   331

NOT AGAIN!
by Jeffrey Klein   337

BIBLIOGRAPHY   343

Contents

CREDITS   345

PHOTO CREDITS   347

CHRONOLOGY OF THE ISRAELI-PALESTINIAN
CONFLICT   349

Acknowledgments

I am very grateful to the hundreds of writers who sent work to me for this anthology. While it was not possible to publish all of the stories that I received, I deeply appreciate the effort that went into everyone's writing.

Many people, some unbeknownst to me, have helped to find the writers for this anthology. To all I send a very heartfelt thanks—this book would not have been possible without you. For your special efforts in providing Israeli and Palestinian contacts, I would like to thank (in no particular order): Charles Davis, of Seattle, Washington; Dr. Thomas R. Trabasso, of the University of Chicago; Dr. Sid Strauss, of the University of Chicago; Dr. Boaz Keysar, of the University of Chicago; Len Traubman, D.D.S., of San Mateo, California; Dr. Michael Roe, Chairman of the Psychology Department, Seattle Pacific University, Seattle, Washington; Nigel Parry, of Birzeit University, West Bank, Palestine; Mary St. Germain, of University of Washington Libraries, Seattle, Washington; Moshe Dor and Barbara Goldberg, of Chevy Chase, Maryland; *Lilith* magazine; Cole Hull, Seattle, Washington; David Lloyd, of Israeli English Teachers Network; Natan Galkowicz, Postmaster for K–12 Schools in Israel; Sylvia Asher, of "Ironi Tet" High School, Tel Aviv, Israel; and Stacy Gilmore, D.D.S., Seattle, Washington.

I would also like to thank all of the people who helped to bridge communication gaps with writers. When I was sty-

Acknowledgments

mied by language differences, border closings, lack of E-mail/fax/typewriters, etc., your help made it possible for these writers to be heard.

Rebecca Alexander, M.A., librarian at the Temple de Hirsch Sinai in Seattle, has once again provided me with invaluable assistance on the Children of Conflict series. Thanks, Rebecca, for being a thorough and very helpful librarian and a good friend.

I have called the librarians at Seattle Public Library's Quick Information Line many times during the course of researching and writing this book. Thanks to all of you for your help and patience. And special thanks to librarian Eileen Hamelberg, of the Humanities Department, as well.

Thanks to Hebrew translator Elizabeth Maor for your quick help with questions about Israel and your on-line friendship. And thanks to Sister Elaine Kelley of Portland, Oregon, for reading and commenting on my introduction.

To Paul McCarthy, who began the editing for this book, and to Jane Cavolina and Brett Freese, who finished it, thank you.

To all at Pocket Books who've been supportive of the Children of Conflict series and who have put your best into each and every volume, thank you.

Introduction

The struggle between Israeli Jews and Palestinians, although one of the most complex and long-standing conflicts in the world, is fundamentally about one thing: both peoples claim the same land as their homeland and, to varying extents, both want to govern it as *they* see fit. Whether they call it Israel or Palestine, the conflict still comes down to the fact that two ethnically and culturally distinct peoples—Palestinians and Israeli Jews—lay claim to the very same sand, stone, rivers, vegetation, seacoasts, and mountains. Add to this the fact that people—of various ethnicities, including Druze and Bedouin Arab, are also occupants of the same land, and it becomes even more understandable that the efforts of numerous world leaders have yet to bring peace to this very troubled land.

As the writers in this book so poignantly describe, Israeli and Palestinian children grow up feeling that they are destined for conflict with their neighbors from the day they are born and that there is little they or anyone else can do about it. To be born an Israeli Jew or a Palestinian is to be born heir to an ethnic identity one is expected to defend at all costs. Until Yasser Arafat's and Yitzhak Rabin's famous White House handshake in 1993 sealing the Declaration of Principles designed to lead to a permanent peace accord, there was virtually no hope of an Israeli-Palestinian peace.

Today, however, despite tremendous hurdles to peace

that have arisen subsequent to the signing of the Declaration of Principles—numerous assassinations, massive bombings with tremendous loss of life, threats to sacred sites, and the continuing struggle over the future of Jerusalem—there is at last a possibility that the writers in this book will see peace in their lifetimes.

Perhaps because of the modicum of hope and trust that the peace process has afforded them, Israeli Jews and Palestinians are for the first time willing to divulge, here between the covers of one book, the intimate details of their childhood and coming of age. From Palestinian refugee camps in the West Bank and the Gaza Strip to Jewish kibbutzim in Israel and the occupied territories, from the Old City of Jerusalem to Ramallah to modern Tel Aviv, Israeli Jews and Palestinians tell us the story of their youth—sometimes happy, more often sad, and all too frequently horrific.

Still, no matter what their ethnic identity, how much and how long they and their families have suffered, and how extreme their differences, the authors of these courageous autobiographies most often reveal a deep longing for peace.

Peace at what price is the question, of course, and here in this book Palestinians and Israeli Jews describe the freedom, justice, and security that they require and the compromises they are willing to make in order to finally turn their dreams of peace into a reality.

I believe that, as young people and adults, most of us are more able to remain open to personal autobiographical stories of childhood and coming of age than we are to history lessons and polemics. Perhaps because we are less likely to suspect a hidden agenda, we can read a teenager's diary of war (Anne Frank's, for example) when we would not care to read a historical/political analysis of the events of the same period. It is my hope, therefore, that in addition to showcasing the work of some very fine writers, the accessibility of this groundbreaking collection of autobiographical stories will invite a wide range of readers and contribute to the mutual understanding that is a necessary first step to peace.

As is true when considering any world conflict, it is not easy to be fair and open-minded while avoiding the trap of a pseudoneutrality based on little more than ignorance. What I know for certain is that Israelis and Palestinians have hurt each other very badly (although not necessarily equally): both peoples have committed countless acts of aggression, terrorism, and torture, and, even today, a little understanding between the two peoples is hard to find.

The authors of these stories do not pretend to kiss and make up. Although often expressing a desire for understanding and reconciliation, they accuse and assign blame: they express hate, anger, fear, grief, humiliation, despair, and the desire for revenge. Nevertheless, if they can suspend judgment for a time and hear each other I think they have a chance of bringing their painful, century-long conflict to an end as we ring in the new millennium. The first step, no matter how difficult, is for them—and all of us—to listen to the stories of one another's lives.

The history of the Israeli-Palestinian conflict has been recorded in thousands of books, and I will make no attempt to recount it in this introduction. Please refer to the chronology beginning on page 349 for the historical context of these autobiographical writings.

The function of this book, the third in the Children of Conflict series, is to provide a forum in which people of two very different cultures can share their personal histories with us and each other. As is the case with all the books in the series, the focus is on the impact of violent conflict on the first twenty-one years of the writers' lives and how that conflict was formative of adult ideas and personalities.

As I chose the writing for this anthology, I was faced with difficult decisions that, no matter how hard I might try to be "fair," might still reflect biases. The number of Jewish and Palestinian writers to be included in the book was one consideration, for example, as was the number of words of each to include. Also to be decided was the amount of writing by male and female writers and whether or not to give special consideration to very young writers.

In the end, the balances I sought quite naturally emerged from the *quality* of the writing. By choosing what, in my estimation, are the very finest of the hundreds of autobiographical stories that I received for consideration, I arrived at a balance that closely reflects the ethnic-religious makeup of the population of Israel, including the occupied territories (i.e., what Palestinians call Palestine and Israelis call Israel). After my choices were made, I discovered that approximately half of the writing was by males, half by females. And, finally, I made the decision to give no special consideration to the ages of the writers, which range from fourteen to seventy-six.

Readers will note that some of the authors of the autobiographical writings in this book have chosen to use pseudonyms. Although none were questioned about their reasons for doing so, it is reasonable to assume that they felt a need to protect themselves and their families from retaliation, which, unfortunately, is a pervasive threat for Israelis and Palestinians alike.

For those who are curious about how I found the people to write these stories, I would say, "with great difficulty." I wrote over two hundred letters to Israeli and Palestinian authors and hundreds more to a wide range of institutions, the media, and personal contacts passed on to me by friends and colleagues. Fortunately, the rapid worldwide expansion of electronic communication has made it possible to make many connections with writers much more quickly than would have been possible even a few years ago. Internet resources played a large part in the gestation of this book.

Another note about the behind-the-scenes work on this book: Readers should know that the writers in this anthology were required to submit their work in English. The costs and difficulties of translation would have made this book a financial impossibility, so this limitation was one with which we all had to live. While I regret that only writers who could provide English translations were eligible for this anthology, perhaps this limitation will inspire other authors/editors to seek out and translate Israeli and Palestinian autobiography written in the writers' own languages. Another regret I have is that I did not receive autobiographical stories by Bedouin Arab and Druze inhabitants of Israel/Palestine. Again, perhaps another author will be inspired to collect these important testimonies.

All stories have been edited for length, common English usage, spelling, punctuation, etc., except those few that have previously been published in English. (Variant spellings have been retained for certain place names, etc.) I have added explanations of words and concepts I think readers may not be familiar with and placed them in brackets. The writers have been given the opportunity to review and correct my edits of their stories.

All available childhood photographs of the writers appear in the photo insert. Not unexpectedly, many writers either never had photographs taken in childhood or the photos have long ago been lost during family dislocations.

And, finally, the order of the stories is more or less chronological. That is, the book begins with those about growing up before the creation of the State of Israel and closes with accounts of recent events by young Palestinians and Israelis still in the process of growing up. Occasionally I've made some intuitive placements because the times of the stories overlap.

As a psychotherapist, writer, and editor of the Children of Conflict series, in which I continue to explore the childhood and coming of age of those growing up in violence, I'm often asked how "damaged" the writers are by the experiences they write about—or, worse, how "dysfunctional" they are, given some elusive standard of "functionality." As a child of homegrown conflict that often went no further than my family's kitchen, I can attest to the irritation people feel at being viewed as "damaged" and having their "functionality" assessed.

But, yes, of course there are repercussions to growing up in near-constant conflict. There are wounds and losses, pain and suffering, unrealized potential. But there are also strengths and wisdom born of growing up in conflict, and I, for one, would never call the writers in this book ''victims,'' ''damaged,'' or ''dysfunctional.'' I would call them experts in coping with some of the most difficult situations human beings can face. And I would call them courageous for being willing to share their secret pain and sorrow, defeats and triumphs, here.

I'm also sometimes asked what lessons I have learned from working on this series about growing up in war and conflict. More than anything, I would say I have learned that so long as we teach young people to rely on their ethnic identities to tell them who they are and who they should become, we will have violent conflict. I believe that ethnic identity is a construction, a concept that is taught to us when we are young, and that it is only when we learn to formulate an identity quite apart from ethnic, sectarian, racial, national, and religious heritage that we will come to have enough understanding of each other to live together.

When country of origin, religion, native tongue, skin color, height, weight, ability/disability, age, gender, sexual preference, etc., are no longer the measures of a person's worth, we on this planet may have a chance of living together in peace. Until that day comes, let us listen to each other's stories and teach our children the meaning of equal opportunity and justice.

This book is dedicated to all of you who are working to bring about a democratic, just, and secure Israeli-Palestinian peace.

Laurel Holliday
September, 1997

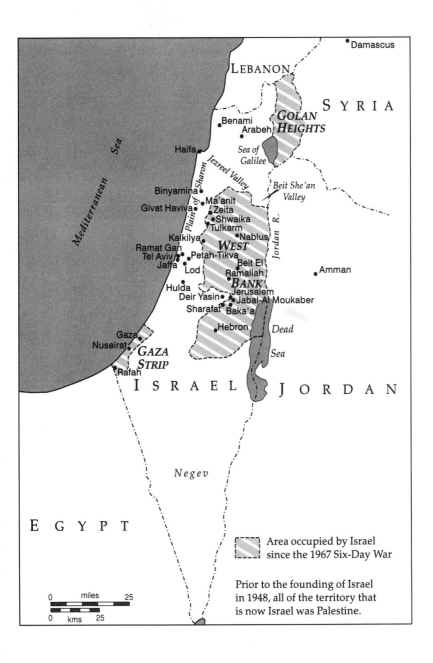

Damascus

LEBANON

SYRIA

Benami
Arabeh

*GOLAN
HEIGHTS*

Haifa

*Sea of
Galilee*

Mediterranean Sea

Jezreel Valley

*Beit She'an
Valley*

Binyamina
Givat Haviva

Plain of Sharon

Ma'anit
Zeita
Shwaika
Tulkarm
Nablus

Kalkilya

WEST

Ramat Gan
Tel Aviv
Jaffa

Petah-Tikva

Lod

Beit El
Ramallah

BANK

Jordan R.

Amman

Hulda
Deir Yasin
Sharafat

Jerusalem
Jabal-Al Moukaber
Baka'a

Hebron

Dead

Gaza
Nuseirat

*GAZA
STRIP*

Sea

Rafah

ISRAEL

JORDAN

Negev

EGYPT

0   miles   25

0   kms   25

Area occupied by Israel
since the 1967 Six-Day War

Prior to the founding of Israel
in 1948, all of the territory that
is now Israel was Palestine.

MOSHE SHAMIR

Seventy-six-year-old Moshe Shamir has been happily married for fifty-one years and has three children and four grandchildren. Born and educated in Israel, he has been a farmer in a kibbutz, a captain in the Israeli Army, and a member of the Knesset, the Israeli parliament. But mostly, Moshe Shamir is known as being a very prolific Israeli writer: his published works include twelve novels, three collections of short stories, and a number of children's books. In addition, twenty of his plays have been produced and published, and three movies have been made from his works. His writing has been featured in many anthologies.

As suggested in these passages of autobiography, Shamir feels very strongly about the importance of the building of Israel. His own parents were pioneers in Israel and he tells me that "the building of a country for a homeless people is, to my mind, the greatest event of the century." He believes that the only way that there will be peace in the Middle East is for there to be "the honest and indubitable acceptance by the Arabs of the existence of a strong and viable Israel among them. . . . At the present, regrettably, I am afraid the Arab/Palestinian aim in what is called 'the peace process' is simply to weaken Israel."

Moshe Shamir is very widely read in Israel and has received every major literary prize there is to be won in that country. His work has also been translated into many languages, and the following novels are available in English: The King of Flesh and Blood, The Hittite Must Die, The Fifth Wheel, *and* With His Own Hands.

My Life with Ishmael, *the autobiography from which the following excerpts were taken, (originally published in Hebrew in 1968), was published in English by Vallentine, Mitchell (London) in 1970.*

No Other Storm

*M*y brother—I knew in his life and in his death. To this day, twenty years after his death, he returns to me in my dreams at night, young and handsome and blond and blue-eyed as he was in life. And in my dream I want to embrace him and I dare not. A dreadful fear roots me to the spot—lest I hurt his wounded body. And within that fear, a terrible joy—that his death is a lie, a lie, a lie. I know what period of time I relive in my dream. It is a quarter of an hour, ten minutes: someone bursts into the Tel-Aviv office of the Haganah, the Underground [secret Jewish self-defense force], tells us about the seven at Yazur and blurts out his name, not knowing that Eli Shamir was my brother; then the man's shock and his saying: "Run to the Hadassah Hospital"—then the moment when I enter the hospital's corridor and my father is sitting on the bench, encircled. Oh that it be a lie, a lie, a lie—and it was the truth. They had summoned Father from his office. It was I who climbed the three floors to tell Mother.

Later, much later, an hour later, someone made the world's most banal and irritating remark to me, and the truest and most needed: "Think of your parents. You must be strong now."

Then, before they took the seven of them away, to lay them out beside the candles and the guard of honor in the barnlike gymnasium, before they took them, I saw him in the refrigeration room of the hospital mortuary—and the dark blue hole in the clear white forehead. And on his face the look: mature, responsible, astonished.

They were killed in an open lorry after it had struck a mine. Injured and burnt they were murdered one by one, shot at close range. What were they doing in an open lorry in the street of an Arab village? They were driving out to inspect the road ahead of a convoy carrying passengers, food, medical supplies, fuel—to Jerusalem.

I was a child among Grade III children at the time of the 1929 disturbances. On a hot day in July the school celebrated Herzl [Theodor Herzl, father of Zionism] Day. We donated a *mil* [small amount of money] to the Karen Kayemet [Jewish National Fund]. The pretty girl from Grade VIII read out Ezekiel's vision of the Valley of Bones. I understood nothing of what she was reading except: "Come oh breath . . ." and then "breathe" which sounded to me like "weep," so I understood it as: "Come oh breath and weep upon these slain . . ." and it made sense. Nice. Really nice. . . .

A week later we received the certificates. That was a real celebration for us. We all came in sandals, and Samul—the Yemenite [from Yemen] devil of the class—came in a blouse! And off we went on our school holidays. . . .

I went to the village where Grandma and the uncles lived. Be'er Ya'acov—a quiet little place surrounded by Arab villages without even a road between, no electricity and no telephone. Just a secluded happy home, quite innocent. An Arab shepherd by the name of Shak'r, who is like one of the family, takes the farmers' cows out in the morning and brings them back in the evening. A friend to everyone, including little me, who steals out every now and then to spend a whole day with him and the cows. Except at almond-picking time which I wouldn't miss for anything, or even better: almond-peeling time. And if they let me help in the fresh-smelling citrus nursery, that's the highlight and a great novelty. Will there be oranges? Mandarines? It is so quiet and peaceful in the village that fire and smoke are remembered as symbols of sweetness and contentment. The smoke of Grandma's baking-oven, with the wonderful smell of burning eucalyptus twigs, or the fire gaily crackling to warm the bath-water on Friday night.

Then suddenly someone is standing by my bed, and it is dark all around, and he quietens me with a kind hand: "Night. Get up. It's all right." By the light of the paraffin lamp in the other room I find my clothes and see my uncle groping in the chest under the bed and taking something out and thrusting it into his belt. Apparently I am still sitting on the bed, goggling in astonishment. Grandma comes in. They dress me. There is no time for my sandals, and they push them into my hands. Tumult in the house, they hustle the women and children outside. Other figures are hurrying about in the cold dark of the village street. They rush to the one and only stone building, on the hill across the street—the schoolhouse. Words are flung in hushed tones. To the southeast, beyond the cypresses in the yard—like a premature sunrise—a pale rosy stain on the fringe of the sky.

"Hulda is burning."

The following day Grandma took me by train to Tel-Aviv (not neglecting the opportunity to bring a basket of lemons to sell at the market). At Lod she would not allow me out of the coach, even though she knew how much I loved running backwards and forwards in the tunnel linking the two platforms under the railway lines. I tried outwitting her by pleading for something to drink, but what had come over her?—no response whatever. Through the lowered shutter I peeped at the Arab boys running about with their newspapers, shouting: "*Falastin . . . La Bourse Egyptienne* [Palestine . . . the Egyptian stock exchange] . . ." When the coach started moving Grandma relaxed her hold on my arm, and then a stone struck the shutter, and the engine whistled.

Grandma said something in Yiddish to our neighbor—and he repeated it three times in emphatic agreement. But at home in Tel-Aviv she closeted herself with Mother to confer in secret and forgot about me and the lemons. I stole out to the yard, and from there to the street. All the children of the neighbourhood were squeezed behind the stone fence of the house at the corner of Hayarkon Street, whispering together in a huddle as I joined them, and looking towards the south.

We were waiting for the daily funeral. This was an Arab funeral that passed along Hayarkon Street every day on its way to their cemetery on the sandhill, to the north, past the huts of Mahlul. Soon the morning would be over—and no funeral. What's the matter with them today?

Over the years we had grown accustomed to those strange processions, and till today I recall the tune they used to sing, just as we heard it and imitated their singing of it: "*La Allah il Allah ua Mukhamad rasul Al'lah . . . La Allah il Allah ua Mukhamad rasul Al'lah. . . .* ["There is no god but Allah and Mohammed is the prophet of Allah . . ."] They used to pass by, every day, winter and summer, a lot of them or just a few, leading the coffin and singing, serious-faced and chanting, moving along with a dancing gait. It was part of the life of the street, a colourful and salient part of the mosaic landscape of our lives—like the skyline of Jaffa and its mosque at a distance, like the drivers of the black, horse-drawn cabs at the corner of Allenby Street, like the fishermen standing on the rocks in the sea, like the hawkers of cleaning-powder—"*Qudsi ramel!*"; like the rag-dealers—"*Weissen Kessalach!*"; like the Bedouin women fruit vendors tinkling their medallions with every nod of their heads and movement of their hands—"*Tut ya tut, taaza ya tut, frishe ya tut—sabress!*" ["Delicious strawberries for sale!"]

The funeral didn't turn up. The children on their holiday rambles discovered that in Allenby Street too the world order had changed: no cabs. At the foot of the casino there was no fishing. We went farther south along Hayarkon Street, daringly—for that was the base of our rival gang in games and brawls—and there, in Yonah Hanavi Street, a young man is strolling up and down with a stick in his hand and making signs to us with the stick that this is as far as we go, and back home please, about face—to Mama, home!

At home Father was already there, and rumours. And what's more the children are not to go out any more. Not even into the yard. As if Father had brought the tension with him. How and why did he come home so early that day? His office, the Government Veterinary Laboratory, was in the German Colony in Jaffa. The Englishman in charge had received a telephone call, summoned the three Jewish workers, and advised them to hurry home. Father went back to his laboratory, calmly covered the microscope, closed the large log-book of tests, inserted something into the pocket of his coat with a quick smooth movement. At home, when he had gathered the children together inside the flat (a two-roomed flat on the ground floor) and then gone himself to stand in the street at the entrance to the building, I saw the knife—not long but highly sharpened—which he used for separating the diseased limb from the body of a sheep or cow in order to examine it.

This was our armoury for the defense of our home.

When we returned to school about two months later, matured by a summer and anxieties, we had an orphan girl in the class. Between the closing and opening of an exercise book—she became an orphan. Her father and mother went to Hebron for a week but were there for four days only. On the fifth, the Arabs came.

They called it a pogrom then. After seven years the name changed to "disturbances."

Hulda was attached, evacuated, and destroyed by fire. Be'er-Tuvia was burned and abandoned. Mahanayim was burned and abandoned. And the list comprises further pogroms in Jerusalem. In Safed. In Jaffa. In Haifa. Men, women and children were slaughtered. Houses were razed. Fields and granaries were set on fire. Citrus groves were uprooted.

And to all those places we returned. All those fields we restored, all those citrus groves we replanted. All the houses we built up. One place alone, the worst hit of all, the most sacred of all, was not brought back to life: Jewish Hebron. Here we had to wait for almost forty years, until 8 June, 1967 [the Six-Day War].

* * *

On the festival of Succot in 1968 a few families went down to Eilat. We found a spot in the fenced-off camping ground of the Stella Maris Motel, pitched our tents, donned our bathing suits, and sent our children to swim in the sea. The spot was at the eastern extremity of the populated area of this oddly-modern Israeli town. It's a town where you walk out into the yard and you're in the desert. The distance from our camping ground to the houses of Jordanian Akaba was no greater than the distance to the center of Eilat. But the quietness over there was like the end of the world.

On the journey, as we hurled along the Arava road, we saw some unusual army activity; billows of smoke, a helicopter landing, parked jeeps on guard with their weapons at the ready. The evening news told us—a mine. One killed. An incident. In the midst of all this, right next to the border, between incident and incident, three days of sunshine and self-indulgence and games and campfires and swimming and shell-gathering. To forget. To sink into a round of aimless activities. When cooking the soup becomes the main preoccupation, that's repose. And the children, we were sure, the children certainly . . .

The children, we were sure, the little ones, were basking in their own Garden of Eden. My son Eli and my niece Merav, a pair of little devils, founded a 'science-group' and were busy collecting things, making discoveries, fishing hopefully but unsuccessfully, sunbathing, disappearing when they were supposed to be eating the soup we spent so much time cooking—in short: utter oblivion, relaxation, a world of eternal peace.

After our first night there, the little ones disappeared early in the morning. On their reappearance to the smell of coffee they were talking together in whispers. No tempting suggestion for passing the time could distract them. Not yet. They still had something terribly important (and terribly secret!) to arrange. My son went looking for paper. A large sheet. White paper. He scratched around and found some, apparently, because the next requirement was a pencil or crayon. What for, eh?—it's a secret.

It went out of our minds, and there were plenty of other things crowding in, one upon the other, to explain the glint in their eyes as the hours passed on that glorious beach. All day the 'science-group' displayed particular interest in the water currents and prevailing winds in the bay. How do fishermen sail here? Does the wind always blow from the land towards the sea? Are there no currents drifting eastward? What, by the way, is the distance by sea to Akaba? I didn't connect all these items, until night came and in the silence, in the shelter of the tent, with his head poking out of his sleeping bag, my son couldn't contain himself any longer: "Daddy, d'you know what we did today? We made paper boats. Merav and I—two boats. And we put them far out to sea to sail away. But first we wrote on the paper, Why don't you make peace with us? Dear soldiers of the Akaba Legion, why don't you make peace with us? Signed, a boy and a girl from Israel. Whoever finds this, please hand it to the Legion, Akaba."

EHUD BEN-EZER

Ehud Ben-Ezer was born in 1936 in Petah Tikva, the site of the first Jewish colony in Israel. Ben-Ezer's juvenile documentary novel, Riders on the Yarkon River, *about his grandfather and the group who founded Petah Tikva, was published in 1988.*

Now sixty-two, Ben-Ezer lives with his wife Judith in Tel Aviv, where he is a writer, a critic, and a literary editor. He has written and published thirty books, including novels, short stories, children's books, and biographies. One of his novels, The Quarry, *was adapted for an Israeli movie. With two exceptions, all of his books have been published in Hebrew.* Unease in Zion, *a book of interviews, was published by Quadrangle (New York) in 1974. And* Hosni the Dreamer, *a picture book for children based on an old Arabic tale, was published in 1997 by Farrar, Straus & Giroux.*

Twice the winner of the Prime Minister's Prize for Literature, Ehud Ben-Ezer recently won the Visiting Hebrew Writer Fellowship in Yarnton Manor, Oxford University, for February to July 1998.

Ben-Ezer, who has written much about Arabs in Israeli literature, believes that the story of the Jews in Israel is one of "unrequited love." He says that the father of Zionism, Theodor Herzl, was convinced that economic prosperity and progress resulting from an influx of Jewish capital into Israel would prove stronger than nationalist animosity. Ben-Ezer says that it came as a surprise to many Jews that the Palestinians were not willing to share their land and embrace them wholeheartedly. Almost as lovers spurned, the Jews were greatly disappointed by Arab rejection and this resulted, Ben-Ezer believes, "in one of our most deeply rooted collec-

tive denials: that of the problem of Palestinian refugees from 1948 onwards. Even the politically moderate Israelis had no hesitations on the subject, due mainly to the Palestinian 'all-or-nothing' position. No individual, no normal nation, wishes to become extinct or to commit suicide.

"Today, however," he says, "the closer the Palestinians come to reconciliation, compromise, and coexistence, the greater the willingness of Israelis to consider solutions to the taboo issue of the refugees." Continued terrorism, Ben-Ezer fears, will bring the peace process to a halt and further escalate the Arab-Israeli conflict.

In this beautifully detailed story of his own boyhood relationship with Arab children, Ben-Ezer captures the wistful longing for understanding and friendship of which he speaks in his adult works.

(See photo insert.)

Thumbprint

Translated from the Hebrew by Jeffrey M. Green

"*I*f you don't learn the value of money," Dad told me at the beginning of the vacation, "you'll grow up to be a loafer and live at other people's expense. Money doesn't grow on trees. You have to work hard to earn it. Work is a good educator. It fortifies you. If you're weak, people will hit you."

He practiced what he preached. The grape harvest on the

farm came during summer vacation, and I was sent to work there.

They wouldn't let a kid like me take part in the harvest itself, which is responsible work and demands attention and expertise. They gave me a pruner for cleaning damaged, withered, or colorless grapes from the bunches, and they sat me down with a bunch of Arab urchins next to a rough board table, laden with crates, that was placed lengthwise under a broad, vine-covered patio on the edge of the vineyard, near the wagon road. The heaping crates of grapes would arrive at our patio from the vineyard. The bunches were a dry, frosty color, and green grapes hung down between the leaves on the vines overhead in constant, unripe freshness.

Those were days of excitement and independence, of light, of the summer. I became an expert in varieties of grapes: black and white muscat, dabuki, and Beiruti fig. Every morning Mom would give me a paper bag containing four thin sandwiches filled with sliced, hard-boiled egg and yellow cheese; fresh cucumber; and a bottle of water. On the first day of my work she put a well-washed bunch of grapes in the bag, so that I wouldn't nibble the sulfur-coated grapes from the vineyard.

By noon I had had more than enough of Mom's clean food. In the shadow of the trees in the nearby orange grove, across the sandy road, near the irrigation faucet whose rusty mouth yawned like the entrance to a deep cave, I sat down to eat in the company of the Arab urchins. Ali gave me a chunk of his round, moist, very salty loaf of homemade bread, filled with cooked rice, and he shared a handful of olives and wild tomatoes with me. They were red and tiny like coral beads. Ali picked them on the side of the road in the morning on his way to the vineyard. Dad said that everywhere an Arab moves his bowels, a tomato bush grows in the summer. Mom absolutely forbade me to eat tomatoes that had grown from human feces. She came from Poland, and people thought tomatoes were poisonous there. But Ali's wild tomatoes were tart and tasty. The manure-enriched soil along the road nourished them with fertilizers that came for free. Every bite left my mouth salty, and in the future I was to feel pungent longings for that savage Garden of Eden—wild tomatoes at noon, wrapped in Ali's bundle with a handful of bitter olives and very salty, moist, home-made round bread.

I shared with Ali the sandwiches my Mom had prepared at home. More than anything Ali was astonished by the rings of hard-boiled egg, sliced to the same thickness. Mom had a special tool made of aluminum and an iron frame, with thin wires you could pluck with your finger. Ali was loath to spoil the pretty shape of the rings, and he looked at them for a long while before eating them. He also ate the washed bunch of grapes with gusto, the Jewish grapes that Mom had sent, and in return he brought me a fresh, cool bunch of grapes that had been harvested early that morning, and which he had hidden in the shade of an empty crate. Then we lay down to rest for a while in the irrigation basin around a tree, the sides of which were still damp and gave off coolness. Dry yellow moss grew on the brown trunk. The side of the basin served us as a pillow. The noise of the water running in the nearby cement channel gave us the feeling of a restful hour on the banks of a river. The orange grove was like a dark forest, and I nodded off until the end of the break.

At four the last bell was rung from the top of the hill on which the courtyard of the farm stood, and from every side—the orange grove, the vineyard, the grain fields, and the vegetable gardens—the Arab workers gathered in bands, some wearing a keffiyeh [Arab head scarf] of simple cloth and others in a takiya, a knitted skullcap. They burst onto the road on their way home to the nearby village, and I was among them, the only Jewish boy among dozens of Arab lads whose eyes sparkled, and oriental melodies trilled in their throats. They raised clouds of dust with their bare heels, and I dragged along with them in my khaki shorts and sandals, waving my hand and opening my mouth wide but wordlessly, so they wouldn't notice that I didn't know the melody. I was excited and ridiculous, joining their laughter without knowing what it was for.

They couldn't understand why I had to work. Had I received a punishment? They all knew that Dad, Hawaja Abu-Udi, was the manager of the farm. So they treated me with great respect and were careful not to hurt me or tease me. A favorite game of theirs during working hours was to throw spoiled grapes in one another's faces, preferably aiming for the eyes. The moment Hawaja Laibo—that was Arieh Leib, the supervisor—looked the other way, they began pelting each other with rotten grapes. The thrower would bend over innocently and hide under the table to protect himself. But if by chance a grape struck my face or shirt, Ali would immediately shout at the thrower and slap him hard. Not even Hawaja Laibo would stop him when he was defending the manager's son.

But what was a Jewish boy doing in the green grape bower, among those for whom work was a necessity, fate?

I didn't know enough Arabic words to explain to them about the educational value of manual labor, and it's doubtful whether I myself believed in it. But they certainly wouldn't have caught my meaning, even if I spoke fluent Arabic.

One morning Dad came to see how the work was coming along, and he gave a short speech in Arabic, which he knew well, including reading and writing.

Many years after Dad's death, I could still visualize him standing somewhat bent, with his sunburned face. He was dressed in a pale khaki short-sleeved shirt, with a notebook and pencil in the pocket. Short khaki trousers came down to his knees, and high khaki socks covered his thin calves. Members of my father's generation went to work in their old low shoes, or in well-enclosed sandals that looked like shoes (but in a photograph from his youth, he is standing barefoot and in underpants in the orange grove, opening an irrigation channel). They wore light-colored khaki clothes during the week, and they didn't abandon that custom even after the British left and khaki became a military color, which Israelis shun in their everyday dress.

Dad held a khaki-colored pith helmet under his arm, colonial headgear that was customary in the British army and administration. He wiped off the perspiration with a khaki handkerchief, coughed from the depths of his nicotine-eaten lungs, and gave a speech to the shebab [youths].

He didn't speak softly, and it sounded as though he was scolding them. His voice was dictatorial. He probably didn't know how to relate to them differently. Even when he meant to praise his workers, he would raise his voice. From the little I could divine in his words, I realized that Dad was giving them a sermon in their juicy language on the proverb from the Talmud, "Better to skin carcasses in the market than to depend on help from other people,'' and he was pointing at me. A murmur of agreement and astonishment was heard then under the broad canopy of vines, and no one dared laugh at Dad's words, either in his presence or after he left.

Thus, every day when work was over, I would march and sing and wave my arms in the midst of a band of boys dressed in rags, boys who didn't know what underwear was. Most of them were barefoot, and just a few of the privileged ones wore rough sandals soled with used automobile tires. I would part from them near the railroad tracks, at the path leading to my house, and for a long time I could hear the sound of their song, as they grew distant, fading into a light cloud of dust on the dirt road leading to their village.

Friday was my big day, the weekly payday, when I would stand in the long line with all the shebab in the courtyard of the farm. Sometimes they would push each other, but around me there formed a kind of circle of respect. The line extended from the water tower in the middle of the courtyard to the doorway of the dark office where Mr. Grisha, the farm book-keeper, received us one by one. The gay clink of coins filled the courtyard, and I would listen and enjoy it, though I still didn't know the value of money, as Dad said. Grisha's nose was hooked like an eagle's beak, and he wore glasses with thin silver frames. His hands were long and grasping. He loved chess, fresh rolls, and married women (so I later learned), and his whole being expressed money. He himself looked like a worn banknote, with the sparkle of coins in his avid eyes.

Each boy in his turn would sink his thumb in the ink pad

designed for that purpose and press it down in the proper spot on the payroll sheet, at the end of the row where his name was listed, the number of days he had worked that week, and his wages. If it happened that one of the boys' black-nailed thumbs deviated from its place in the column, Mr. Grisha would quickly seize it, redirect it, and press it down hard in the right spot. I would move forward in line until I stood on the threshold of the office, knowing that in a moment everyone would hold their breath in amazement. No, I'm not modest. My great hour was at hand, and the true height of my worth would not stand out in contrast to my backwardness as a manual laborer.

I attended school!

Though I was younger than them all, I took the pen from Mr. Grisha with a practiced hand and traced my name on the payroll sheet in a precise, fancy signature. There it would shimmer, the only Hebrew writing in a column marked by the thumbprints of Ishmaelites. Not only that, my wages were higher. They received a shilling per day, which was five grush, whereas the manager's young and learned son received six grush per day!

I hated the sun, the sweat, and especially the plague of wasps. Huge yellowish-brown wasps would swarm to the arbor from every direction to suck on the ripe grapes, which were bursting with sweetness, and to slake their thirst on them. They flew underneath the green canopy of vines, which was stiflingly hot, whizzing over your face with an annoying and threatening buzz, or sauntering like madmen on the bunches of grapes in the crate. Their sting was very painful, many times more than the sting of a bee.

Not only that, my fingers became sticky and dark with the sweet juice of the grapes and from the dust that clung to them. The pruner quickly became filthy, its handles stuck to my fingers, and my tender skin swelled up and blistered. My hands stung at night, and the wounds didn't heal.

Dad was pleased that I was getting hardier. I was reading less, my eyes didn't hurt me, and my dizziness had gone away. Besides, at my age hadn't Dad supported himself from a vegetable garden, going down by himself to sell the produce in the big village market?

But Mom wanted to spare my health and didn't conceal her opinion.

Dad got angry. There can't be two heads in a single turban, he cited the Arab proverb, and two people who disagree cannot educate a single child, because in the end he'll grow up into a mixed-up idler. She had to decide which of the two would educate me, alone, and bear the responsibility.

Mom was determined. Dad shouted silently. In his anger, his tan face burned black with blood. It seemed as though he was about to have a stroke. She didn't understand education, he said. Damn her domineering ways! He wouldn't do everything she wanted. It simply would not come to pass!

Mom started crying. At that moment it was decided without words that I would no longer go to work, but this was formally announced the following morning, when I discovered that no one had prepared sandwiches for me. Dad gritted his teeth and said that he was resigning from his job, and that from this day forth, Mom alone would educate the boy. He wouldn't lift a finger, for better or worse.

MOSHE DOR

The author of some thirty books, including poetry, interviews, essays, memoirs, and children's books, Moshe Dor is one of Israel's major writers. Having worked as a journalist for close to forty years, he served as cultural attaché in London, Distinguished-Writer-in-Residence at American University, Washington D.C., and president of Israel's chapter of PEN from 1988 to 1990. He has been the recipient of both the Prime Minister's Prize for Literature and the Bialik Prize, Israel's top literary award.

Now sixty-five, and the father of two sons and two grandsons living in Israel, he splits his time between Israel and the Washington, D.C., area. Three of his most recent books are Coals in the Mouth, Silence of the Builder, *and* Why the Whale Smoked a Pipe, *all published in Hebrew.* Khamsin: Memoirs and Poetry by a Native Israeli *(1994) is available in English from Lynne Rienner Publishers, Boulder, Colorado.* Dor is also the co-editor of a newly released anthology, *After the First Rain: Poems on War and Peace* (Syracuse University Press in collaboration with Oryad Press, 1998).

The haunting and powerful memoir that follows was written in English especially for this book.

Marked by the Teeth

*I*n a sea of golden sand, the Moslem Cemetery was an enclave of dark conjecture. It was surrounded on three sides by little white houses, ours among them, in what came to be known as Northern Tel Aviv—on the west, beyond the steep dunes, spread the Mediterranean—but still the cemetery managed to retain its atmosphere of mystery. Even in those distant years of my childhood many of the tombstones were already crooked and marked by the teeth of the damp sea air. To get there on your own after sunset took supreme courage, and even invading its premises in a group, after nightfall, was considered unhealthy.

Rusty iron gates, tottering on their hinges, and low sandstone walls, breached in various places, guarded the cemetery. Nobody dreamed of desecrating the graves. It was a holy site, overgrown with prickly cacti, oleander bushes and forlorn tamarisks, and the ghosts of endless Arab dead. Years later, during the War of Liberation, the resurgent Israeli Army put up official signs to warn off marauders, declaring the sanctity of the place. In point of fact, the ground all around the cemetery was already sold by the Palestinian owners to the Jewish National Fund for full price, and more. Somehow no one drew a line at the cemetery to exclude it from the transaction. It was assumed nothing would disturb the peace of the dead.

But not far away, while strolling on the beach with his

wife, Chaim Arlosoroff was shot to death in June, 1933. It was a summer night resplendent with stars and breeze and the rustling of the sea. According to testimony, the killers were two men "speaking a broken Hebrew with a thick Arabic accent." Did the two men really want to rob Arlosoroff and rape his wife? Or was it a political assassination, hatched by Palestinian extremists? No one knows. Arlosoroff, only thirty-four when gunned down, was already the head of the Political Department of the Jewish Agency for Palestine and a brilliant leader of the Jewish Labor Party in the Land of Israel.

I was a baby when the murder took place, but my father admired Arlosoroff, knew him personally and shared his moderate views, supporting the search for common ground between Jews and Arabs in Palestine. When I grew up my father took me again and again to the very spot where the great man was killed. When I was even older, I read his collected works, published in a memorial edition by the Labor Party, and found he wasn't only immersed in Jewish-Arab politics and social problems, but also dabbled in poetry. But by then more innocent blood had flowed. And somehow, at least to me, it was all connected to the Moslem Cemetery, making it even darker, more sinister.

Jaffa, the Arab city, lay south of Tel Aviv. At the beginning of this century, a group of Jewish residents decided to build their own town. They moved northwards, planted a stake in the dunes, and founded Tel Aviv—"Hill of Spring." Tel Aviv grew in leaps and bounds, becoming the first Hebrew town where the Holy Language, rejuvenated and modernized, ruled the streets. Jaffa stayed in the background. One beach stretched between the two towns. The same Mediterranean whispered or roared to the west of both. For years an uneasy truce was maintained, easily broken. The sharper the conflict between the two national movements, the denser the suspicion and hatred. Clashes broke out, blood was shed. Eventually a full-scale war erupted.

But I put the cart before the horse. I am still a child, playing on the beach near my home, digging in the moist sand, erecting citadels of pure fantasy. I can see Jaffa far to the south, its minarets shimmering in the haze.

At that time I was not aware of the complex relationship between the two cities. For example, I didn't know of the bloody riots of May, 1921, when Arab nationalists from Jaffa massacred Jews living along the dividing line. Among the victims was Yosef Chaim Brenner, one of the creators of modern Hebrew literature, whose writings expressed deep sympathy for the ordinary Arab. The pogrom happened eleven years before I was born, but Brenner was a writer I deeply admired—a kind of tormented Hebrew Dostoyevsky. The photo of his maimed body, full of stab wounds, is etched in my memory like a personal trauma.

The rioters from Jaffa attempted to break into Tel Aviv proper, wild with hatred and lust for imaginary riches. They were stopped by Haganah [underground Jewish self-defense organization] volunteers and Jewish soldiers of the British Army in Palestine. There were later violent episodes, culminating in the 1936–1939 "Disturbances" (the "Arab Revolt," according to the Palestinians) that swept over the whole country, leaving an ineradicable swathe of blood and tears. Jaffa was a center of Palestinian nationalism. But at that time I knew only the beauty of caravans of camels slowly making their way along the beach.

The camels were usually laden with sacks of zifzif, a rough, gravelly kind of sand dug out at the sea shore and used for building. The Arab drivers sat astride the camels, rising and sinking with a sea-like motion, their heads nodding. Bells were tied to the camels' necks, making sweet, unearthly music. The camels' eyes were big and sad and moist. It was all like a scene from *The Arabian Nights*, which I came to love passionately once I mastered reading and discovered some of these tales translated into my language. In the summer, when dusk was late in falling over the hot, indolent land, the caravans sometimes traveled at night. The shapes of camels and men melted into each other under the enormous starry sky, but the melody of bells lingered long after the beach was deserted. Years later I came to read an anthology of Russian poetry in Hebrew translation and found poems written by Ivan Bunin, a future Nobel Prize laureate, during his visit at the turn of the century to the Holy Land. One poem lovingly, with subtle pen strokes, depicts a caravan of camels moving in the night and "the driver, like a dead man, nodding/his star-crowned head."

The southern streets of Tel Aviv blended into Jaffa itself, partaking of its colors and smells. But the more one went north, among white houses gleaming in the sun, their little plots of geraniums, the evergreen ficus hedges, the remoter Jaffa became, physically and psychologically. One could see, in times of relative restraint in Jewish-Arab relations (oddly enough, the years of the Second World War were like that), Palestinians shopping in Tel Aviv. But they preferred to conduct their business closer to home. The few Arabs who penetrated deep into the Hebrew city were essentially peddlers, buying or selling junk. They shouted boisterously about their goods, not in Hebrew, not in Arabic, but in Yiddish! Knife sharpeners or sellers of vegetables, oranges, ka'eks (Arab sesame bagels) and sugar cane came too. They all moved freely about the town. In fact, their presence continued nearly up until the fall of 1947.

Arab vegetables and oranges were not as good as those grown by Jewish farmers. Our agriculture was more advanced, using fertilizers and original techniques. But "their" veggies and oranges were cheaper. "Buy Hebrew products, cherish Hebrew labor!" placards and editorials urged, part of the Zionist campaign to return the Jewish people to cultivating the soil in their historic motherland. But the difference in price was a great incentive, at times overcoming collective loyalties and norms of behavior. As to ka'eks—I loved them. I can still savor their crispness, the texture of sesame, and the flavor of za'atar. When you bought a ka'ek you also received, in paper rolled into the shape of a cone, some za'atar to dip it into. Za'atar—resembling oregano—is an omnipresent seasoning in the Middle East. But for me, buying that ka'ek— when I was able to raise the money—then dipping the pieces of it in za'atar and slowly, ever so slowly, munching it, was more than a culinary bargain. It was a ceremony, the beginning of an exotic journey. And then there was sugar cane. Crunching the cane into pulp in my mouth, feeling the sweet liquid flow down my throat—what a treat that was!

Some time ago I was walking in the neighborhood of my Tel Avivan childhood. The golden dunes are no more. The sands have been paved over by asphalt road, and hotels and apartment buildings block the view of the sea where I used to roam and dream. And where the crazily leaning tombstones of the Moslem Cemetery slumbered in half light, half shadow, soars the Tel Aviv Hilton, adjoined by a beautiful municipal park, Gan Ha'atzmaut (Independence Garden). Both hotel and park overlook the Mediterranean. A few years after the War of Liberation the Moslem Religious Authority of Jaffa gave permission to dig up the cemetery, gather the bones and re-bury them in a common grave in a corner of the park-to-be. The grave has a small monument to mark it, with the cemetery's history carved in the stone.

I stand there, deep in thought. It is a summer evening. There is a breeze blowing from the west, driving off the remnants of a hot, hazy day. The fiery ball of the sun slowly descends into a turquoise sea and the monument is already cloaked in shadow. At this brief moment there is no fear, only a great sense of peace, as if reconciliation has finally been achieved.

And then it is dark.

YEHUDIT HENDEL

Yehudit Hendel grew up in Haifa, where she remembers Jews and Arabs living together without hatred. She married Zri Mairotich, a painter who was one of the leading artists of Israel. After his death, she moved to Tel Aviv, where she is living now. She has a daughter and a son.

Hendel began writing when she was very young, and her publishing career spans more than forty years. She writes novels, short stories, and essays, and has eight published books to her credit. One of her more recent works is a novel, The Mountain of Losses, *published by Hakibbutz Hameuchad/Siman Kriah (Tel Aviv) in 1991. Much of her work has been adapted for stage and screen, radio and television. Currently she is working on a collection of short stories.*

Hendel is a slow and precise writer, carefully crafting every page. She says she is drawn to writing about extreme situations of pain and suffering, but she chooses to depict the great drama of life with small details. She rarely leaves home, she says, and writes mostly about her own neighborhood. Her books are years in the making, and Hendel says she devotes herself completely to the journey of writing each one. "I have no rest," she says, "till the text reaches a condition when it breathes some human truth and behaves like a living body."

In this story about her deep connection with an aging Arab man that began when she was a young girl, she displays the contribution of small details to understandings of the human heart.

The Arak of Abu-Anton

Translated from the Hebrew by Barbara Harshav

*I*n Haifa, we lived on the roof, that is, actually inside the roof. It was an old stone house, built in the oriental style—broad, spacious, a house of thick, heavy stone walls with arches and vaults and high wide windows and doors, and a big square hall in the middle where rooms and balconies went out to all four sides. So there was the sea and there was Mount Carmel and there was the street and there was the courtyard.

Because it was a tile roof with a turret, slanting on all sides and in all directions, and the ceiling and windows too were all arches, in the little children's rooms—which were really at the edge of the roof, the edge of the slope—there were little portholes on the ceiling, facing the sky, straight up, as on a ship, with the constant sense of something very open, something of a constant journey. And because it was an old house, the banisters of the balcony would rust, and always had to be painted, also as on a ship, and the tile roof too was dozens of years old and pigeons and crows flew over it and stones were thrown on it and branches, so every year there was a broken tile somewhere and the strip of pitch on the turret was ripped, and every year the rains came in, and every year we repaired the roof.

* * *

There was an Arab named Abu-Anton who would repair the roof for us. He was a little man, short and skinny, with legs like two broken sticks, a very unstable, tottering gait, and a great desire for rain. When October came he would appear, ring the doorbell, smile, with yearning on his face, yearning for the roof. When we would invite him to drink coffee with us he would say, "Later." And it was clear that desire burned within him to go up to the roof, and there, on the slanting roof, where it was truly a mortal danger to walk, with his two broken-stick legs and his very unstable, tottering gait, he began running around on the inclines and skipping on the slopes as he leaped from tile to tile and from slope to slope and from gutter to gutter, stroking the gutters and touching the tiles with a kind of inner affection. And when he would find some broken tile, his face would beam with joy. He would sit down, pick up the tile. Put it back. Pick it up again. Put it back again. Move it. He had a very wrinkled face, and when he laughed, the wrinkles deepened. And whenever he raised a tile, he laughed.

The roof waited for him all summer long. The tar exploded, he would say happily; it was a hot summer. Afterward, after that strange, high tour, leaping skinny on the roof as I stood trembling on the balcony, he agreed to come into the house, and we drank black coffee, and we talked a little. Once, when we were talking like that, I told him that when I was a little girl we lived in Nesher, near the cement factory. Our house was on the mountain slope, facing the quarry, and next to it was the Moslem cemetery. The windows were open, and I was afraid of the cemetery, and my mother told me that there was nothing to fear from the dead. And the tombstones? I asked her. Nothing to fear from the tombstones, she said. They're made of stone. You think there's no life in stone? I asked her. The wind changes the shape of the stone, I said to her. Oh, no, said my mother, only time does.

He sipped his coffee and smiled a small smile that lit up his face. Yes, nothing to fear, not only from the dead, from the living, too, he said. He picked up his cup and slowly took another sip. Then he asked, Where is she, your mother. She died, I said to him. Of what, he asked. Typhus, I said. He moved the cup on the table and looked at me in silence. My father died of typhus too, he said. Afterward, he asked how old she was. Forty, I said. He gave me a long look, playing with the cup on the table and keeping his small, dark eyes on me, eyes that grew wider and now seemed close together, near one another, as if they were one long narrow eye. He still kept looking at me in silence. My father too. I was a child. I don't know exactly how old he was, he said after the silence. Then he finished his coffee and started talking about the next rain, of course. He said that we would wait until the next rain. The water comes through, he said, it comes through in unexpected places, you never know where, and it catches the branches, the tiles, the birds' nests, and at the first rain, he would come, he would come at once, just as the rain would come—he would come. And with the first rain, every year, he came at once, came and presented himself, as to a hidden call, went up on the roof and wandered around there for a long time in the rain.

The first rain—that was always something unusual. On the dry tiles and the patches of the mended concrete, the rain made a roof on top of the roof, a roof of water, a kind of dome of water on the orange rust-colored arches with the strange patches, a kind of transparent, moving crust, which would break at once, easily, and inside it was warm and cozy and homey. He had a black flapping windbreaker, slightly torn, and every year I remember him in his torn black coat flapping on the roof in the wind and dripping water, and his black rubber hat that dripped water, and he still wasn't satisfied. After the strange, meticulous tour, he would sit down on the slope, on the side facing the sea, would sit there, on the roof, wrapped up in the black coat, the black hat, in the rain, his arms folded within himself, moving only his head, black and dripping, like some gigantic crow.

And it was impossible to get him down off the roof in the rain. When the rain was long and continuous and we would start shouting: Abu-Anton, Abu-Anton—he didn't move. He laughed, raised his hands, and signaled to us: What can you do, the rain. Clearly he had been waiting fervently for that hour all through the long dry summer, to sit there, wrapped up in the strange torn coat, alone on the roof in the rain, looking at the sea, all dripping. Sometimes he would open his mouth wide and gulp the water. Sweet, he said, sweet, just as in the verse: The water from above which is sweet.

There is a saying: Why does the rain come from above? So that the high one will drink it low. And so he sat, drinking low. That rain was his arak [liquor], and he gulped it fervently, lustfully, with his whole body, shaking with the cold and the water and wandering around up there on the roof like some strange large bird. Sometimes he would suddenly sit down by the turret, very close to the turret, and folded up like that, black himself, he looked like a little turret next to a big turret, a kind of small, living, moving turret.

This story was repeated every year. He grew old before our eyes. Every year the legs were more crooked, the face more wrinkled, the smile more weary and the eyes more small, but they never went out. And when he would stand in the door, eager for rain, the older he grew the more nimbly he leaped on the roof. With a more fervent desire, with a kind of passion to get through one more winter, one more first rain, one more sitting in the torrent descending straight down on him from the sky, black on the red tiles, every year the melody would be repeated. When he found out the roof was dripping and would have to be repaired, and it would be possible to run around up there, and to come for another check, and to sit there again, close to the turret, higher than high and lonelier than alone, in the water coming down on him from the sky, closest to the sky, right inside it, inside that huge net inside the air, the sky pierced like a sieve—he would come. Just as there are people who have fear of heights, he, Abu-Anton, had a passion for heights, his arak.

We loved him, of course, and we waited for him every year, of course. We would fix him pita, olives, coffee. One winter October came, and he didn't come. Rain fell; he didn't come. We waited one day. We waited two days. He didn't come. We had no address. We didn't know where to search. We knew that he lived somewhere in the Arab quarter in the lower city, near the small church next to the Italian hospital. And one day we went down and walked from house to house near the church and the Italian hospital, and on the other side of the street, and back, but we didn't see the little man with the torn black coat. And no one knew who was Abu-Anton, no one knew any Abu-Anton, and we didn't know if he was sick or dead. Once I said: He died in the summer. No. No, they told me, couldn't death wait until winter?

But death, it seems, couldn't wait until winter, and we never saw Abu-Anton again. And we found a Druze from the village of Dalyet-el-Carmel who came to repair the roof, but it wasn't the same roof and it wasn't the same rain, and through the skylight, every winter, year after year, I would seek that strange bird-man, sitting and laughing on the roof, with the rain coming down on him, moving his head so the water would trickle right on his face, as not to lose a drop of the sweet water, the water from above. He had introduced himself as a roof repairer, but for me he was the rain-man, burning with the passion for rain, with a lust that crept into his bones on the roofs.

Many months later, as we were sitting in a café in the lower city, we suddenly asked, by chance, if anyone knew the roof repairer. The roof repairer, they said, he died. And it turned out that he really had lived there on the ground floor, with a few steps up to his apartment, and he was going down a step, and he stumbled on a branch, and fell, and injured his head, and lost consciousness, and a few days later he died.

That was strange, amazing. We were shocked. That man who, every year, every winter, leaped in the rain on the high roof—fell on the low step.

1986, Tel Aviv

REUVEN MIRAN

At fifty-four, after having lived with his wife and three sons in Israel, Africa, Great Britain, Holland, Belgium, France, and Italy during a twenty-five-year career with the Israeli Foreign Service, Reuven Miran now lives in Binyamina, Israel, where he devotes himself to writing full-time.

The author of eight works of fiction for adults and three for children—all published in Hebrew—he has also written playscripts and screenplays. In 1995, his book of short stories Turtle Soup for Breakfast *won the ACUM Ashman Prize for Literary Achievement, and he received the B.B.C. World Service Prize for short stories in 1996.*

"The Dark Villages" is a haunting eyewitness account of the events and emotions surrounding the U.N. vote in favor of statehood for Israel on November 29, 1947.

(See photo insert.)

The Dark Villages
Translated from Hebrew by Elizabeth Maor

A light wind blew, whispering over the tops of the ficus trees, rustling through the branches and the tangled leaves, passing over the red tile roofs of the settlement's houses. The setting sun spilled amber light on the hills in the east and on the white houses of the Arab villages beyond the cactus fence. Shadows of clouds fell on the brown fields between the villages. The colorfully-robed men and women who had been working the fields collected their tools and began to return home in the fading light of the setting sun. Herons wheeled overhead, the wind carrying their cries eastward.

I watched the darkness descend on the orange groves at the edge of the settlement. For a moment a last ray of light touched the top of the water tower and then it too disappeared. The lamps were lit and shed their pale radiance on the sand. From afar came the night-cry of a jackal.

"Robby, does your head still ache?" asked my mother.

"No," I answered. I closed the window and stretched out on the bed.

"I'll take your temperature again in a little while," she said.

I was silent. Outside, on the road, a car was straining to get through the sand. Doctor Martin, I thought. He always gets stuck in the same spot. I lay on my back and looked at the ceiling. From the kitchen came the sounds of frying. Oil sizzled in a skillet and dishes clattered.

Then I heard my mother saying, "Doctor Martin, do you need help?"

"No thanks, I'll do just fine by myself. It always happens in the same place."

Aha, I thought, I was right. But I didn't say anything. It was the third day I had been sick. Doctor Martin came into my room and examined me and said that it was the beginning of strep throat. I didn't have a high temperature but he said it would be better if I stayed in bed until I was well. "It's winter," he said, "and you never know what these things can turn into."

From the road outside I could again hear the whine of the engine as the wheels of the car spun around. Then suddenly the sound deepened and began to fade in the distance. He's out, I thought to myself.

My room was small. Opposite the bed was a bookcase, and my father had hung a shelf over it for my toys. In the corner, above the desk, there was a limp Jewish National Fund calendar showing the date: November 29, 1947.

I was hungry and went into the kitchen. My mother was frying eggs. She had already prepared the salad.

"Robby, slice some bread, please," she said.

"Any mail from Dad?" I wanted to know.

It seemed that with the coming of night the wind had gotten stronger. Something moved under the roof and then fell silent. A branch beat against one of the shutters. I could hear the jackals howling in the orange groves to the east of the settlement. I set the table. Since my father had gone to the Galilee, my mother and I were alone in the little house. She had explained that he was an officer in the Haganah [underground Jewish self-defense organization] and right now he had to be away from home—far away—and that it was important. I understood.

"Mail? No, no mail."

I wanted to stroke her hair, but instead I poured out two glasses of water.

She sat down at the table. "Bon appetit," she said. We ate in silence. The wind had almost died down.

"I think it may rain," she said. Her eyes were very blue

and I liked looking at them. Someone knocked on the door. "Come in!" she called.

"I bet it's Mrs. Limoni, come to borrow eggs as usual," I said.

The door creaked as it opened. I could hear the sound of footsteps.

"Robby," said my mother, "remind me to oil the hinges."

Mrs. Limoni stood in the door of the kitchen. "Good evening," she said. She was about fifty years old and very short and fat. She had been born in Jaffa and spoke Hebrew fluently, but with a Russian accent. She and her husband lived next door, on the other side of the lone palm tree which grew on the border between her yard and ours. They had no children.

"A dozen enough?" my mother asked with a smile.

"Thank you," Mrs. Limoni answered, "this time I've come about something else."

"What happened?" The fork dropped from my mother's hand and she looked pale. My father? Someone else?

"The UN vote is tonight; it will be on the radio."

"I completely forgot," my mother said, and the color returned to her cheeks. It was OK, nothing bad had happened.

"How could you forget something like that?" Mrs. Limoni sounded almost insulted, but then she smiled. "So, smart guy," she said turning to me, "you picked a time to get sick!"

I could feel myself blushing. I couldn't answer.

"How does he feel?" she asked.

"Better," said my mother.

"I hope he gets well soon," sighed Mrs. Limoni. "Have you heard anything from Chaim lately?"

"No."

"I guess they're busy," Mrs. Limoni said. "They have a lot to prepare for."

"How's everything?" my mother finally asked.

"Thank God," sighed our short fat neighbor in her Russian accent. "I just hope everything goes well." She left and we went back to eating supper.

"What are they voting on in the UN, Mom?" I asked.

"On the Partition Plan, on the division of Palestine into two countries, one Jewish and one Arab," she answered.

"Where will the Jewish country be?" I took some salad and carefully sprinkled salt on it.

"Here, in the Plain of Sharon where we live, the Coastal Plain, the eastern Galilee, the Jezreel Valley, and the Negev. Do you want tea?" She left the table and went to put the kettle on.

"Yes." I waited for a minute and asked, "Who's going to vote?"

"All the member nations."

"What about the British—will they agree to it?"

"If the majority votes for partition they'll have no choice."

"So then they'll finally leave?"

"Yes, they'll go back to their own country."

"I hope that happens," I said. I didn't like the British soldiers who invaded the houses in the settlement, looking for concealed weapons and men and destroying the fields and fences and orchards. And I had a feeling that when they left my father would come home.

"What about the Arabs? What do they want?"

"They're against the plan," she said. "They want the whole country for themselves."

I didn't say anything. When I was younger the Arabs used to come from the villages in the surrounding hills to sell their produce in the newly built market. I had liked to watch them. They were quiet and polite and smiled at us children. And sometimes they would give us a piece of fruit or a vegetable to eat. Then one day they stopped coming, and now we weren't allowed out at night to visit friends unless an adult went along with us. Sometimes we heard shots being fired on the other side of the orange groves, and death notices of people everyone knew had begun to appear in the newspaper which was tossed into the yard every morning.

"If they want the whole country for themselves," I said, "I don't think Dad will come home for a long time."

"Go to bed," my mother said. "I'll bring your tea to you there."

I went to my room, turned on the light, and lay down on the bed. The room was chilly and I covered myself with a green wool blanket. Outside the wind had died down. My mother brought me my tea and I drank it slowly in sips. The radio was in my parents' room and I wanted to sleep in their bed. I asked my mother and she agreed immediately. We went into the big bedroom and I curled up next to her, wrapped in the blanket. The room was dark, and only the green glow of the radio dispersed the gloom. From the brown Bakelite box came noises, static, songs, and people's voices. It was late and I felt my eyelids getting heavy. I wanted to tell my mother something but before I could, my eyes closed and I fell into a deep sleep.

The hand on my shoulder was warm, and the voice saying, "Wake up!" was familiar and mingled with the voices coming in from the road.

"Wake up, Robby, wake up!" said my mother.

"What happened? Did something happen, Mom?" I asked.

"We've got a country, my son. We've got a country of our own!" She hugged me hard and I could feel the tears falling from her eyes onto my forehead and rolling from there onto my cheeks. I had never seen my mother cry.

I could hear people singing outside. Someone called out that they were organizing dancing in the public square. The lights were on in all the houses. "Let's go outside," I said.

"But you're sick," said my mother. "Doctor Martin would never approve."

"I don't feel sick."

"Oh dear, I forgot to take your temperature."

"We'll do it when we get back," I promised.

We got dressed and went outside. We ran into Mrs. Limoni on our front doorstep. She fell upon my mother and kissed her on both cheeks. Her eyes were wet with tears, like the eyes of most of the people we met. Someone had brought a loudspeaker and was playing songs and marches. People milled around, hugging each other and laughing and crying and walking back and forth without going anywhere. In the near-dark the dancers had formed a circle, their swaying bodies faintly illuminated by the light of the lamps. Blue and white flags had suddenly appeared as if from nowhere. Without warning a large hand fell on my shoulder.

"What are you doing here?" asked Doctor Martin. "Do you want to be sick?"

"I'm already sick," I answered. "What else can happen to me?"

Doctor Martin smiled and patted my head.

"We'll go home in a minute," said my mother, but Doctor Martin wasn't listening. He hugged her and planted loud kisses on both her cheeks.

"We've got a country," he said in a laughing voice I had never heard him use before. "We've got a country. What do you have to say about that?!" And he left us and went on, mingling with the rest of the crowd.

We've got a country, I thought on the way home. We've got a country. Thirty-three member nations voted in favor, thirteen against, ten abstentions, and one didn't even come to vote. And I missed the broadcast because I fell asleep. Now finally the British will leave and Dad will come home.

My mother and I walked hand in hand. The sand in front of the house was damp and our feet sank into it. We wiped our shoes before going inside. I moved the branch near the shutter and tied it to the trunk of the tree with a cord I found on the porch railing. "Now it won't hit the shutter if there's wind tonight," I said.

My mother opened the door which she had left unlocked. The hinges grated and I reminded her to oil them. Just then noises came from the other side of the dark orange groves to the east. There was a burst of gunfire. We stood on the threshold.

The gunfire ceased as suddenly as it had begun. But the night-black orange groves were there, and in the Arab villages on the hills beyond them, silent in the dark, no lights had been lit in celebration.

ANAN AMERI

Author and sociologist Anan Ameri, Ph.D., was born to a Palestinian father and a Syrian mother in Damascus, Syria, in 1944. Her family lived in the western part of Jerusalem until the 1948 war, when they were forced to leave their home. This unforgettable story relates a three-year-old's emotional responses to a year-long separation from her parents while they found a safe home for her in East Jerusalem.

Ameri says that the turning point in her life was the 1967 war, during which she volunteered in Palestinian refugee camps, first in Jordan and then in Lebanon. Since that time she has been a political activist/community organizer and college professor. From 1984 to 1993 she was the president and director of the Palestine Aid Society of America. In 1995/96 she was awarded the Peace Fellowship at the Bunting Institute at Radcliffe College. In 1997 she was the acting director of the Institute of Jerusalem Studies in Jerusalem for a time and then moved to Detroit, Michigan, where she is the Arts and Cultural Director of ACCESS, the Arab Community Center for Economic and Social Services.

Ameri is the author of one book, the co-author of another, and she has also co-authored several articles focusing on the Middle East. She began writing short stories in 1994.

Early Lessons of Separation

*I*n the old city of Damascus, at the age of three, I sat on the doorstep of my grandfather's house, waiting for my parents to come and get me. I sat at the doorstep of this three hundred year old home, separated from my parents, and separating myself from my relatives who lived here. I sat on the outside end of the long, dark, narrow, L-shaped corridor. On the other end was a square, sunny courtyard with colorful tiles, fruit trees, lots of flowers, and a fountain.

It was a big two-story house built for a large extended family. But I only remember my grandfather and two of his daughters—the unmarried ones—living there. In the summer they would spend their evenings in the courtyard eating watermelon, playing cards, and enjoying the scent of the jasmine and the gardenia as it got stronger in the late hours of the night. My grandfather would play cards with me too. He would let me win and then give me a new silver coin for winning. He always had new shiny silver coins.

When my parents had gone to Jerusalem they promised they would be back soon to get me and my sister. They were not back yet. Every morning I would sit in my favorite spot, looking towards the end of a street so narrow no car could come through. I looked there for a car to stop and for my parents to get out of it. Each car brought excitement, hope, and disappointment.

Some days I would quietly cry. Other days I would go

inside, angry at my parents and tired of waiting, only to come out after a few minutes, hoping that this time they would show up.

Aunt Nahida, my mother's older sister whom I loved dearly, must herself have been worried about my parents and other relatives. She must also have been aware of my anxiety and the extent to which I missed my parents. Often she would come to the doorstep to comfort me, bringing me something to eat or drink—a piece of fruit, a candy, a sandwich, a glass of milk, or fresh squeezed tomato juice. She would gently try to get me inside the house, promising that my parents would come soon.

"When?" I would ask.

"Tomorrow," she would say, quickly adding *"Inshallah"* (God willing).

Why did my mother and father leave me here? Why did they not come and get me as they promised? How come they did not even bother to call?

My aunt was a teacher, but that did not help her answer my questions. How could she have explained to me, a three year old child, that my parents did love me, despite the fact that they had taken off, leaving me and my sister behind? How could she have made me understand that there was a war in my country, Palestine? How could she explain that my parents brought me to stay with her because they were concerned about my safety and the safety of my sister, their only two children?

My aunt did all she could to compensate for my parents' absence. I can still feel her love. She would often put me in her warm lap and tell me stories or sing to me until I fell asleep. When I was anxious and angry she would calm me down, assuring me that my parents did love me and that they would be coming back soon.

Soon it was not.

I do not remember exactly how long I stayed in Damascus, separated from my parents and separated from my puppies, the only vivid memory I have of Palestine. In the west side of Jerusalem, where we lived before 1948, my parents had gotten me and my sister two puppies. We named them Lulu and Murjjan. Lulu was white and Murjjan was light brown. I thought they were very pretty. I can still remember how excited and happy I was when we got them. During the day I would play with them and my greatest joy was when I learned how to get them to chase me as I ran around our home. At night I would plead with my mother to let them sleep in my bed.

"They need to be potty trained," she would say.

When my parents came back to Damascus to get me, almost a year later, I was so angry I went into my bedroom and closed the door. I did not want to see them or talk to them. Only my Aunt Nahida was able to talk me into letting them in my room.

A few days after my parents arrived we packed our belongings, loaded my father's small car, and said farewell to my grandfather and other relatives. By that time I was not sure I wanted to be separated from my aunt Nahida. But I was.

I sat in the back seat of the car. Finally we were going home. My father, who was driving, did not seem to be very happy—nor did my mother. He was trying to explain to me and to my sister that although we were going home, it was not going to be exactly home. It was going to be a different house. We would have different neighbors who had children we could play with.

"What about Lulu and Murjjan?" I asked anxiously.

"No, they will not be there."

"Why not? Where are they? What happened to them?"

"Lulu and Murjjan were taken by Israel."

That was how I was first introduced to the word "Israel."

I cried. I wanted my puppies. My father promised to get me new ones.

"But I don't want new ones. I want my dogs! I want Lulu and Murjjan!"

My father tried to explain why they had to leave Lulu and Murjjan behind as they fled for their lives. I did not understand. And although my father was once a teacher like my aunt, he could not make me, at the age of four, understand.

Now I am about to be fifty. Still, I sometimes feel that I cannot really understand what happened in 1948.

MUSA JAMIL JAFFER (PSEUD.)

Born in Jaffa, Musa Jamil Jaffer grew up in a refugee camp in Ramallah, West Bank. As a young man, he left home and went to work in North Africa, where he saved enough money to go to the United States for higher education.

Jaffer taught school in Chicago, wrote almost weekly articles for Chicago papers, and hosted a Palestine radio show between 1969 and 1975. Currently he is in the import-export business in Connecticut.

In this story of his flight from Israel in 1947, when he was six years old, and his childhood spent in a refugee camp, Jaffer depicts the misery that he and his fellow refugees were forced to endure.

I Survived the War

*M*y earliest memories reflect the criteria of a child. For instance, I remember the time a British soldier gave me a chocolate candy. I remember how he looked and how he was seated on a stool at the bar my father owned in El-Manshyyieh in Jaffa. Yet I don't remember much of anything about my mother being wounded by a bomb when she was shopping at the market even though I was older at the time.

I do remember though the serious conversations between my father and mother when they were trying to decide if we all should leave or stay. Many people were leaving their homes in Jaffa because of mobile loudspeaker warnings of the danger of bullets and bombs. It was 1947 and the British were leaving. We were told that very soon we would have nobody to protect us if we were attacked by the Zionist gangs.

I remember my father deciding that he should use his small pickup to move us east. Every time he made the decision he would later change his mind after talking to neighbors who urged him to stay. Ultimately, though, reports of killings and massacres reached us on a daily basis and my father loaded as much as possible for our evacuation of Jaffa.

It was a cold day in December, 1947. I remember being wrapped in a blanket and tucked into a heap of old clothes and linens on the back of a truck my father had hired with my sad-faced brother and sister. We were moving toward the east. Why we were moving I had no idea, except that I overheard my father explaining to my mother that it was dangerous to stay. The Jews were attacking everywhere. I was only six years old and I had no idea what was happening or why. I asked my father about some of the children I used to play with. What about Majid and Anwar—are they moving too? Yes! Yes! They will join us later. Join us where? Where are we going anyway? A sad look on my father's face is all I got for an answer.

Boy, it was really cold on the back of the truck. My mother was lucky since she was sitting in front. In a few minutes we stopped to let some people ride with us. I guess everybody was trying to run away. We stopped again and again, until there was no more space left in the back of the truck. I marveled that my father had arranged for us to leave in the pickup while thousands of other people were walking on the road, carrying with them whatever they could from their households.

When we arrived at the first town we unloaded our hitch-hikers and continued on to the city of Ramallah. My father kept telling the driver to go to this street or the next street. He was looking for a place for all of us to stay. Nobody had such accommodations. After a long search and inquiries we ended up in a corner of a garage that my father secured by swearing that we would vacate the premises in a few days and that we would disappear during the day because the garage was a place of business.

My complaints to my father about the poor accommodations changed nothing, but he assured us that it was a temporary situation and that we should pretend that we were enjoying a picnic. A picnic! He must have been joking. The smell of the place hardly compared to the picnics we used to have in the open fields, the sandy beaches, or under the trees. What about the dirt, the wet oil spots, the cockroaches? Our blankets were all that separated us from the hard floors. And, please, let us not talk about the toilet facilities! I could hardly compare our bathroom in Jaffa to the sharp-edged tin bucket which we all used to dispose of nature's calls.

I woke up the next morning to the sounds of an argument between my father and mother. My father was trying to con-vince my mother that everything would be fine since he had just come from a mass rally at the Oudeh hotel in Ramallah and King Abdullah had promised that things would change and that all refugees would be returning to their homes very soon. Meanwhile he said that, until the time of that return, we should all report to a nearby camp where everything was waiting for us from tents to food.

It did not take long for my father to win that argument with my mother because, as a last resort, he practiced his manly superiority over my mother, telling her in a sharp tone to shut up and do what you're told.

Thanking the garage owner for his hospitality, my father tried to offer him some money for our stay, but he refused vehemently, swearing that he would have asked us to stay with his family if he'd had space.

In less than twenty minutes we were standing at the gate of the camp, waiting in line for our turn to register with a man seated behind a desk on the street in front of the camp. It was very hard for a child my age to understand the human drama of all these refugees who were screaming and weeping and demanding their return as they looked for loved ones they had lost in the tragedy.

As I later saw in movies, the arrangements were like going to jail with each convict being given a number, some blankets, utensils, and then being directed to his cell. In our case it was a tent. The tent had four mattresses for adults and two small ones for my sister and baby brother. My other brother and I accompanied my father, carrying aluminum dishes as we waited in line to get food. Then my father took us on a short tour of the camp and pointed out the common public bathrooms. They were wooden shacks, hurriedly installed and fitted with long water pipes in a modest attempt to meet the hygienic needs of the refugees. But of course the only point of comparison with most modern facilities was that they were separated into men's and women's shacks.

A strange wooden structure at the outskirts of the camp was called a school. Nobody expected our school to look like a normal school but what we had was out of this world! To start with, there were no classrooms. There was only a large room where the teachers would get their age groups to sit around them as they explained that they would only be covering general subjects like arithmetic and geography. The teachers had to make sure that while they were teaching they kept their voices low so as not to interrupt the other teachers in the same room.

It took me a few days before I realized that the site of this "picnic" was becoming our home. Marwan and Sami, who lived a few tents away from us, told me that the promise of our going back to our homes in a few days was not true. I did not believe them. What did they know compared to my father?

It took us a few weeks to understand how we must behave in the camp. The play area was restricted to a spot outside the camp so as not to disturb the inhabitants. We had to wait in line to use the public toilet facilities which did not have toilet paper. To clean our faces we had to help each other by pouring water from a tin can into each other's waiting, cupped hands. The other alternative was to wait in line at the wooden shower shacks with your bar of soap and towel. A narrow canal was dug to channel the used water into a larger canal. A larger canal received the used water which had all the toilet shacks connected to it by narrow channels. In short, it was our sewage system.

My mother's cooking facilities were like what you would use on a picnic. My father was able to purchase a few bricks with which he built our oven. Of course there was no electricity. Wood and old tree branches were our only cooking fuel. My father gave us clear instructions to bring home any tree branch or lumber we might come across. We had to do our homework as soon as we came from school because it would have been too expensive to use the kerosene lamp.

After a few weeks my father gave us square boxes with belts that we used to hang around our necks to display a few items that we were to try to sell. We had to help earn income for our survival. In these boxes we used to display cigarettes and all kinds of candy. I remember how I used to explore the whole city on foot looking for potential customers. My father used to encourage competition between me and my older brother. I used to beat my brother in total sales almost every day.

Of course there were sacrifices in spending our time being young peddlers. We lost the joy of playing with the other kids since by the time we came back from our daily mission it was time to go to sleep. And, by roaming around so much, my brother and I used up our cheap shoes and the holes in the bottom of them grew wider every day. My poor mother used to scold us for having wet socks, accusing us of stepping into puddles. She did not know that water used to creep up through the holes in our shoes.

The worst season at the camp was the winter season when everything became muddy. Thank God the rain was limited to a few days for rain meant an emergency at the camp.

Water always found its way into the tent and mud and wet-
ness became a part of our house. Thank God that my father
was able to elevate the mattresses by making wooden frames
under them. One advantage was that the sewage canals were
flushed with the extra water pouring through them. The
worst part was that my brother and I lost all our sales on
those days—money we sorely needed in order to survive. . . .

GUNTER DAVID

Gunter David was born in Berlin, just as Hitler was rising to power. He and his family fled to Paris in 1933, and then, when he was five years old, they moved to Tel Aviv. Just before the creation of the State of Israel in 1948, David came to the United States to study journalism and acting. Over the course of twenty-five years he was a writer for several major city newspapers including The Baltimore Sun, *Philadelphia's* Evening Bulletin, *and* The New York Times, *host of a daily radio program on consumer affairs, a foreign correspondent who covered the Yom Kippur War for the* Philadelphia Daily News, *and a contributor to several national magazines.*

A resident of Philadephia for the last twenty-five years, and married to his wife Dalia for forty-five, Gunter David is father to three children and grandfather to five. He is currently in private practice as a psychotherapist in Philadelphia and devoted to his new career as a fiction and creative nonfiction writer. He received first prize in the literary short story category in the 1997 annual Philadelphia Writers' Conference.

In this story David explores the hard choice he had to make as a teenager between his desire to remain in his homeland and his desire to realize his dreams.

(See photo insert.)

Going to Jerusalem

"**D**on't sit by the door. You could take a bullet," my father warned me.

"Go with God," my mother said. I felt her tears on my neck, there, in front of the apartment house, under the tall, bare tree, its brown leaves scattered on the sidewalk by the cold December wind.

"Take care of yourself," my father said. We shook hands. I buttoned my coat and walked to the corner of Shenkin. The bus to downtown came in a moment, and I quickly turned and waved. They waved back, holding on to each other, alone together.

I was going to Jerusalem. Beyond Jerusalem lay America: Times Square, Broadway, Hollywood, palatial homes, swimming pools, cars, nice clothes, malt shops, jitterbug, jazz. That was America to me.

I was eighteen years old.

The dispatcher at the cab stand on Rothschild, just off Allenby, waved me into the back of the big, black car. It was empty, smelling of tobacco. Two jump seats were unfolded, awaiting passengers. I settled into the middle seat in the rear. I knew it was selfish, but I wanted to be safe. At least, as safe as possible.

I put my hand inside the breast pocket of my jacket to

make sure the new British Passport 224866, issued by the government of Palestine, was safe. Soon it would contain a visa granting me entry to the United States.

No war. No Arabs. No shooting. No bombs.

I'd wanted to live in America ever since I started going to the movies. I used to imagine all of America as one big movie set. Chaim Rosoff, who lived next door to our third floor walk-up in Tel Aviv, called America the "Goldene Medine," the Golden Land. "It's where dreams come true," he used to say.

Soon I would dream there too.

The dispatcher interrupted my thoughts.

"Move over," he commanded. "Sit by the door. Let the girl sit in the middle."

"But I was here first. I want to sit in the middle."

"What's the matter? You're too scared to sit by the door?" He laughed, a dark, swarthy man with thick eyebrows and golden teeth.

"If he's scared, let him sit in the middle." A husky voice announced an attractive girl, about my age. Her cheeks were red from the wind, her dark eyes shining with laughter.

I moved to the door.

In short order, the rest of the passengers entered the cab. The girl next to me placed a bag in her lap, extracted two knitting needles attached to yarn, twisting snake-like from the bag, and began to knit. She shook her long, light brown hair free of her jacket. A bearded young man, wearing a skull cap, sat on her other side and began reading. Two middle-aged women occupied the jump seats, and a young couple sat up front. No one spoke.

The driver was the last to arrive. When he turned around, our eyes met.

"Avraham!" I exclaimed.

He smiled.

"Since when are you driving a cab?" I asked.

"Why would you be going to Jerusalem?"

"I . . . well . . . I'm going on an errand. For my father."

"I'm filling in for the driver. My sick uncle."

"Yaallah, let's go!" shouted the dispatcher. Avraham turned the key in the ignition. We lurched ahead.

Avraham mustn't find out why I was going to Jerusalem, I thought. He mustn't find out that I was leaving for America. I knew what he would say. He'd say, "You're a quitter. How can you leave us behind? Your chevre [community], your friends, your people? How can you walk out on this fight for our independence? In a few months we'll have our own state. For the first time in two thousand years. And you won't be part of it."

I knew how I would respond. I'd say, "There'll never be peace with Arabs. There'll always be killing. I live only once. I want to live where there's peace. Where I can get somewhere. I have a right to live my life my way."

We had had these discussions before, Avraham and I, when we were in high school. He was a Zionist, born in the Land of Israel. I was born in Germany, and my family fled from Hitler. "Sands, flies, and Arabs," my father said a few months after we arrived in Palestine.

I could hear the sounds of voices and running feet that awakened me one night in 1936 when I was six years old. My parents were carrying blankets and pillows out of our apartment in North Tel Aviv. From my window I saw flames, like moving golden sheets, illuminating the southern horizon, toward Jaffa. Scores of men, women, and children were huddled in the open red poppy fields in front of the house. People were bringing them food and supplies.

"The Arabs attacked Jews on the border of Jaffa and Tel Aviv," my father explained when he returned. "They shot them and set their houses on fire." He sat down on a chair in the kitchen and wiped his face with a handkerchief. "I was just there this afternoon. . . ."

It was the start of the Meoraot, the Disturbances, that were to last until the outbreak of World War II. Many a night I would hear the crackling of gun shots and scamper under my bed. In the morning I would examine the outside walls for bullet marks.

I thought of it all as we moved forward, down Allenby and other city streets, to the Central Bus Station. There we joined a convoy of buses, taxis, and private cars. Rumors had it that members of the Haganah, the Jewish underground, accompanied the convoys for protection against attacks by the Arabs. Scores of young men milling about alongside vehicles seemed to give credence to the rumors. I had been briefly one of them, but received a medical discharge after being diagnosed with a heart murmur. Now I would be protected by them—I who was leaving them behind.

* * *

The flat lands outside Tel Aviv whizzed by, apartment houses soon giving way to Jewish settlements surrounded by wire fences and guard towers. The road to Jerusalem lay before us, gradually twisting and climbing up the mountains of Judea. Stone houses of Arab villages, carved into the mountain sides, appeared after a while. Arabs and Jews lived practically side by side. They might as well have been deserts apart.

Avraham drove steadily, at a fast clip, somewhere in the heart of the convoy, a bus in front and another in back of us. No need to linger in enemy territory. We'd been traveling for about an hour when one of the women in the jump seats began eating a sandwich.

The girl next to me looked at her and laughed. "Some people always think they'll starve," she said to no one in particular.

The woman turned around.

"You know, sweetheart, you're much too skinny. I bet your mother tells you that you don't eat enough."

"My mother's dead," the girl said quietly. "Killed when Arabs attacked our kibbutz."

"I'm sorry." The woman reached out and touched the girl's hand. "Forgive me."

A sign by the side of the road proclaimed, "Latrun. Military Installation. Government of Palestine."

The bus ahead of us slowed down. The woman and the girl settled back in their seats. Avraham stopped the car.

"Roadblock," he explained.

From my window I saw British soldiers fanning out

among buses and cars, banging on doors, shouting, signaling drivers to stop. Two of them, one on each side of our taxi, opened the doors up front. The polished shotguns on their backs glistened in the sun. The soldiers examined the faces of the driver and the couple. Then they looked on the floor of the car. They slammed the doors shut and opened the back doors.

The man with the beard continued reading, never acknowledging their presence. The young woman knitted as she had been doing since we left Tel Aviv. Were they looking for weapons, I wondered, or for the Hagana? Someone from the Irgun, or the Stern Gang—the other Jewish underground organization?

"Step out, please," one of the soldiers told the passengers in the jump seats. The two women leaned on the backs of the seats for support, the one still holding her partly eaten sandwich. When the women had left the taxi, the soldiers examined the floor. They folded back the jump seats. They looked at the floor under our feet. I felt exposed. They looked at our faces. I had nothing to hide, yet I could feel my heart racing.

The soldiers backed out. The women returned. The soldiers slammed the doors shut.

"*Mamzerim*," [bastards] murmured the girl next to me. "At least they could have flipped back the jump seats."

"Quiet," said the woman with the sandwich. "Don't make trouble."

"Why don't they go search the Arabs for guns and leave us alone," Avraham said.

*   *   *

Another convoy arrived from the opposite direction. A taxi came to a halt parallel to ours. Avraham stuck his head out of the window.

"How was the trip from Jerusalem?" he shouted at the driver.

"All quiet," the man answered.

"Thank God," said Avraham.

The bus in front of us moved forward.

"All quiet," the driver had said. And I was thinking in the stillness of the car that for Yossi Mendelson it also was quiet. Permanently.

He was my best friend. Our mothers were best friends. They grew up together in Germany. They stayed friends in the Promised Land. Yossi's father was a rabbi. Each Passover my parents and I traveled to Jerusalem to participate in the Mendelsons' Seder.

Yossi was an only child, as was I. He was tall, like his father, red-haired and freckle-faced, like his mother. He had twinkling green eyes from some ancestor unknown to me. He loved to tell jokes and to laugh and sing.

One evening Yossi and his father were walking home after prayers at the Western Wall, down the cobblestones in the ancient, narrow streets of the Old City. A single sniper's bullet hit Yossi in the chest. He died the following day.

We heard about it on the news broadcast on Kol Yerushalayim, the Voice of Jerusalem. Two days later my mother and I attended Yossi's funeral. When they lowered him into the hole in the ground, his skull wobbled in the shroud. My mother held my hand tightly. His mother sobbed. His father shed silent tears. I could feel nothing.

Later that day, in the Mendelson's apartment, sitting in mourning on a wooden stool, as was the custom, Mrs. Mendelson looked at me and then whispered in my mother's ear. On the bus taking us home to Tel Aviv, my mother told me what her friend had said to her:

"Let him have his dream. Let him go to America."

My mother's eyes filled with tears.

It was in the springtime, when the way to Jerusalem was green with budding trees and a rich brown with freshly-plowed fields, both Arab and Jewish. It was then we buried Yossi. Now, in the chill of winter, I was returning to the place where he no longer lived.

The convoy had made its way down the Mountain of Judea into the valley below. A bus and a car, and a bus and a car, perhaps a dozen altogether, followed one another as if holding on to a lifeline. Soon the mountain rose on both sides of the road.

"Not much more to go," said the sandwich lady.

"Don't give us the Evil Eye," said the woman in the other jump seat with a laugh.

The young man with the beard and the skull cap was asleep. The girl next to me was knitting. I closed my eyes and thought of Yossi, that I wouldn't be seeing him ever again.

The crackling sounds of my childhood. Scores of them at once.

I wanted to hide under my bed.

"Get down, everybody!" shouted Avraham. "Ambush!"

My face hit the floor.

The rat-a-tat of a responding machine gun deafened my ears.

Someone leaned over me. A barrage of something sharp rained on my back. On my head. Was I hit?

I saw my parents holding on to each other as they waved goodbye.

I saw Yossi in his grave.

No. It was I.

I felt the car speeding. Voices shouting. Buses rumbling.

"I got hit. My arm." It was Avraham's voice.

"Can you drive?" a woman asked.

"Yes, for now."

Sounds of ripping fabric. A gasp of pain.

Then it was quiet.

"You can get off the floor now," the girl next to me said as she put components of her submachine gun back into the knitting bag. Empty shells were all around me, empty shells that had bounced off my body as their contents zapped through the air.

The second woman in the jump seat was bending forward, bandaging Avraham's arm. A first-aid kit lay next to her on the seat. Avraham grasped the steering wheel with both hands.

"Just a bullet scrape," she said. "You'll be fine."

I caught his eye in the rearview mirror. I must have looked grim. He smiled.

"I'll be okay. Just doing my duty."

So he was in the Haganah detail! As was the girl next

to me. The woman administering first aid probably was a Haganah nurse. They risked their lives. And I . . . I was going to America.

I leaned back in my seat thinking of how I'd just been spared. Thinking of my father's warning, not to sit by the door. The bullet that scraped Avraham—it could have struck me!

Suddenly my father's voice echoed in my mind. "Sands, flies, and Arabs."

I thought of Mrs. Mendelson's message to my mother: "Let him have his dream. Let him go to America."

I closed my eyes. What to do?

The trees and houses on the outskirts of Jerusalem were a welcome sight. The convoy rolled down Jaffa Road, the city's main thoroughfare, to the Central Bus Station. We all shook hands, congratulating each other on having survived. "Shalom. Shalom. Peace be with you."

A man on a stretcher was carried from one of the buses into an ambulance. The only motions were those of the men carrying him. His eyes stared ahead. I felt a needle in my heart. He was probably dead. Did he have a mother? A father? Wife and children? The ambulance door was shut. The vehicle pulled out of the station. The siren was not turned on.

"Now tell me why you're really in Jerusalem," Avraham said, as we stood on the sidewalk outside the station. "Your father wouldn't send you on an errand in times like these."

I looked at him and said nothing.

"You're leaving, aren't you? Your visa's come through."

I nodded. I couldn't lie to him now.

He grabbed my arms.

"If you leave, you have no right to come back," he said. "Because we're all doing our duty. Risking our lives for a common goal. And you're walking away from it. For your own selfish reasons."

He released me. Then he turned back into the bus station where another convoy was assembling. He would be in it, of course.

I sat on a nearby bench, my head in my hands.

America, the Goldene Medine, where dreams come true.

Eighteen years old. To be on my own, in the land of opportunity, with no father and mother to tell me what to do. To have my whole life ahead of me. Who knew how far I could go in America? And then, some day, I would be back. Yes. Of course. I would be back.

Times Square, Broadway, Hollywood, palatial homes, swimming pools, cars, nice clothes, malt shops, jitterbug, jazz.

No war. No Arabs. No shooting. No bombs.

I hailed a cab to the American consulate. A sudden rainstorm rumbled down from the skies. After a while the cab came to a stop. The driver turned around.

"This is as far as I go," he said. "The consulate is inside the Arab quarter. You don't expect me to drive there, do you?"

"How'll I get there?"

"Walk." The driver laughed.

* * *

On that afternoon of December 26, 1947, a visa was stamped into my passport. Arab bullets bounced off the armored car that subsequently took me and other passengers to Lod Airport. I arrived at LaGuardia on January 12, 1948. The Jewish state would be established four months later.

I've visited Israel many times. But I've never seen Avraham.

I've never looked him up.

WADAD SABA

Wadad Saba came to the United States on a scholarship when she was twenty-one years old. Only recently retired from a thirty-five-year career as a professor of music at Seattle Pacific University, she has been very active in teaching voice and opera in the Seattle community. In addition, she has been a frequent vocal soloist and served as musical director in several Christian churches.

Forced to flee Jerusalem in 1948, when she was fifteen, Saba is passionate about the plight of the Palestinian people, which she depicts in her story. She says, "The Palestinians are a disenfranchised people whose country is still subject to the 'iron fist' of occupation by Israel." She believes that the current government of Israeli Prime Minister Netanyahu is "a threat to any negotiated peace as he continues to violate the Peace Accord and international law."

(See photo insert.)

A Christian Palestinian's Story

I can assume that only those readers who have lost their home and their country will really understand the trauma I experienced when, two months before my sixteenth birthday, I found myself forced to start life all over again with a new identity in a new residence.

I was born in Jerusalem, Palestine, and lived there for almost sixteen years preceding the creation of the state of Israel in 1948. You see, for centuries there was no country known as Israel. My country was known as the land of Palestine, spoken of so prominently in the Biblical record, and that land clearly belonged to its native inhabitants, the Palestinians. But Palestine was literally stolen from me and my countrymen and renamed Israel in 1948 with the help of the Western world, who felt guilty for allowing the Holocaust against the Jews of Europe and were not eager to have them immigrate to their lands.

I am a Palestinian Arab and proud of it. My parents were Christians and I was raised in the Anglican church of St. Paul's in Jerusalem where my grandfather, the Reverend Salih Saba, had been the rector.

I grew up in a multi-cultural and multi-religious society. There were people living in Palestine who came from all over the world. My home in the part of West Jerusalem known as the Greek Colony had a high concentration of Greeks. Within walking distance was the German Colony where I went to kindergarten and first grade in a German school run by Lutherans. Our neighbors and friends were Muslims. My father's best friend and his physician were Palestinian Jews.

Palestine at the time was a British mandate and when World War II threatened to involve the Middle East, the British government shut down my German school, rounded up all my German teachers, friends, and classmates and sent them to undisclosed "detention camps." I never heard from them again!

This was my first experience of loss and disruption in my

life. I was seven years old and had no idea how much more was still in store for me. From the age of nine to sixteen, I attended a private Catholic school for girls where some of my friends were Jewish while others were Muslim and Christian. The last two years at St. Joseph's High School, I learned that some of my Jewish classmates were going away on weekends to Zionist kibbutzim for military training which they eventually were to use against me, my family, and my people.

At the age of thirteen, I remember walking to a neighborhood movie house and being shot at by Zionist snipers. One day at school when I was fourteen, we all had to duck under our desks when an Israeli tank drove by the school and sprayed the classrooms of Arab children with gunfire.

I remember spending many nights in terror, afraid that my father and mother would be ambushed by Jewish terrorists on their way home from visiting friends in the neighborhood and cringing each time I saw my dad pick up a loaded gun for self-protection when he left the house.

I remember studying by candlelight many nights to avoid making our home a visible target for terrorist attacks.

I also remember playing the piano at noon on July 22, 1947, and being startled by a horrendous explosion that shook our house. It was the King David Hotel, headquarters of the civilian government of Palestine, that was blown up by the Irgun Zvai Leumi gang, an underground Zionist terrorist organization headed by Menachem Begin who later became Prime Minister of Israel. Two hundred and fifty civilians were killed in that attack, many of them friends of my family. The sense of loss and grief I experienced are indescribable.

I remember the horrific news of the April 10, 1948 massacres of the village of Deir Yassin where 254 Palestinian men, women, and children were raped and slaughtered by the Stern gang with whom Itzak Shamir was involved. He, ironically, also later became Prime Minister of Israel.

This infamous massacre signaled a change in the history of Palestine. It was, by the Israeli leadership's own admission, a deliberate attempt to terrorize the Arab civilian population and drive them out of their homes and towns. With the continuation of such attacks, their plan succeeded. Millions of Palestinians fled their homes in fear, hoping to return when peace was restored. Fifty years later, they are still waiting!

As the situation became more and more intense, my parents decided they would send us children (four girls) to spend a few weeks with our aunt in Cairo, Egypt, and then send for us when things settled down. I left Jerusalem with my three sisters on a bus on May 11, 1948 bound for Cairo, and on May 15th Israel raised its flag, declared itself a state, and closed its borders.

The United States under President Truman recognized Israel as a legitimate country and Palestine simply and suddenly disappeared from the map. Because the borders were shut down, we were unable to return to our home in Jerusalem.

For two years the only news we had about our mother and father were occasional cryptic Red Cross messages. It was 1950 before Mother joined us in Lebanon and 1951 before we were reunited with my father in Beirut.

My father was a successful established businessman in Jerusalem representing Firestone Tires, Diamond Trucks, and automotive spare parts. When Israel declared itself a state, it "requisitioned" all my father's assets as enemy property. This included looting the huge inventory in his store and seizing several shipments still waiting to be unloaded. He told me that even his bank account with Barclays Bank was frozen by the Israeli government. All attempts to recover his losses through the Israeli courts were fruitless. In despair, and knowing that this long separation from his four daughters was unacceptable, he decided to leave Jerusalem and join us in Beirut. In order to do so, he was forced to sign a release saying he would never seek to reenter his homeland and that he would not claim any compensation for his home, his business, or his bank account.

What a price to pay! Father's spirit was broken and he never quite recovered from this ordeal. Still, I consider myself as one of the lucky ones among the millions of displaced Palestinians. My family was able to relocate in Lebanon because of my mother's Lebanese origins, and we were able to find work and gradually get on with our fractured lives. That was not the case for the majority of Palestinians who till this day are living in refugee camps under conditions that make the slums of New York seem like resorts. Or they are eking out an existence on land in the West Bank and Gaza, experiencing the daily inhumanity of military occupation and oppression.

When I first left Palestine, and saw what the Jewish immigrants from Europe were doing to my country and my people, I naturally was filled with anger and hatred. As a teenager, I would have gladly picked up a gun and shot the first Israeli I saw. It took some years before my faith in God was rekindled and my acceptance of the love of God impacted my feelings of hostility, making me realize that hatred is an unproductive emotion. Nevertheless, to this day, my sense of outrage has never left me. It has become more intense the more I learn about the continuing horrors of Israel's occupation of the West Bank and Gaza. I find myself motivated by a heightened sense of justice to work for the end of these horrors. God requires justice, mercy, and righteousness! I believe that as a Christian I must stand up and speak out wherever these values are violated.

As a Palestinian in exile, I was unable to return to my homeland for many years. Finally, with an American passport, I made my first journey back to Jerusalem in 1990, forty-two years after leaving it. I cannot describe the torrent of emotions and reactions that flooded my mind and heart upon seeing my beautiful hometown again. It is such an incredible place —even the air is special! But the heartache I felt when I observed what was going on there was overwhelming. I remembered Jerusalem as a beautiful, quiet city worthy of its name, "the City of Peace." It used to be surrounded by rolling hills, covered with wild flowers, where we as children went to watch the sunrise every Sunday and pick wild anemones and cyclamens. Seeing the city again, ripped apart by pain and tragedy, surrounded by ugly concrete settlements, and teeming with submachine gun–toting Israeli soldiers and civilians, I wept.

While I was there I determined that I would find and visit the home in which I grew up, which I knew was occupied by Jewish settlers. After all those years, I had no trouble remembering exactly where it was located, and I had a friend drive me there. Upon seeing my home, tears welled up in my eyes as my heart thumped at a rate I don't care to experience again.

I had heard of many incidents of Palestinian Americans returning to their occupied homes only to be greeted with stones and insults. I wasn't ready for such an experience.

I noticed that the first floor of the two-story house had been converted into a grocery and flower shop and that someone was living upstairs. I bought a nice bouquet of flowers, hoping it would offset any feeling of hostility or confrontation, and I cautiously climbed the stairs. A tall, handsome, elderly woman answered the door and I began to tell her in English who I was and why I was there.

"Sorry," she said, "only Hebrew! Sarah, come!"

Her thirty-something daughter came to the door and translated what I had to say to her mother, whereupon they invited me in warmly and brought Arabic coffee and cookies as my friend and I sat in the living room—which used to be my bedroom—and engaged in a most incredible dialog.

The mother wanted to know how and why I left my home. I told her in detail about my childhood, the terror of war, the escape to safety, the loss of all our possessions, the three-year separation from my parents who had fled from the house and sought refuge in a Lutheran hospice. All of this was translated into Hebrew by Sarah.

Then I asked Sarah how she and her mother came to possess my home. She started by saying that her mother came from Iraq. I turned in amazement and asked the mother if she spoke Arabic. Yes, of course she did. All of a sudden the conversation did a round-about and what I told the mother she translated into Hebrew for her daughter.

She had come to Jerusalem from Iraq and housed her family in a small dwelling that she found vacant. But some days later, an armed soldier ordered her out at gunpoint since it was a place he wanted for himself. He promised to find her another home and that home was mine.

When I got ready to leave, I asked for permission to take some pictures of the house with its familiar colorful Italian tile floor, its old weathered wooden shutters and its gorgeous white stone structure. Sarah brought out her camera too and took pictures of me and my friend with her and her mother. She put her arms round my shoulders and with a slight tremor in her voice said, "Isn't it awful what people do to people? Next time you come to Jerusalem, please come visit your home again."

Tears were the obvious response for both of us. For one brief moment, by the grace of God, the walls of partition dissolved and traditional enemies responded heart to heart.

Hope of reconciliation, yes! But I was overcome by sadness as, on my way back from the house, I passed Israeli soldiers kicking Arab boys, overturning fruit carts, beating up children to the point of breaking their bones, forcing Palestinian shopkeepers to close their shops, and bulldozing and wrecking Arab homes.

Wadad Saba

This oppression of my people is still going on today and in many ways it has intensified. I fear it will continue as long as we allow it to do so. People must see each other as people . . . and work together for peace *and* justice. One cannot occur without the other!

YITZHAK BAR-YOSSEF

Yitzhak Bar-Yossef is married with three children and lives in the small town of Ra'anana near Tel Aviv. He writes for the Hebrew daily Yediot Aharonot *and is the author of two novels and four short story collections.*

The following excerpt is from his autobiographical novel, A Token of Love, *published in 1995 by Am Oved Publishing House, Tel Aviv. As is true of other Bar-Yossef works, there is a fantastical element in this excerpt that appears in the midst of very detailed and realistic writing. Underneath the flight of fantasy, however, is a message about the Arab/Israeli conflict.*

Asked for his thoughts on the prospects for Israeli/Palestinian peace, Bar-Yossef said, "I believe in compromise and hope that we and the Palestinians will be wise enough to accomplish the Peace Agreement and end the bloodshed. Peace is our only hope."

(See photo insert.)

Yehezkel

Translated from the Hebrew by Suzy Shabtai

I sit daydreaming about him for hours. "When will we go to Jerusalem, to grandfather and grandmother's, to Uncle Yehezkel?" I ask mother.

"That's enough of your fancies," she snaps. "What's all this Uncle Yehezkel business? His name's Noah, not Yehezkel."

But I don't care what everyone else calls him, I call him Yehezkel. I shut my eyes tightly and shout inside me as loudly as I can so that my voice will fly up into the sky and reach him: Yehezkel, come and take me away, like before when we went up on grandfather and grandmother's roof, when we flew together over Jerusalem. If you can fly over Jerusalem, why can't you fly here, to this sad house in Tel-Aviv and take me away from here?

Yehezkel calls me to follow him. On the roof is a broken tile and Yehezkel looks out of the gap and indicates that he will let me look out soon too. I know what he wants to show me. Every time we go up to the roof he shows me the same thing: the Old City, beyond the border. At the end of grandfather and grandmother's street there's a path between the buildings, and behind it an empty area which you mustn't go into because there are mines there, and behind that is a place called "Mandelbaum Gate," and there are policemen there, and I always keep away from policemen. But what a border is I don't understand. I know there's a rusty barbed-wire fence, and if you get close you can get tetanus as well as bullets from the Jordanian soldiers posted on the Old City walls.

Once there was a man who wanted to cross the border and he lay all day between the rusty fences. They could only get him out at night, but his blood had already spilled and there was nothing to do with him but bury him. The Jordanian soldiers are sent up on the walls when they are small, and they never come down as long as they live. They are sent food up on a rope, and once a year the king comes and puts a gold coin in every soldier's basket. Only the one who collects a hundred gold coins can come down.

And did anyone collect a hundred coins, I asked. Yes, said Yehezkel, there were plenty who collected a hundred coins, but they were already used to living on the wall and they didn't want to come down.

And when they die, what happens to them? Yehezkel didn't know, and he said he would go to the National Library and look for the answer.

I thought he was angry with me for asking him hard questions, and I said, "They must lower the bodies in baskets, the way they send food up," but he got annoyed with me and said, "You don't understand anything." And before I could answer, he left me and went down. He forgot I was up there and moved the ladder away from the trapdoor.

I shouted, "Yehezkel, Yehezkel, don't go!" But he had already gone. I heard the big front door close, and it was quiet down there.

I shouted "Mother, Grandmother, Grandfather, Yehezkel!" but no one heard. Mother and grandmother had gone to the market and grandfather to the study house, and I was left in the *boidem* [garret].

I didn't know what to do, so I sat down on a tank and waited for something to happen. It became hot. I was thirsty. I opened the lid of grandfather and grandmother's big water tank. A boy looked out at me from inside the tank, but I wasn't afraid because I knew it was me. I remembered it from the cisterns in the big yard of grandfather and grandmother's building. Once a year, before Passover, they open the metal lid of the cisterns to clean them and check the water, and I look inside and see myself deep down.

The neighbor's granddaughter, whose name is Malka, which means "queen"—and she's really as beautiful as a queen—likes to look into the cistern. Opening the cistern, we see ourselves, one head next to the other, and I want to frighten her and I pull faces, and she laughs and pulls faces back at me and sticks her tongue out, and I laugh back at her too, but then one time she suddenly disappeared from the cistern. Her mother shouted at her and gave her a slap in the face and pulled her back. She dragged her up the stairs to her grandparents' apartment, next door to my grandfather and grandmother's, hitting her all the time. Afterwards, I heard her crying and Mother told me it wasn't nice for a boy and girl to stand so close together even if it was a game. Since then they haven't let us play together, not even jacks or hopscotch on the big balcony.

And I thought about all this when I was sitting on the water tank in the *boidem*, and I looked in and saw myself, and I wondered if I would see Malka too, and I made faces the way I did before, hoping she would suddenly appear. Nothing interesting happened, so I banged on the tank to see the circles that spread over the water.

Yehezkel says that these circles are the speech of spirits we can't see, and if he says it, it means he knows, because Yehezkel knows everything. Every day he goes to the National Library and to museums, and he can tell me about the olden-day caves in Jerusalem where our ancient kings are buried, because once we had kings too, not only the Jordanians. When they buried the kings they put in jewelry and treasures of gold and silver, and to keep thieves away they sealed the caves with huge stone doors, which can be opened only if a bonfire is lit at the door and then the stone opens of its own accord, but that's the biggest secret of our ancient kings and only Yehezkel knows it and I, too, who heard it from him, and if I tell anyone, that's the end of me.

I got down from the tank and I looked through the open door of the *boidem* again to see if someone had come but no one was there, and I began to get a bit scared because there are big mice in the *boidem,* and mice are even worse than our landlady's chickens; the chickens only drink your blood but mice eat your bones. I climbed up on the tank again and looked in, but I only saw myself. I banged on the tank to see the circles of the souls and I tried to hear them talking the way Yehezkel promised me that if you listen patiently you can understand their whispers.

And then I realized that no one would bring me down from the roof and I would stay there forever. Yehezkel would go to the caves of the kings and take all the treasures. Mother would go back home to the Montefiore Quarter. Father wouldn't come to the funfair. Malka would play only with girlfriends. I knew that I would begin to cry soon, and I thought, if I cry into the tank mother and grandmother and grandfather will drink my tears.

When we arrived in Jerusalem, Yehezkel was waiting for us at the train station. He promised he would take me up to the big *boidem* at night; we'd remove some tiles from the roof and look at the sky through his telescope. I didn't believe him because he often made me promises he didn't keep—such as to take me to the secret tunnel which you walk through all night until you reach the other side of the world, where the people go around upside down, their legs up and their heads down.

Grandfather shook his head; the wisdom of the Gentiles. And that telescope—ach! A plaything for the light-minded! Why should one look at the sky when we have the sacred Law here with us in the big bookcase. Should we scrutinize the deeds of the Holy One, blessed be He? But Yehezkel said that it was a mitzvah, a religious duty, to examine the deeds of the Creator. Didn't the Holy Torah say, 'How manifold are Thy deeds, O Lord. All in wisdom hast Thou wrought'? And he pulled me to the other room, opened the big wardrobe with the three doors and the mirror on the middle door, and showed me a long tube in a black box which had a round glass on its end.

In the evening when Grandfather went to the study house and Mother and Grandmother walked Aunt Sureh to the end of the street, Yehezkel took the ladder, leaned it against the wall underneath the *boidem* trapdoor in the ceiling, took the telescope out of the closet, locked the apartment door from the inside so no one could disturb us, and climbed up. To be in the *boidem* at night—I had never ever believed there could be such fear, but if Yehezkel went up there, then I would too.

Only after I was already among the pipes and the water tanks and the masses of empty bottles which rolled around there did I remember the mice, and I screamed when something touched me, but Yehezkel, who had by then taken out several tiles and positioned the long tube in the new space, called me to come quickly, come quickly, come see the moon. "There's mice!" I shouted, but Yehezkel didn't answer me.

He grabbed me by the waist and hoisted me up so I could reach the telescope. When I looked at the moon he said, "You see how beautiful—that's the Little Light."

"And what's behind it?" I asked.

"Behind it is the sky."

"And what's behind the sky?"

"Behind it is more sky and more sky."

"And after that?"

"After that—it's forbidden to wonder what's after that," said Yehezkel, and he fell silent.

I wanted him to go on talking. It was so nice to be held by him. He hugged me tight so I wouldn't fall, and I was aware of how small I was and how big he was, and I thought that this was the best time to ask him whatever I wanted to ask and request from him whatever I wanted because he would agree to anything, but I didn't know what to ask for. It was so nice, I thought I was melting, falling asleep; everything was soft around me and the cold wind touched my face. Yehezkel's arms held me close to him. I could hear his breathing and his heart and my heart, and I thought, I know what I want, I want Yehezkel to be my father. And I said to him, "Do you know what I can see? I see you and me going to the moon."

I was sure he would say I was just lying and be angry with me, but he put me down and looked through the telescope and said, "I see too."

Now I thought he was lying, and I said, "Let me, let me see."

He lifted me again and I looked at the moon and I said, "I can see the two of us."

* * *

The picture I most like in Yehezkel's books, which he keeps in the wardrobe next to the telescope, shows a vast underground hall with walls of huge stones like the Western Wall, the one which has people weeping at it in all the pictures, and I don't understand—if it's such a sad place, why do we have to go there?

"It's Wilson's Arch," says Yehezkel, who has to explain the picture to me again and again. "And those are the archeologists who discovered the place a hundred years ago. . . ."

I lay on the couch under grandfather's wall clock and looked at the picture. . . . I asked Yehezkel when we would go to that place, but he shook his head and said it was impossible; it was over the border.

He sat down next to me on the couch and said, "When you're older, we'll sneak in there. I have a secret way."

"You're just saying that," I flared up. "You don't want to take me because you think I'm a baby who doesn't understand anything and that I'll tell your secrets. Even my father, who couldn't care less about me and never lived at home with us, me and Mother—and it's because of him Mother's sad all the time—even he takes me to all sorts of places where you've never ever been. . . ."

Yehezkel didn't answer me. He lay next to me with his eyes closed and his face as white as the wall, and I was scared and sorry that I annoyed him, but my eyes were heavy and I closed them the way he'd closed his, and I felt we were both flying out of the window above the geraniums that Grandmother grows in empty olive oil cans, flying over the market, and over the big study house whose lights burn all day and all night, and soaring over the Italian Hospital, which is the most beautiful building I know, and we are high above the border, and that was the first time I understood what a border was because we could see our policemen and the soldiers of the Jordanian king on both sides of the rusty border fence, and everyone looks at us, and the Legionnaires aim their long rifles at us, but their commander, who has a chain of one hundred gold coins on his chest, signals them not to shoot, and they lower their rifles and fall on their knees and bow down to us, and we continue to rise higher and higher, and the world is tiny and far away beneath us, and then we stop above a small black point, and Yehezkel dives down through the air, moving it with his hands as if he is swimming, and I swim after him and in an instant we are in the huge hall, exactly as in the picture, except that the men are lying on the ground and their torches are extinguished, and the only light in the darkness is the small candle that Yehezkel holds.

"Why don't they get up?" I ask.

But Yehezkel signals me with a finger on his lips not to ask such questions and whispers quietly, "They're all dead. You remember I told you the picture was a hundred years old."

"And a person who's dead can't ever come back to life?" I ask.

"Never," Yehezkel says.

"It's not true," I say. "At Mother's funeral they said that all the dead would come back to life."

"But your mother isn't dead yet," said Yehezkel.

"Mother isn't dead? I remember that she died. I remember that I was at the cemetery and I saw them put her in the ground, I remember that everyone cried, and you cried too."

"You're wrong," Yehezkel says. "Open your eyes and you'll see your mother."

I opened my eyes, the huge hall vanished, we were on the couch in grandfather's room, and Mother stood there with a slice of bread spread with olive oil for me the way I like and snapped at Yehezkel, "What are you filling his head with rubbish for? Why don't you take him for a walk instead of lying on the couch all day and telling him stories."

After Mother shouted at Yehezkel for filling my head with rubbish, he took me for a walk. . . . He came to a stop in front of the big post office building and asked me, "Do you know who built this?"

"No," I said, even though I did know from the other times we'd been there.

And Yehezkel spread both his arms in the air as if he wanted to embrace the entire building and said, "Austin Harrison!"

"And the stones were brought from near Jericho," I said.

"How do you know?" marveled Yehezkel, the scatter-brain, the absent-minded professor. He'd already told me everything at least a thousand times. How when he was still a child and lived with my mother and Aunt Sureh, who were also small, and Grandfather and Grandmother near the place called Damascus Gate in the Old City of Jerusalem, he ran away from home and instead of going to the study house he would go and stand at the scaffolding of Rockefeller Museum. The Egyptian contractor's workers, who were constructing the building's special domes, already knew him and once even let him get up on a camel.

After they unloaded the stones from the camels, the convoy set out on the way back to Jericho and he was on one of the camels in a big sack which had previously held stones, and they came to the Mount of Olives, but the English policeman who escorted the convoy saw him and made him get down from the camel and gave him half a grush [a small coin like a penny] to buy a lollipop.

After we looked at the post office building from outside, we went inside and walked around the huge halls. It was cool and pleasant inside and you could slide on the marble floor.

Years have passed. I became a big boy, a soldier. I climbed no more with Yehezkel to the roof of my grandfather's home in Jerusalem. In fact, I didn't have to: after the Six Day War in 1967 there was no border, and I could just walk through the alleys of the Old City. There were no Jordanian soldiers on the walls— only Israelis (including me). And Yehezkel, he was joyful: again he could visit "his" Rockefeller Museum in the east part of the city.

Then, the peace talks began: there were rumors that Israel would withdraw from the Old City of Jerusalem and would give back Rockefeller Museum to King Hussein, the king of Jordan.

Grandfather and Grandmother despaired of marrying Yehezkel off and tried to at least find him a steady job. He worked a while in a bakery, then as an electrician's assistant, and a bookbinder. He helped the milkman distribute dairy products in the neighborhoods around Meah She'arim, worked a little in a carpentry, and spent several years at French polishing until he found work in the archives of one of the ministries.

He began to see stars and lightning. At first no attention was paid to it. His boss said, "This is a government archive, not a planetarium," but when he caught cold and went to the doctor for cough medicine, he casually mentioned the stars (and in the meantime, worms and flies had also begun to cruise and hover in front of his eyes); in half an hour he was in the emergency ward, and from there he was taken straight to the operating theater.

"We'll be very lucky if we manage to save the retina," the professor told me when I came to visit him. I walked along the corridor, I looked into the rooms, until one of the nurses led me to his bed. His head was turned aside, his eyes covered by a big bandage. . . .

A few days later I come to visit Yehezkel again. He sits upright at my approach, his eyes still bandaged, and says excitedly, "Did you hear what they said on television? They signed a peace agreement and they'll give everything to the Arabs! And the Arabs want everything. They want the Old City of Jerusalem and they want the Rockefeller Museum. . . ."

"No one's giving the Rockefeller Museum back to the Arabs," I say to him, but he doesn't calm down.

I speak to the professor, but he answers angrily, "Impossible!"

I go back to the ward and Yehezkel sits up in bed again and says, "Did you hear what they said on television?"

"Come, I say to the old woman [a friendly attendant], we're going for a walk."

We get Yehezkel into a wheelchair as if we're taking him to the lavatory, and at the end of the corridor we rush out, commandeering a private ambulance, straight to the Rockefeller.

The moment we get inside I put his hand on the engraved stone inscription in the lobby so he'll know it's the Rockefeller Museum, but he doesn't need it; he knows he's there.

"You see, Yehezkel," I say to him, "they didn't give Rockefeller back to the Arabs."

And we walk around with him, and he's happy, so very happy.

That Rockefeller—it's endless. We race from hall to hall, we open doors, we close doors, and he, with the bandages on his eyes, tells us what we are seeing—this is from the Gezer dig, this is from Megiddo, and this is from Ashkelon, and that skeleton there with the beads around its neck is a prehistoric man from the Carmel caves.

But the old woman and I have no strength left to look at all these old bits and pieces; we're already walked off our feet, and I say to him, "Yehezkel, we have to go back to the hospital; the professor will be worried about you." And I push the chair toward the exit, but then I don't know what comes over him—he suddenly sits up in the wheelchair and reaches out to the display case we're passing; he opens a drawer, snatches a small fragment of pottery—something like a small jug—puts it into the pocket of his robe and suddenly smiles. We haven't seen him smile for so long that only for this it would all have been worthwhile. But even so, I don't think it's proper to open the museum's cases like that, and I say to him, "Yehezkel!" in a tone meant to convey: what you did isn't very nice.

But he pretends he's fallen asleep. He lowers his head to his chest and snores, his hand holding what he took deep in the pocket of his dressing gown.

We race outside, put him in the ambulance waiting for us in the parking lot, and drive straight to the hospital. When we put him back in bed, I see that smile on his face again, and I bend down and see his eyes shining through the bandages.

He takes out of his pocket the item he palmed from the Rockefeller Museum. I swear, I've yet to see such a beautiful thing: a statuette of a woman, but broken from the waist down.

It's better so, I think, because this little lady is naked. It's enough that her breasts are exposed.

"If they give Rockefeller back to the Arabs, at least we'll have her," Yehezkel says.

YAEL MEDINI

Author Yael Medini lives in Ramat Gan, Israel. With the exception of seven years when she earned her bachelor's degree in English and her master's degree in educational psychology and taught in several Hebrew schools in New York, she has lived in Israel (Palestine prior to 1948) since she was born in 1930.

As she relates in this story based on personal experience, Medini served in the Israeli Army during the War of Independence that began in May 1948. As she began her service, she was troubled by fond memories of a time not very long before when she was friends with an Arab family, and she was uncomfortable with her new role as an enforcer of Arab dislocation.

Ironically, she was headquartered in what she believed might have been the Arab family's house before they were forced to flee their village. Despite the fact that her commander strenuously objected, Medini courageously came to the aid of a member of the Arab family even though their peoples were at war with one another and some Israelis might have viewed her acts as treasonous.

Yael Medini has had six books published in Hebrew, among them fiction for young people, and she has had several short stories published in English in anthologies and magazines.

Paradise on the Border

*M*y father said, "They meant it when they invited you to spend this Shabbat with them. But you're old enough to realize under what tension Ezra's working. I trust you to behave yourself."

My mother said, "Batya loves you and wants you to be with them. But you're old enough to understand under what tension she is too, because of Ezra and because of life in general in Benami. I trust you to help her in whatever way you can."

It was 1943 and I was thirteen. And it was wonderful to be finally alone on the bus going down from Jerusalem, free from those constant parental dos and don'ts. After an almost two-hour drive we reached the central bus station in Tel Aviv. There I boarded the bus to the inner coastal plains for a ride of about another hour.

"Rachel!"

Batya spotted me in the bus even before it came to a full stop in Benami. I quickly grabbed my suitcase and alighted straight into her outstretched arms. We embraced and kissed. How I loved her young spirit, her ready laugh, her everything.

Little Miri, her five-year-old, and a big black dog nudged their way to separate us. I kissed the little girl perfunctorily and told her I brought her a book.

"Oh," she made a face.

Her disappointment made me realize a toy or a sweet would have hit the mark better. I added, "It has beautiful pictures with many, many colors."

"Let me see!" she demanded.

"You'll see it when we get home," Batya said. "And, first, thank Rachel and introduce her to Sa'ar. He feels left out."

Miri said, "Thank you and this is Sa'ar. We told him to expect you. Just pat him on the head and he'll be happy."

During the short walk to their place Batya told me that Sa'ar, who ran ahead of us, was a recent gift made to them by one of the Arab sheiks in the area in gratitude for having his teeth fixed.

"I didn't know that you've become dentists," I said.

"What happened was that, one, the sheik had a terrible toothache; two, Ezra talked him into giving Benami's dentist a try; three, when he finally came he was too frightened to get on the dental chair; so, four, I shamed him in front of everyone. Afterwards he didn't have enough words of thanks. And Sa'ar was just the dog we've been looking for. Come here, Sa'ar. Yes, we're talking about you, pal. I won't forget about your bone."

When we got to their place, I opened the suitcase and took out Miri's present. Before we even opened it, she grabbed it and rushed to the next room. I followed her.

She was already in Ezra's arms, thumping his chest with the book. "See what Rachel brought me," she shrieked.

Ezra put her down and shook hands with me while Sa'ar circled around us. "It's good to see you," he welcomed me with his good-natured and timid smile.

"What's up?" Batya eyed him with concern.

"O'Reilly paid us a surprise visit."

"And?"

"It hopefully worked out all right."

I felt that Batya and Ezra wanted to speak by themselves, so I enticed Miri to go to our room where I told her I would read to her from the book. She was delighted and Batya gave me a glowing smile.

We sat on her little bed. While declaiming nursery rhymes about birds and animals, I cocked my ear to the other room. Batya prodded Ezra with questions which he answered with clipped sentences. Names in Hebrew and English and Arabic were mentioned along with "guns," "pistols," "bullets," and "grenades."

I knew this had to do with the tensions that my parents had hinted Ezra and Batya were living under. They did not spell it out in so many words, but I knew what it was about in general terms. Ezra was a sergeant in the British police under whose Mandate we were living. But that was only one of his three roles—the only one for which he donned a formal uniform. In his second role he was the area commander of the Haganah Jewish underground force. And in his third role he was in charge of the desired amicable relationship between the lone Jewish village of Benami and the Arab villages surrounding it. Juggling these three roles was naturally taxing. Sometimes it developed into a bitter conflict.

This business of Major O'Reilly's surprise visit, for example. . . . The British supplied the police station of Benami with arms. When necessary, Ezra would "loan" some of them to the Haganah men for their clandestine training. But when the British Major came for inspection, anything missing had to be accounted for. If his credibility with the Major was harmed, Ezra would automatically lose his prestige with the

Arabs. Also, the Haganah men would lose their source of weapons with which to train. He was walking on thin ice.

The atmosphere in the next room was palpably strained. To make matters worse, somebody suddenly came to tell Ezra there was an urgent telephone call for him at the station.

Midway our supper he came back. His face was relaxed and the look he gave Batya meant that one more fire was put out.

He washed his hands and joined us with a hearty appetite. Miri stole into his lap and he fed her like a baby.

"The apple of her Abba's eye," Batya said lovingly.

"You're in luck," Ezra said to me. "We're going to take a hike tomorrow. To Arabeh. I have to talk to Mohammad and the people there and try to settle a certain 'affair.' "

Before I had a chance to express my happiness, Batya said, "I will not go. I never want to see that Mohammad again as long as I live." She even stamped her foot for emphasis.

Ezra shushed her and explained to me, "The 'affair' has to do with a shepherd of Arabeh who let his flock graze on Benami's land a week ago. One of our farmers saw it and instead of calling me, he got on his horse to drive them away. The Arab rounded up the flock and started running back. The farmer didn't stop at the end of Benami's land but kept running into Arabeh land. He only held off when one sheep slipped and broke two legs. Now, a sheep is like a very valuable piece of property. Two days later one of Benami's chicken coops was broken into and was found ten chickens short. The footsteps of the thief led to Arabeh. So now each side wants to press charges. Pressing charges means a court case and that not only means legal expenses but a lot of bad blood—a wound which rarely heals. The best thing is for both sides to come to terms somehow peaceably. And this is why I want to go up to Arabeh and speak with Mohammad, the *Muh'tar* there, who is also an old friend."

"Not of mine anymore," Batya pronounced.

"Don't be childish, Batya," Ezra dismissed her objection. "For heaven's sake."

"Is it I who am childish?" Batya protested again and turned to me. "This *Muh'tar* of Arabeh, this chief of the village, this so-called 'old friend,' this Mohammad—do you know what he did three months ago? He upped and took a second wife because his first wife failed him. And how? She only bore him five daughters. Despicable."

"Batya—" Ezra tried to stop her, but to no avail, for she was on the warpath. "As if it's Amina's fault! As if it's a fault at all! Are girls less important than boys?"

"Not in this house, they're not!" Ezra held Miri close to his chest. "But Mohammad is free to act as he wants."

"And so am I."

"Batya, your not going there won't make him change his mind about the second wife. Besides, it's going to be such a nice outing for the girls. And it's not in your nature to be a party pooper."

"You can take the girls yourself."

Ezra's face became serious. "Listen. Mohammad will know how to interpret your absence. For everybody's sake, we most certainly don't need for this to come between us. And you're fun to be with generally and particularly on an outing. So, be reasonable, my one and only wife. This is not a request but an order."

* * *

In the morning we set out on the narrow asphalt road that went through the middle of the village. Miri and I rode on Lava, cushioned comfortably in the saddles Ezra had prepared for us. He held her by a leather rein. But this was an unnecessary precaution for the mare was old and trustworthy. Her hooves touched the ground with a sure and measured foot. Batya went on her other side holding a box of cookies she had baked for Amina. Sa'ar shot around us in circles barking as if to announce our progress.

It was a glorious Shabbat, the way a Shabbat can be towards the end of winter. The sky was deep blue, the sun warm, the small gusts of wind caressing.

At the end of the asphalt road we followed a dirt path into the forest. Now the sky and sun showed through the speckled canopy of pine trees and the air smelled of pungent resin. Batya gave Ezra her box of cookies to carry and started to hunt with Sa'ar for mushrooms and truffles. They ran a contest as to who would spot them first. They scampered hither and thither, he yapping and she giggling, and the basket was filling up nicely.

When the forest started to thin out, Batya propped her basket next to the trunk of a tree from where she would retrieve it on the way back. Ezra helped her to camouflage it with dry pine branches and needles. Sa'ar was asked to pee around it for a safe measure and he dutifully obliged.

When we eventually came out of the forest we faced a moderately high hill crested with small houses. Ezra pointed to them saying, "Up there is Arabeh."

We climbed a path that led up the hill. On each side of us

was terraced land with olive trees growing on it. Their leaves were a fresh silver, and you could just make out their tiny clusters of buds. Here and there were red spots of poppies and anemones.

"Rachel," Batya raised her face to me, "what do you smell?"

"Fresh growth and . . ."

"And?" she needled me.

"And something else—I can't quite tell."

"Sweet, smelly, stuffy?"

"I guess so."

"It's dung and baked pittas," she laughed. She was light-hearted. Her objections to the outing seemed to have been forgotten.

At that moment a barking chorus started on the hill. It was like the call Sa'ar was waiting for. Because he answered it with a loud bark and lurched forward up the hilly path and disappeared. The chorus from the top became louder, reinforced now by Sa'ar's strong baritone.

Ezra said, "Sa'ar is receiving a warm welcome from his family."

"Is this where he came from?" I asked.

"Yes," Miri said turning to me. "This is where his father and mother live. He must have missed them."

Now Sa'ar was running back down to us surrounded by a pack of dogs. The barking became a pandemonium. Lava neighed and wiggled her mane. It seemed that she wished to be recognized too. Ezra and Batya calmed the canine glee club. The dogs then did an about-face and ran before us like they were heralding royalty. As we reached the top of the hill an Arab man came towards us.

"Mohammad, *marhaba* [hello]!" Ezra greeted him.

The man returned the greeting, "*Marhab'tein Hawaja* Sergeant Ezra!"

The two men then shook hands and kissed three times and offered each other more blessings. It was then Batya's turn to greet Mohammad. But she and the Arab did not shake hands. They only greeted each other politely in Arabic and Mohammad touched his forehead in a gesture of respect. Ezra then helped Miri and me down from Lava and Mohammad patted Miri on the head. When I was introduced to him he treated me like he treated Batya. Being thirteen, I was already a young woman in his eyes.

We then followed him along paths that led between the small plain houses of the village. Whoever chanced to meet us stopped to greet Ezra and Batya. They were obviously popular. Nobody seemed to bear them any ill will because of the "affair."

We stopped by a big tent. Its flaps were raised and its floor was covered with colorful rugs. A few men were sitting on them cross-legged, smoking or sipping coffee from small cups. Batya said to me, "Now men and women separate."

She turned to Ezra and said, "Take your time. Now that I have come here, I don't want to be rushed."

Ezra said, "As long as you come back."

She said to him, "You're one of a kind, Ezra Cohen."

"And so are you." Ezra winked at her and followed Mohammad into the tent where the Arabs rose to greet him.

"Lava will stay here like the good girl that she is," Batya said as she patted the mare's neck. A little Arab boy put a heap of hay in front of her and she started to nibble.

Inside the tent the Arabs formed a circle on the floor and

Ezra and Mohammad, also cross-legged, took their places among them.

"Let's go now," Batya urged us. She was carrying the box of cookies in her arms while Miri clung to her skirt on one side and I walked on the other. Sa'ar, who walked in front, seemed to know our destination. His head held high, his panting inaudible, his steps measured, he acted the dignified leader and protector.

After passing some houses, Sa'ar stopped. And we did the same. Batya handed me the box and called out, "*Sitt Amina!*"

A curtain parted in the doorway opposite us and a gaunt woman covered in black from head to toe appeared. "*Sitt Batya!*" she said.

The two women rushed into each other's arms. They kissed and held themselves together for a long time. Tears filled their eyes and mixed together when they streamed down their cheeks. They spoke hurriedly in Arabic, their words intermingling.

Miri and I and Sa'ar stood there as if forgotten.

But not for long. For Batya and Amina dried their tears and beckoned for us to come to them. Sa'ar went first and nuzzled Amina's feet. Then Amina kissed Miri and touched her face to show how beautiful she has become and tapped her head to show how tall she has grown.

When Batya introduced me she said I was from Jerusalem.

"El Quds," Amina said and held me close to her. Her bosom was fleshless. I felt every rib there. She kissed me and I felt her parched lips.

She invited us inside. The house was one room, clean and

orderly. A stack of mattresses was piled neatly in the corner of the room, a thin rug in the middle, a few low square straw chairs on it. Two oil lamps hung on the walls, one opposite the other. There were no windows in the room. Instead, there were niches like very deep window sills. One served as storage for folded clothes and pillows and blankets. The other one held dishes, kitchen utensils, notebooks, and books.

There were three girls in the room and they all stood erect next to the wall. Batya kissed each one of them and spoke with them a little. They all knew Miri and kissed her.

Now Batya introduced me, saying that I was from El Quds and that my name was Rachel. They nodded at me and repeated my name. It sounded different in their mouths. Maybe, I thought, it sounded like that in Biblical times. Their names were Zeineb, Fatima, and Aisha. They ranged from three to seven.

Batya opened the cookie box and offered it to the girls, but not one of them budged. She offered it to Amina, but she only thanked her. So she opened it and put it on one of the low chairs.

Then she said we should take a little walk. She took Amina's hand and motioned us to follow them outside.

Sa'ar resumed his leading comportment and every once in a while turned back to see that all was in order. Batya held Miri's and my hands. Amina, who walked on my other side, took my hand in hers. Her grip was strong and her skin like sandpaper.

The two women did not stop talking. At one point, when Amina looked at me with exaggeratedly gaping eyes and pulled her ears sideways as far as she could, I realized that I kept turning my head from her to Batya, trying to understand what they were saying. She then posed a question for Batya to translate for me. "When will you start learning Arabic?" she asked.

"In two years," I said.

By and by we turned into a narrow lane between two houses and presently we were outside the village.

"It's going to be very steep here, so be extra careful," Batya warned me and took Miri in her arms.

Before I knew what was happening, I was hoisted in Amina's arms. Was she strong! It had been many years since I had been held like a baby. Amina now took the lead. She walked cautiously on the slippery rock. When it ended abruptly, she lowered me slowly until she was sure I stood firmly on my feet. Then she led me by the hand until we stood on a threshold of a ravine.

I gasped. It was covered with a carpet of cyclamens. "Batya! Look!"

Batya was now near me with Miri and Sa'ar. She said, "You once told me that the cyclamen was your favorite wild flower."

In the fields outside Jerusalem cyclamens grew in clusters in and around rocks. Here they filled the whole ravine all the way down to the cactus hedge that bordered the area. It was a sight out of this world. I never saw cyclamens in such density. Their dainty curled petals on their delicate stems bloomed in several hues of pink, from the palest marble pink to the richest purplish velvet. And each one of their lush green leaves was imprinted with the same delicate lacework in a light shade of bluish-grey.

"This is paradise," Batya said.

And Amina said, *"Il janneh,"* and I understood it to be the same word for it in Arabic.

"Can you smell the cyclamens?" Batya asked. "You have to close your eyes to do it."

We all did that. Even little Miri. Even Sa'ar. It was a moment of veneration.

"Why do they grow here with such abundance?" I asked Batya.

"It's a secret of nature," she said. "It's probably a combination of factors. The rocks, the kind of earth, the amount of rain and dew, the angle of the slope, the side it faces. Isn't Arabeh lucky to have this paradise!"

I crouched on my knees to caress the cyclamens. Amina crouched next to me. She took off her black kerchief and spread it on the rock. One by one she picked cyclamens and laid them in the middle of the kerchief. When she was satisfied with the heap they made, she united its two pairs of opposite corners in knots, one on top of the other, making the bundle secure and airy at the same time.

"For you," she said in Arabic as she handed it to me, and I did not need any translation to understand her.

I asked Batya, "What's behind the cactus hedge?"

"A not-too-steep drop down to the wadi. If you listen carefully you can hear the water running there."

"It comes from the hills?" I pointed to the range of hills opposite us.

"No, it comes all the way from the far-far mountains. Do you see them? Those brown-grey mountains all the way to the east."

"Which mountains are they?"

"The mountains of Samaria. And now it's time to go. We shouldn't keep Ezra waiting."

"Time to leave paradise," I said, "like Adam and Eve."

Once back in the village, when Sa'ar discovered we were following a different route, he did not take the lead anymore. He walked meekly by Batya and Amina who resumed their intense talking. I took Miri by the hand behind them and tried to engage her in conversation. Somewhere along the way Amina nudged Batya and nodded sideways. I turned to that direction too.

It was just another small house. But at that very moment the curtain parted in its doorway and a plump young woman appeared on its threshold. She was made up like a harlequin. Her eyes were outlined with blue and black mascara, her cheeks were covered with rouge, and her thick lips were fiery red. Her yellow kerchief was bordered with coins. Bead necklaces hung down her ample bosom and her dress was shiny green satin. One foot of hers, shod in a sandal bedecked with tinsel, was already outside the house. But then her eyes met Amina's. Met? It was a collision between innocent gullibility and two sharp daggers. Instantaneously the young woman cowered and disappeared behind the curtain.

It barely took two seconds.

Amina and Batya looked at each other knowingly. Then they started to walk again. They were quiet. They had their arms around each other's shoulders.

The long outing tired Miri and she fell asleep after five nursery rhymes. I closed the book quietly and listened. Batya and

Ezra were speaking quietly in the kitchen. I joined them. The earthy smell of mushroom omelettes still hung in the air.

"Not sleepy yet?" Ezra asked with his timid smile. "Would you like a cup of cocoa?"

He was relaxed. Already on the way home he told us that the conversation he held with the elders of Arabeh was successful. An agreement had been reached. The ten chickens would be returned and the payment to the vet for setting the legs of the sheep would be shared by both villages. To celebrate the agreement a "sulcha"—a big feast with a roasted lamb—would be held to which everybody would be invited.

"I keep thinking of Amina and the new wife," I said. "The look they gave each other—I shall never forget it all my life."

Batya said, "No woman could ever forget that."

"It reminded me of the stories in the Bible about Abraham and Sarah and Hagar, about Jacob and Leah and Rachel."

"Aren't we lucky to have come a long way from that," Batya mused. "Amina's a wonderful woman, so wise and intelligent and diligent. She lost her beauty and looks because of her hard life. And look at the way she insisted that her two older daughters, Mariam and Hannan should go to school and achieve what was denied her. She told me how Mohammad reacted:

"All right, let them go to school. But who will do their share of the work?"

"So she took that upon herself also. As if she doesn't do enough. But even if she weren't this exceptional human being, to demote her like that because she didn't bear a son. It's so cruel."

"How is she taking it?" Ezra asked.

"Amina's way. With a stiff upper lip. But her heart is bleeding."

"Where is the new wife from?"

"From Nablus. From a wealthy family. The matchmakers said that all her sisters had only boys. Your friend Mohammad paid a pretty penny for her. She looks like a human peacock."

"You saw her?"

"For one second. She looks stupid to boot."

"What's her name?"

"I didn't care to ask." Batya was getting excited. "I hope she bears Mohammad a son who will grow up to be as callous as he is."

"Did you ever consider, sweetheart, the shame Mohammad is bearing for fathering only girls?"

"I won't stoop to such considerations. The callous, stupid, primitive man."

"It's their culture."

"It's a crappy culture."

"Batya—"

Ezra was angry. He could not brook vulgar language. But by the same token, he would not allow himself to rebuke his wife in my presence.

Quiet tension weighed down the kitchen. The only noise came from Miri's calm breathing in the next room.

"The cocoa's delicious, Ezra," I said, "as usual."

"You know you can always count on me to make a perfect cup of cocoa."

"People count on you for more than that."

"Oh Rachel, you made Ezra blush," Batya said.

The tension broke.

"You succeeded in reaching this agreement today," I said.

"Yes," he said with modesty. "With a bit of wisdom and patience, Jews and Arabs can live peacefully together."

But it was not to be.

Five years later, on May 14, 1948, the British Mandate expired and its army and police forces pulled out of the country. Simultaneously the Jewish State of Israel was proclaimed. Within a few hours the armies of the neighboring Arab countries invaded it. Our War of Independence had broken out.

I was eighteen then and was serving in the army, of course. Toward the end of my basic training I bumped into Commander Michael. He was five years older than I and we knew each other from school. He told me his unit was ordered to man a stronghold on the border and lay mines around it. He was in the process of recruiting four girls to handle the kitchen for the boys. He was looking for sturdy characters and hard workers. He had already found three. I volunteered to be the fourth and he accepted me.

A fortnight later we were on the truck that took us to our post. I heard the boys saying that we would be stationed in Arabeh. I made sure I heard the name right. Yes, I did.

I said, "But this is an Arab village."

"No more. It's ours now. And it's empty. The Arabs have fled."

"Where to?" I asked.

"Across the nearest border, I'd assume," the boy next to me said. "Eastward. To the hills."

The road was familiar to me. When we passed through Benami the children of the village waved to us. They were proud of their soldiers. When the asphalt road ended, the truck could not go through the forest, but skirted it until it stopped at the foot of the hill of Arabeh. We unloaded our belongings, ammunition and kitchenware and carried it all up the path.

It was the same season as five years before, the end of winter. The olive trees on either side of the path were in their early bloom, but the earth around them was not tended. Poppies and anemones dotted the fresh grass, but whole sections of the terraces were broken. The air was sweet, but no smell of dung or baked pittas permeated it. No canine chorus welcomed us. And no Muh'tar appeared to greet us.

Our kitchen unit of four girls was allotted one of the one-room houses. Was it Amina's? I could not remember very well but it looked like it. A broken oil lamp lay on the floor along with some clothes, blankets, a torn pillow, a notebook, and crayons. The place, obviously, had been left in a hurry.

I heard about the evacuation of Arab towns and villages during the war, but this was the first time I came face to face with it and I felt uneasy. This feeling was shared by my three friends. We collected all the odds and ends, wrapped them in a blanket, and put it aside. Someone found a stickless broom outside and swept the floor.

Commander Michael came by to see how we were settling down and brought us a gas lamp. Tomorrow, he told us, a tanker of water will hopefully make it up the hill, but we should forget about using the precious water for washing the floor. We should now make haste to the makeshift kitchen. The boys were starving.

After supper we all congregated in the one-room house—very much like ours—which Michael had turned into his headquarters. His table was a plank of wood on two saw-horses and on it he had a field telephone, a pair of binoculars, a pad of paper, some folders, and writing utensils. He stuck a map on the wall and pointed to where we and the other strongholds of the area were, tracing his finger along the wadi down the hill that was the border.

After that the four of us straggled dead tired back to our room and rolled out our sleeping bags. There was not the usual laughter and gossip. It was as if we did not want to disturb someone. *À la guerre comme à la guerre.* War is war. This phrase, repeated ad nauseam ever since the beginning of the war, went through my mind. I rebelled against it, but I had no solution for this predicament.

Next day I told my girlfriends about my chance acquaintance with Arabeh and that I wanted to show them something special.

My feet guided me to the narrow path between the houses and then up to the slippery rock. When I cautioned my friends to be careful, I echoed Batya's words.

The ravine was indeed a carpet of cyclamens. Everyone was stunned into silence. Then they broke it with exclamations. I told them it was called "Paradise." The name was unanimously adopted. We picked bunches of cyclamens for our room and to surprise the boys.

But that night, when I hit my sleeping bag, I found it hard to sleep because of a fleeting scene I thought I saw while in Paradise. It was a piece of printed cloth that darted behind the trunks of the cacti of the hedge. Why didn't I say anything about it before? I didn't know. I closed my eyes and concentrated. Did I see it? Did I imagine it?

The next day while we were washing up after breakfast, I excused myself and I ran to Paradise. I went all the way down to the hedge and looked around but saw nothing. I went back to our room. An hour later I went there again. This time I went down another path. I tiptoed along the hedge and scrutinized the area behind the cacti. Nothing. I started to climb up. Abruptly, I turned my head. The printed piece of cloth darted behind the trunks of the cacti. I was sure of it. It even grew a pair of spindly legs.

Is this dangerous? I wondered. Should I cry out? No. This could not be a grown man. This could only be a child.

I returned to the hedge and asked softly, "Is there somebody there?"

No answer.

I repeated the question in Arabic.

After a moment of silence there was a kind of whisper.

"Who is it?" I asked.

"Only me," came a whisper. "Please, *Sitt* soldier, don't tell anyone."

Is this child a Trojan horse?

"Please, *Sitt* soldier, don't tell anyone," the whisper repeated.

"What do you want?" I whispered.

"Nothing. Just to look. You're good. God will show you mercy."

"Look at what?"

"At the village."

"Please don't hide from me. Let me see you. Come out

from behind the cacti. Nothing bad will happen to you, I promise."

A girl of about eight appeared from behind the thorny leaves. She was thin, shabbily dressed, and had bright black eyes.

"Did you live here?"

"Yes, by Allah."

"Do you know Mohammad and Amina?"

"I'm their daughter."

I forgot all the daughters' names except the one that resembled its Hebrew parallel. "Are you Mariam?"

"No. Mariam is my oldest sister. I'm Zeineb. The youngest."

"And I'm Rachel. I was here five years ago. I came with Ezra and Batya and Miri to visit you. Do you remember them?"

"Of course I remember the good people. May God protect them. But I don't remember you. Please pardon me, *Sitt* Rachel."

"It doesn't matter. Do you know that those good people don't live in Benami anymore?"

"Yes. They came to tell us. A year ago. They moved to El Quds. Sergeant Ezra was going to become a bigger officer."

"He did."

"My *Ummi* and all my sisters cried when they came to say goodbye. Even my *Baba* had tears in his eyes."

"How is your *Baba?*"

"Crying all the time now."

"And your *Umm?*"

"She says she would cry if she had the time. She's working harder than ever now."

"And the other wife?"

"She died."

"What happened?"

"She was big with child. When we had to run away from the village, she slipped. She was badly hurt. Two days later she died. And the baby also died. It was a boy."

"Did she have other children before?"

"A boy. Hassan. My brother is four years old now."

"Your brother?"

"We have the same *Baba*."

"Tell me, Zeineb, how was it between your *Ummi* and the other wife?"

"At first they hated and then they loved. Especially after *Baba* wanted to take another wife."

"Why did he want to do that?"

"Because after Suhah had Hassan she was very ill and weak. *Ummi* started to take care of Hassan the moment he was born. And we all helped her. He is our prince. *Ummi* loves him like her own son."

"I remember your *Ummi* Amina. You look like her."

"People say that."

"Maybe she remembers me."

"She does. I'm sure, by Allah. *Ummi* never forgets anything."

"Where do you live now?"

"Behind those hills. It's bad. It's not home. People ask what's to become of us."

"I hope something good will be done for you and very soon."

"I hope so too, *Sitt* Rachel, by Allah."

"And you come here often?"

"Every day if nobody is looking. I want to see our Paradise, our house. Even from afar. What do you do up there in our village?"

"Nothing. Just staying there. Guarding . . ."

"Do you guard the village for us?"

"For all of us," I stammered.

Then the reason for which we were stationed up in Arabeh hit me and I said, "Listen, Zeineb, you should not come here."

"Why?"

"It's dangerous. They are beginning to lay mines all over the fields. Do you know what mines are? They're hidden and they explode if you step on them and they can kill . . . And there are soldiers with guns. Shooting."

"I'm not afraid."

"You should be, Zeineb. This is a border here. You shouldn't roam around here anymore. Promise me you won't."

"I won't promise, *Sitt* Rachel. I'll come again and again— every day if I only can."

"Don't do that, dear girl. You don't understand. You could get killed."

"No, I won't get killed. As long as I live I'll never die."

"Listen, I want to send your *Umm* some cyclamens," I said. "But how shall I do it?"

"I know how."

In a moment there was a swoosh in the air and Zeineb's kerchief landed not far from me. She had cleverly tied a stone to one of its corners to give it weight. I spread it on the ground and filled it with cyclamens. When I was done I tied its two pairs of opposite corners in knots, one on top of the other, making the bundle secure and airy at the same time— the way Amina did for me five years before—and then I threw the bundle over the hedge.

"*Shukran, thank you, Sitt Rachel. Ummi* will be so happy to receive the cyclamens from our Paradise. I'll go now and come tomorrow."

"No, dear girl, this is serious. I'll also come here tomorrow with my commander. He'll catch you."

"No he won't. I can hide from all the commanders of the world."

"*Ma'sala'ameh.*"

Then I heard her patter of feet going down the slope.

I climbed up the path and went straight to headquarters. I simply walked in with, "Michael, I must talk to you at once."

He was taken aback. He motioned to the officers and soldiers who were with him to clear out.

"Why, Rachel, what's the matter?"

I saw apprehension in his eyes. He was the ultimate authority in this God-forsaken place, and a grave responsibility weighed on his shoulders. He needed a girl in hysterics on his hands like he needed a hole in the head.

"Sit down. We'll have coffee in a minute. Here, have a sweet in the meantime. Do you want a day off?" His patience was as thin and transparent as cellophane.

I forced myself to tell him the story in a restrained tone of voice.

His first reaction was to raise his voice at me. "You shouldn't have done it. It's against regulations."

"What was against regulations? Trying to see who was there on the other side of the hedge?"

"You should have called one of the boys, preferably one of the officers."

"Would that little girl stand there and wait for them?"

He was stumped. He got up and paced the floor. "What have you got us into—" He threw his arms in the air.

"You know I meant no harm."

"Am I a commander of a stronghold or am I running a summer camp for Arab children? I cannot stop the war."

"There must be a way to get to the parents of this girl on the other side, to keep her from running about. There's the U.N. . . . those committees . . ."

"Finding those parents is like finding a pin in a haystack. There are swarms of Arab refugees behind those hills."

"Call somebody. Call headquarters."

"What is this Arab girl to you anyway?" he blurted out and then immediately added, "Sorry."

Sorry? I knew what he was thinking: God damn you Rachel and your Arab girl. He picked up the receiver from the field telephone. He turned the handle several times, repeating, "This is A-947," like a mantra, and then he hung up. "No use." He looked at his watch with exasperation. "It will be another hour before they hook us in."

I realized that I must get to somebody above him. I must, must, must! I said, "O.K. Don't forget to call in another hour. Now I have another favor to ask."

"What now?"

"I was supposed to go to the movie tomorrow, but I'd like to go tonight."

"To get things off your mind?" he asked, turning sympathetic.

"Exactly."

"Can the girls do without you?"

"I'll take care of it."

"Then there's no problem." He consulted his watch again. "You have to hurry. The truck is supposed to push off in fifteen minutes."

We finally stopped in Benami in front of the storeroom turned into a movie house. I was the first to jump down saying I needed to take care of something before the movie. I decided not to go to the village central office or to the police station. Using the phones there excluded the possibility of a private conversation. The only other phone in the village was the Dorfmanns', the doctor and his wife who settled in Benami after they fled from Hitler's Germany.

I knocked at their door and Dr. Dorfmann answered it. I remembered his stern face, but he could not, of course, identify me from my short visits to the village.

I said, "Pardon me, Dr. Dorfmann, but can I please use the phone?"

He looked me up and down. Was it my uniform? My polite speech? The fact that his angelic wife came and stood by him. Solemnly, without a word, he showed me inside to where the phone was in the corridor. "It's long distance," I then said.

"Make it as short as possible," he ordered. "My phone has to be accessible, especially at times like these."

I dialed the operator and put in my call. Then I had to wait. Frau Doktor Dorfmann brought me a glass of lemonade and a few cookies. I gulped everything down and only then realized I should have resisted the cookies. Food was rationed and soldiers ate better than civilians.

When the phone rang I jumped. But Dr. Dorfmann beat me to it. He said, "Dr. Dorfmann," and listened for a moment before he handed me the receiver.

"Who is calling?" It was Miri's voice.

"Miri, it's Rachel. I have to talk to your Abba. It's urgent."

I heard her cry out, "Abba, it's Rachel and she says it's urgent!"

Next I heard Ezra. "Rachel, shalom. What is it?"

"Ezra," I said, bursting into tears.

"Rachel, where are you?"

"Ezra," I tried again, but I could not get through my tears.

I heard Ezra say, "Batya, come quickly. Something happened to our Rachel."

"Rachel, listen," Batya said. "Swallow your tears and breathe deeply. Do it again. Do you hear me?"

"Yes," I mumbled.

"Do as I tell you. You're not a small girl, but a soldier. So obey my orders. Your parents told us you look smashing in your uniform. But you know as I know that the main thing is to feel strong inside. And you also know that Ezra and I would do anything in the world for the people we love. Now your tears must have dried and you can tell me what's the trouble. Tell it all and at once. One-two-three—Go!"

When I hung up I melted into tears again.

Dr. Dorfmann said, "Next time, if you want to speak with the family of Sergeant Cohen, just say so."

I wanted to say that I hoped there would not be any next time, but it was as if my strength to shore up my tears was all but spent.

"We're happy and honored to make your acquaintance, Private Rachel," Frau Doktor Dorfmann said as she took me by the hand to sit me down in an easy chair. Then she held my face in her soft hands and looked at me with her gentle blue eyes.

"Oh, these terrible wars," she said softly. "What they're doing to people."

SHAMMAI GOLAN

Born in Poland, where he experienced the Nazi occupation, well-known Israeli writer Shammai Golan emigrated to Israel when he was twelve years old. He lived there on a kibbutz and later attended Hebrew University.

The author of both adult and children's books, Golan has received many literary prizes, including the Agnon Prize and the Prime Minister's Prize for Literature. Currently he is serving as Counsellor of Cultural Affairs for the Embassy of Israel in Moscow.

"One of the places that an Israeli young man becomes acquainted with the Arab-Israeli conflict is, to our grief, in the Army," says Golan. In this very graphic and powerful account written just after his release from the Israeli Army, Shammai Golan describes his horrifying and painful encounter with death.

Ten Centimeters of Dust
Translated from Hebrew by Richard Flantz

*T*he rock's cold. Maybe because of my forehead leaning on it. The rock's probably white and gleaming like the stones of the path at Tel Hai. On the way to the Roaring Lion. The walls of the school on the Weiss land across the Yarkon [River] are also white. Uri wrote Nahum and Rina on the wall with black chalk. And it wasn't true. I wiped if off with the sleeve of my shirt. And the wall remained white. Now Uri's sleeping. If not for this hairy stalk sticking into my mouth, I'd move my neck and call to Uri. I'd peep upwards too. Where are all the clouds sailing now with the beginning of autumn. It's important to know. Maybe I'll lie like this a day. Two days. Maybe until the Messiah comes. If he comes. I'll be dead by then. I'd like to know death when it comes. This damned stalk. If I could pull it out. But my hand's holding on to my ribs and lungs. And to the escaping blood. Dripping warm and sticky through my fingers. Which had held the Uzi. The Uzi's a good weapon. Effective. For defense. For attack. In face-to-face fighting. But today's Friday. And there's peace at the borders. And I'm only on watch over their road. They fired. Suddenly. Why'd they fire, suddenly? In war one fires. People get wounded. Killed. Nimrod told us. In the War of Independence. Father listens and plucks his beard while Nimrod tells. He always plucks his beard when Nimrod tells about the war. Father says, It's good they didn't fire at you, son. That what he says, it's good they didn't fire at you, son. And plucks his beard. Since Nimrod came back from the war Father has grown a beard and goes to synagogue on Saturdays. Now they're partners in the business. Textiles. Materials, in Nahalat Binyamin Street. You'll be a partner too, Nimrod promised me. Soon as you finish the army. You'll finish before you know it. Today it's not like in my days. Today it's a chocolate army, with after-duty leaves. Only mother has a red hand. When she prepares the fish for Shabbat. She still keeps the bladder for me. Doesn't believe I'm a soldier already. And today, Mother, what will you do with the bladder today. Maybe you'll give it to Nikki the cat. And

126

Nikki will play with it. Just like that. With her claws. And the air will seep out slowly like from a hidden hole in a balloon. My lungs are perfectly in order. I'm breathing. With difficulty though. That's because of the blood. I'm all wet. Maybe it suddenly rained. Sometimes it rains in September. Even before Yom Kippur. And I'm already damp. And flowing. All is flowing. And all is vanity. And you can never enter the same river twice. The Philosopher teacher. A great sage. A philosopher. I entered the Yarkon lots of times. At "Seven Mills." White froth on the stones. Only the water's yellow. Like the bilharzia [intestinal parasite, often water-borne]. The eucalyptus over the water are green. And the leaves fall over my body. Soft. Purple. Like the water under my belly. Soft. Warm. How long can one flow like this. An hour. Two. Three. Until the clothes rot. And the rock's suddenly black like the sky on the back of my neck. I know it isn't night yet. How long does it take for the air to leave the body. And the blood. Uri knows. Uri. What's more important for the body: blood or air, Uri asked the nature-study teacher. He's sharp, is Uri. The teacher—she laughs when Uri asks. She always laughs when Uri asks. Her body laughs too. Her breasts. Her legs. Only I can't laugh any more. Not on these rocks. Not on this moist earth which was so dry until they opened fire. Suddenly. And this stalk aimed at my mouth. In the end it'll succeed. And that'll be the end. If Uri'd just move my head a little I'd forgive him for Nahum and Rina on the wall. But Uri doesn't answer. U-ri. Maybe I didn't call out loud. Uri has to hear. An old school friend has to hear.

You suggested I come out on this watch. To substitute for Lees. Lees' wife's about to give birth. And Uri's the squad commander. He could have given an order. She could give birth any day. Any hour. Any minute. And on Friday there'll be no one to take her to the hospital. She'll bear a boy, Lees promised. A big boy with spiked shoes on his feet. Lees laughed. Lees is a bastard. He knows I love running in spikes. Go, go to your son Lees. Run quickly before I change my mind. Just make sure he goes to high school near the Yarkon. Arthur's the trainer there. As long as he doesn't drink the water in the Yarkon. That yellow bilharzia. Streaming quietly from my body. It's good that Leonora's far away. And can't see me here. Like this. Wet. All the same, I'd go to her. If I could. It's still early. I feel the heat on my back. Or is it a wound from a metal splinter. I could make it there before her parents got back from the city. She's still at school. They finish early on Friday. Uri would have written Nahum and Leo . . . it's a long name. She promised to change it. In Israel one doesn't need a long name. One syllable. Two. Nilli. Or Nikki. Or Leah . . . or Lenni . . . or L . . . Lll . . . I'll whisper by the door. To go up three steps, that's a lot. And on top of that, to press the doorbell twice. Le-o-no-no . . . no . . . this damned stalk. An oat stalk, for sure. A wild oat. With antennae like spiders' legs. She'll open the door. Like on my last Shabbat leave. She was wearing a floral house robe.

The birthday flowers of an eighteen-year-old girl. Flowers of all colors. Red and pink and purple and orange. Every flower between two stalks. Not oat stalks. Not oat stalks. I wanted to know the flowers. Her body was white beyond the flowers. You're awfully hairy, she said. Her fingers were gentle. I laughed into the recess of her neck. Now I can't laugh anymore. The pain in my chest. But you can also laugh in your heart. But laughing in your heart is like crying. And when you cry the wounds hurt. I know. When your whole body's a wound. Nimrod said: if at all, then let it be a small wound. Like in a blood count. After that you can lie in a white room. White nurses. Leo's flowers were colored and I didn't get to know them. They were many. Her parents came home too early from the Nitmans'. They threw the cards on the table and said, Nitman doesn't feel well. Nitman's a bastard. Not feeling well on a Friday. Nitman and this stalk. Nitman and Stalkman. Nittalk and Stalk. Just let me get out of here and I'll go and see Nitman. Let him know what I think of him. To get out of here. And she'll change her name to Ll . . . That's a nice name. Ll. Like *Layla*, night. *Lachem* [to you], reads the Bible teacher. To the glory of Bible reading. His tongue rolling in his mouth, red and round, *lachem.* The chemistry teacher in her white coat. With her chemical face. Running tests in the classroom. Don't breathe. Open the windows. Chlorine is a sharp substance. It burns the eyes. The chest. The ribs.

At first it almost didn't hurt. As if a stone had hit me. Uri's a great clown. He's thrown a stone at me again. So I won't fall asleep. He's sure I want to sleep. Who did you sleep with. Uri cares. All week long you want to sleep. Uri's a squad commander. He knows everything. Anyone gets laid on a Saturday wants to sleep all week long. But you're on watch, yells Uri. You've got to note down the movements of all vehicles on their road. Now tell me who you slept with. Give me her name. So he can write it on the rock. Inscribe it for a lasting memorial. I didn't lay her, Uri. I had to tell him the truth. I've never done it, Uri. Maybe you haven't either. Now he's fallen asleep. Or fainted. Suddenly. Suddenly there was a noise here. Then huge flies came. Transparent ones. Buzzing around my ear. Bzzz. And it was already too late. I didn't even open her robe, Uri. Upon my life, I didn't. I just saw her white body through the buttons. I tried to open one button. She refused. I said, We're from the same school. Yes, she said the same *gymnasia*. She says *gymnasia* funny, like her mother. With an *s*, not a *z*. Ss, not zz. The two sounds I can still pronounce. And Ll. You're sleeping, Uri. I'd wake you if I could. I'd tell you everything. Maybe he really is tired. He brought the mortar alone. And I brought the machine-gun. Alone he carried the mortar and the shell cases. Six in each case. Two in each row. With two he'll cover his legs and with two he'll fly with two. Done. I don't have to remember everything. I'm already a soldier. And Uri's the squad commander. Fire. I yelled when they suddenly started. And Uri didn't have time to fire. Pity. The flight of a mortar shell is beautiful. I'm seeing beautiful things today. Like a black swift. Hits from two-inch mortars aren't precise, Uri explained. The base is too light. Unstable. Uri spoke like an important person before he fell asleep. Falling asleep in the middle of the day. Maybe he fell asleep before they started shooting. Maybe because of the heat of the dry earth. I can't. I can feel how it sucks every drop out of me. I'm drying up. And resting. In the middle of their day of rest I'm resting. My rest ought to be tomorrow. Nevertheless I'd get up and go. At least I'd get up to see who started this *fantasia*. The shots came from there, from across the road. As if they'd paused from smelling the aroma of the baking *pittas* [pita bread] and the burning dung, and just fired at us. Now only the flies remain. I can hear them. Bzzss. They stop. Fall silent. Now they're sucking my blood. Like the earth from below.

Making the desert flower. The teacher Zussman: We too are pioneers. All the lessons I'm learning today. I must wake Uri. Get up, Uri. Explain. He'll explain everything. He knows. Even questions in geom . . . another hard word. Like L . . . L . . . eo . . . no . . . ra . . . ra. Ra. Ra. I want to run away from here and go to my L . . . When she sat down to show me her *gym-na-sia* album I saw her body. Silky and white. She promised me that today. But today Lees' wife will give birth. And I'm lost. This stalk knows I'm lost. Not like Nimrod. When he was wounded he thought of his mother, he told us. Of the homeland. Of Mother Homeland. Nimrod laughed when he told us. I need my mother now. She could help. Mother. But all I have left is a strip of earth under my eyes. Maybe ten centimeters long. Five wide. And this hairy stalk. Growing into my mouth. It's God, God the Omnipotent. And I'm giving Him drink. I can't help it. It goes of its own accord. Maybe Father could help me. But today's Friday [Sabbath eve]. And Father keeps God's commandments. He even warned me against punishment from heaven. *If* I could only look at the sky. It's surely like looking into the opening of L-eo's robe. Today, she wrote. The Nitmans promised to be well. Lees' wife has already given birth. But the opening of the sky is closed with ten centimeters of earth. And Uri's sleeping. He could have told me about his girl friends. With his laughing eyes, he would have told me. There's all kinds of kinds, there's even real blondes. Uri knows. I have to know too. Before it's too late. Just as soon as I get out of here. Even if I have to crawl, I'll get to her. Down this hillslope I'll roll down to the road. True, the road belongs to them but their Sabbath day is over. They won't start another *fantasia*. And so I'll get there, the short way. And from there along the path through the *wadi* [river bed] to our road. I have to make it before the Sabbath begins. Father's already closed the shop. He's angry. What do you care how I come, Father. I'm going to Le-ana. The Sabbath's just beginning to descend. On the vale of Genassereth. That's what the songs say. Not on the ruins of Bir. To flee from here. Three steps. And a bell. Let Lees come back. Or send his son. I'm ready. First we'll check the legs. The toes. They're resting. At absolute rest. I can't move them. Uri. Uri. He must help me. The stalk has succeeded. It's penetrated deeper. Salting my tongue. The neck too, I can't move it. My fingers can flutter. And my legs are two rods. I'm going to Le . . . o . . . I'm tired. But I must get across the road. Uri tell me how will you write Nahum and Leo . . . Only tell me how to get there. When my legs won't move. Mother on the other side shouting Stop, Nahumke. She's in the doorway of the little shop, bright inside the darkness. Stop Nahumke she calls to me and vanishes among the cars and again floats up between the wheels of the trucks like a large lifebelt. That one can rest on. Even in the middle of the road. I only have to get there. With Uri I'd be there in a flash. Even with paralyzed legs. Uri knows how. He's been through squad commanders' course. Here. Among the rocks. At Bir. At squad commanders' course you learn everything. I'm a little general, Uri said, the Brigade Commander said that we're little generals. So tell me Uri how to walk when the blood keeps on flowing out of me. Of course. There's a material that stops the blood. A special kind of material. The Nature-Study teacher told us. She knew. All the teachers are teaching today. All my teachers from all my times. A long school day. And in the evening Le's parents are going out. To play cards. Rummy. On Saturday nights they play poker.

Pok. The name of the material that stops the blood is . . .
I've forgotten today. Maybe I can take my test tomorrow.
Tomorrow will be too late. The Sabbath is descending. It's
late. Make an effort, Nahum. Uri. Now he's mad at me. I'll
tell you her name. I'll wake you with her long name. And
we'll go and answer all the questions the teachers ask in
class. Le-o-no-ra. And now, aloud, Nahum: Le-o . . . I'm lost.
Everything's lost. I didn't hear my voice. But I'm breathing.
The soul can't run out just like that. I'd see it go. Even if it's
white. Like the vapor rising from the Yarkon in the morning.
How do they know that a man's dead, Mother? They put a
feather beside his nose and look. If the feather moves, it
means he's alive. But when does he die, Mother? Mother
didn't tell me about the hairy stalk beside the nose. And it's
already inside me. This damned stalk. I must move my head.
Arthur, the trainer, is looking at you. Raise your head.
Higher. Higher. I'm not a pupil anymore, Arthur. I'm a soldier. And today I have a leave coming. Lees will be back
early. And on Friday school comes out early and Le will be
home. Her parents are going out to pok. To pok. Head up,
Nahum. But where are the spikes you brought me. To
Nahum, the outstanding sprinter, you wrote on the ap-
pended card. And the way home is long, long. You're a soldier, Nahum. A man. You can manage on your own. Like
Nimrod in the War of Independence. Your brother was a
hero, in the Palmach, says Father. Today he's partners with
Father. Delivering cloth in a van. Independent. He collects
money and buys ice cream for his kids. Maybe he'll come
here too. In his van. He knows how to dress a wound. He did
it often, he often told us, and laughed. You seal a wound
with spiderwebs and soft bread. Nimrod told us, laughing.

Spiderwebs and bread. I see the spiderwebs beside me. The spider advances slowly. Weaving the net. At night it will suddenly cover everything. Uri. Uri. He doesn't answer. I didn't hear my voice. Didn't hear a sound. You have a nice voice. Le said, it's very masculine. Like your hairy, muscular chest. If father were here he could turn me onto my back. I'd look at the sky like him. Perhaps I'd see God Who comes with the Sabbath. From the vale of Genassereth. But Father isn't here. Only I am here. And the hillock of dust. And this stalk. I could swear that there's exactly ten centimeters of dust here. I'd measure it with a ruler. To prove it. That's important. To be sure of one thing. It's important. To know. How the sky closes in ten centimeters of dust. To know.

BASIM ABDORAAD (PSEUD.)

A teacher, Basim Abdoraad lives near Jerusalem with his partner. Other members of his immediate family are spread out all over the world: Jordan, Lebanon, the United States, and Canada.

In this lyrical story beginning with a metaphor of a contorted fig tree, Abdoraad shows how his growth has been affected, his possibilities denied, by the seizure of his family's house and land.

"Palestinians are still under Israeli control," he says, "militarily and economically, and are denied self-determination and development. Real peace can be achieved only when the basic causes of the injustice and unrest are addressed and when double standards are no longer applied to the issues. For a beginning, Palestinians who wish to return should be allowed to do so, and confiscated properties should be returned to their owners."

Tracings

*T*he fig tree outside my door: it is a temperamental old thing, knobby and contorted, stumped in many branches. It does not seem happy—drops much of its crop and only incidentally makes an effort to ripen any. But how honey-sweet is what it holds when it wants to, the largest and most delectable of figs. I wait for its offering to come. It is October now, and the huge fruits if not picked begin to split, showing late-ness and dissatisfaction.

It has been a long time since I tasted the fruits of Pales-tine—years of unwanted absence in childhood, youth, and adulthood without rest in place after place, luckier than oth-ers in moving more and not tasting one painful exile more than another. So I take the task of reaching the ripe figs seri-ously. I climb up through the twisted branches, balancing as an agile child on the thinnest limbs, to reach the farthest point possible in search of a single pear-shaped fig.

As I peel the fig and taste its seedy sweetness, I get a better view of the hills surrounding Ramallah and down to the west the haze of the coast of the Mediterranean. Beyond the cypresses the hills are dotted with olive trees, and the ones on the terraced hills draw my attention. At a distance it is difficult to see a difference between the natural step ter-races made by geological formations and the terrace-like steps created by our farmers as retainers for silt and water on the slopes. On the human-created terraces the stones laid side by side in solid haphazardness make the walls distinct from the rock formations. Still they blend, unimposing, un-controlling.

Those terraced hills connect me to the distant past, to my ancestors, to the thousands of years when the Canaanites tilled this land and long before, to the mild and benign ef-forts to create more cultivable habitation, inspired by the nat-ural rock embankments. And the olive trees on the terraces are my connection to myself and my beginning. (O terraces, terraces, how maligned are ye. Our farmers have raised ye stone by stone, labored years and years, so that others without effort except myth-making, can claim turning the barren hills into gardens.)

This is olive-picking time. The olives are far off, but I feel them in me, around my skin, in my bone, all over. I look to the south, toward Jerusalem. That is where I began: my mother rubbing the thick, dark-green oil of the olives into every pore, smoothing the wholeness of the land into my being, straightening my legs as she moves down them, massaging them to make sure, as they say, that the child will walk straight. My mother.

Memory's work is strange. It remembers and forgets. There is what it can't forget even when thought too young to remember. I have a picture in my mind, as clear as yesterday and today, of a time when I must have been less than three and living in our house in the Baka'a area of what is now called West Jerusalem. I see the museum-furniture my father built with his hands, the beautiful carved tables, the grass outside, the onion-skin-colored eggs I searched for in the grass on an Easter day, the shade of an olive tree in the garden. (How untortured was that shade.)

Down the street, into a field, the grass is much taller—too tall to believe now. Then down farther with my brother and sister I see the railroad track, but no trains—only a donkey caught by a train, down on its side, crucified, unmoving.

And then a change which I remember, but after which I remember little: the spent cartridges in the streets that we went out to collect, sitting on my mother's lap in a bus with the windows protected by metal grills, hectic activity, my parents storing heavy valuables futilely, my father grabbing his handcrafted cane and one picture album, and a truck loaded with strangers. And then I remember almost nothing.

* * *

April 10, 1948: this is history. The British government was still in charge with its mandate. (What was thy mandate, O great Britain?) The leaders of Palestine were not willing to accept a compromising partition plan when the Palestinians were an overwhelming majority, and their visitors, European Jews with a design, were intent on more.

April 10, 1948: the massacre committed at the village of Deir Yasin, not too far from our Baka'a in Jerusalem. Men, women, children—it did not matter to those who did it. Men one could say were resisting, but women and children and old women and old men . . . The village was erased and an insane asylum built on that hill in its place with all that money. (Where are thy bones buried, O massacred, to erect a memorial? Bodies piled upon bodies, someone must have seen those who did it whose conscience might awaken and tell us where in that one erased village, among all those erased villages, the bodies are piled in common burial in the belly of the land, still unknown, unclaimed.)

The official Zionist movement said illegal zionist gangs did the slaughter, but the equipment and the weaponry were too well-coordinated for that. The effect was what was desired. That crime showed how some could use the injunction to be "more crafty than the serpent"—and the trusting did trust and fell victim. Word of mouth and disinformation inflamed this and other terrors into the bigger design. In places where rumor did not have the desired effect, coercion was applied and trucks and buses tore the defenseless from home and land. By land and sea, trailless and deprived, rushing into unknowns, hundreds of thousands of Palestinian civilians went into exile and loss.

Our truck took us down the valley of death into the Jordan River depression. That winter in the Moab Mountains was cold: a family of nine in a 3x3-meter shack, at least better than the tents of most, snow unusually thick, no return.

It's the earliest solid memory, before the change, that grips me now with the need for retrieval. This is why I am coming back. This is why I am coming back.

Amman, Jordan, is my first stop from Toronto (via Amsterdam airport, where all the cleaning women I saw were Arab) on the way to my holy memory and city. Amman is a logical place to begin since in it are the graves of my mother and my father. It also has some remnants of my family still: my eldest sister and two brothers. My sister and brother are at the airport. My sister, a widow now, is tall and majestic, her eyes and face reminiscent of my mother's. She is dressed in the latest European style. My brother has greyed and balded and developed a potbelly. Our hugs and kisses are warm but don't feel really intimate. Intimacy grows from proximity. The reflexes are there, and the common memories, but I have been away too long, and they have been here, accepting the reality of no return, even when they are not ready to.

I do not feel completely at home in Amman, despite having lived there fifteen early years. The place has expanded on its seven hills into an organized and clean city. But I cannot disentangle its real worth from my feeling that my childhood was forced to be there. My sister and brother lavish all the hospitality on me for which our culture is famous—elaborate welcomes and meals and offerings. While I appreciate these gestures, I cannot help looking at them with half-stranger eyes. I think about how many cultures have been victimized because of their own goodness, their giving natures. How many worlds have been lost when the powerful abuse goodness and take everything.

I am more interested in traces. I ask for pictures, old pictures. My brother gives me a faded cardboard box with a mix of photographs. "Take any of the pictures you want," he says. I sift through the box and take out three pictures, all of the family before my birth. We discuss my plans to go across the border, and I ask what I could do to find our house in Jerusalem. My eldest brother is very good about keeping documents. He searches and gives me copies of papers for two properties: one in pre-1948 Jerusalem my father had purchased some years before the exodus, the other near Sharafat, south of Jerusalem in the areas that became the West Bank after 1948.

My path takes me down the Jordanian hills toward the Jordan River valley and the Allenby Bridge. (Why do they still call that bridge Allenby? O, General Allenby, you implementer of colonialist plans—you, one first cause of our woe.) I then pass through the Dead Sea depression and up the Palestinian hills on the other side, toward that city upon the hill, my birthplace, Jerusalem. This was the same journey my father and mother were forced to take—in reverse direction—back in 1948, clutching their seven children and what their arms could carry, forced by terror, both to be buried in a strange land.

At the Allenby Bridge, the Israeli woman at passport control examined my Canadian passport, compared the picture and my face, checked the visa form and my passport again. She was perhaps twenty-two, confident-looking, and apparently well-trained. Her curly blonde hair had been combed into careful disarray. Her features were East European. I thought she could be friendly. I try to assume people are friendly.

"You can't put Palestine here. You have to write Israel."

"When I asked "Why?" she replied, "This is Israel, not Palestine." She was referring to the item on the visa form for country of birth. I thought that was a factual question, so I simply put down "Palestine."

"But I was born in Palestine, before Israel was established. See, here's my birth certificate with State of Palestine on it."

She did not seem interested—or was she surprised? By this time, her supervisor approached to participate in the argument. "It doesn't matter. You can't write Palestine. It doesn't exist."

But it did exist—in my mind and in my heart, not to mention history. I didn't want to say that they had taken the country (land, buildings, all) by swindle (they'd say they had bought some things here and there, as if that gives them all and everything). I did not want to say that they are still living in our old buildings, that they didn't purchase those for sure. I did not want to say that they should at least be gracious to a harmless visitor who only carries memories. The issues would then turn into argument and counterargument, where myth and reality are mixed, where lies become pseudo-truths that all the books of history cannot unravel. And if we get into any of that I might not even get a visa.

How painful to be a visitor in one's own country. Later, as I walked away to the taxis, I felt I had one consolation: they did not know all my plans for coming back.

Summer, 1954. Before I am left with my aunt for the summer, my father takes me to the line (they called it the green line after the colored marker used on ceasefire lines between what became Israel and the West Bank. From on top of a church tower in the Old City he tries to point out to me the area of our house in Baka'a and, farther to the southwest, the two dunums of land he had purchased to build on. He explains why he has come to East Jerusalem this time. There is a cooperative society offering plots of land south of the Old City toward Bethlehem, near Sharafat. The fees are reasonable so he can now afford them. "We want to think of the future. I don't know that we can get those two dunums and the house back. But at least we can get close and perhaps build something here."

Another roadblock, and another. On my way to Jerusalem now to follow up on those documents, I go through several more Israeli military checkpoints. One would think they are justified as necessary for security, and some may be so. But I wonder when I can easily avoid some of the checkpoints by taking a slightly longer route. I see the lineups, the barriers with huge Israeli flags, the road spikes, the intentional slowing of the whole procedure. The stance of some soldiers, the posture, gives pause: feet spread apart, rifles cocked ready for the slightest excuse, a smile or sometimes laughter stained by an assumption of control, a glee of power, an executionary conceit. These soldiers are almost all very young, not older than twenty-five. And what is the real function of roadblocks such as the ones set up regularly to arrest Gaza students studying in West Bank universities. Cars are stopped arbitrarily—students searched, copybooks and documents thrown about. Transferred to Gaza, those young women and men lose years and the opportunity to get a quality education in another part of their own country— humiliated and frustrated, many, as intended, never return to schooling. Just beyond one roadblock is another colonialist enclave of recently arrived Jews, given automatic privileges (called "settlers" and "pioneers" to gain respectable identification). They are happy, it seems, to learn how to construct military outposts and how to engage in practices of intimidation, abusing nearby farmers, uprooting olive and fruit trees in Palestinian farms and so making life less possible.

I am in the Israel Survey Office in West Jerusalem to ask for a map of the block and plot, using the numbers from the papers my brother gave me. The numbers are still in use, but the two women there tell me the map is not available now and that I could come back in two weeks. "Is there any map I could use to look for these block and plot numbers?" One of the women points to a general map on the wall. I do find the block number, and I drive there right away to inspect the area. The location is beautiful and strategic, but sprawled all over most of the block is the central depot of the Israeli bus company, Egged. Would it ever be possible to retrieve this plot of two dunums?

I think now of the other piece of property near Sharafat in the occupied territories of the West Bank. Surely it would be safe. There are no useful municipal records left in East Jerusalem for such a search, so I pay a visit to the very modern land office in the municipal building in West Jerusalem. I explain and give them my documents.

"Sorry, we have no records that will help."

Is it possible that a piece of land could disappear? Later, in my apartment I examine the document carefully. I see a list of three officers from the cooperative society that issued the document. I inquire from well-connected people and discover that two of the officers are deceased and one is still living in the Old City. He tells me the story of the plots near Sharafat.

In 1969 the Israeli government issued a confiscation order. Appeals by the society to the United Nations, the United States, and other governments—even to the Pope—were fruitless. On the whole area, including our plot, is now situated the colony of Gillo, a complex of block apartment buildings.

What remains to be seen is purely sentimental in value—our old house. A retired man who knew my father offers to drive me to the house. We find that the Israeli inhabitant is disabled. When I explain why I am knocking on the door, he says, "I'm sorry, I moved in only four years ago."

I notice the garden is not as well-kept as it is in my memory. I forget to ask if anything—albums or other old items—could have been left behind. The olive tree is no longer there. I wonder if there might still be time to plant a seedling.

I begin to better fathom the feeling of my tribe in those strange lands from which I have returned. It is a look in the eye that is desolate, that tells how much they need to belong. It is a conflict in their nature: the disinherited in a land of disinheritors. They may seem free from their oppression but are still slaves to their predicament.

The cycle continues: two modes of existence remain, one controlling, the other enduring. The roles sometimes change. The persecuted persecute. Mythic imperatives justify, multiplying. Falsity holds up masks of truth; cruelty beneficence. Simplicity is lost in a world severe and unyielding. Will it be whole—will it to be whole.

LEAH AYALON

A librarian at the Jewish National and University Library in Jerusalem, Leah Ayalon is the author of several published collections of poems, a short story collection, and a novel. Her most recent publication is a novel entitled The Immortals, *published in 1996 by Keter Publishing, Jerusalem.*

In this carefully crafted account of the fear she experienced as she grew up in Jerusalem, Ayalon discloses that, even as a mature adult and despite her hopes for peace, she still has "a deep fear of the Arabs."

Hopes Are Hopes

*D*uring my childhood, Jerusalem, where I was born, was a small town and it had an end which one could reach. Looking back, it seems to me that not many people are privileged to be able to touch something with an end.

I lived in a home cared for and protected by my parents: my mother a Jerusalemite from the Old City within the wall and my father also a Jerusalemite. Still, I was deeply afraid of the Arabs.

The border was very near—almost no further than the distance of an outstretched arm—and very tangible. In many places the border was in the form of barbed wire stretching along in large rolls, mines buried deep under them, and big signs warning of danger and death. I told no one about my fear of this border, and I took care not to come close to it.

The places on the other side of the wall—the palace of the High Commissioner, the Tower of King David with its ornamental fringes which one could see because Jerusalem is surrounded by hills, and especially the Wailing Wall which could not be seen—all these aroused such a feeling of longing.

I imagine to myself that the words "... and our feet stood in your gates, Jerusalem, the city rebuilt and united," were written in my days because I see myself as having the right to stand with my feet in Jerusalem, at the entrance to the city on the carpet on which an arched cat is woven, yes, under the arched entrance to the city. But the many memories which I collected in my small box of lilacs—and my head is certainly a box of lilacs—are hard to forget.

I used to stand on the balcony of my uncle's apartment under the roof of the building, a place from which one could not see any border, but in between its embrasures [an opening in a parapet through which a gun can be fired] were hidden Jordanian snipers with red kaffiyahs [Arab scarves] on their heads and with drawn rifles in their hands. And, despite my restless character, I stood on the balcony as if at an easel, ready to studiously paint the city, the surrounding hills, the olive trees, the rocks—all these without a threatening wall and sniper posts dividing the city.

Sometimes I thought that I had no reason to be afraid in a city like Jerusalem, but things turned out differently. Once during an energetic family walk in the company of two older male cousins of mine, my parents, steeped in talk, walked ahead of us at some distance. Near the Montefiory windmill, opposite Mount Zion, my cousins began suspecting that Jordanian snipers were hiding behind the wall, following us with their eyes, and that they would probably shoot and kill us.

I was shaking with fear. Until then I think I wasn't aware of that kind of fear— of evil eyes following us and conspiring against us. My cousins teased me by covering their mouths with their palms and whistling loud. My fear grew stronger and I was sure that the Jordanian snipers, hearing our voices as they watched the three of us walking innocently along the pavement, were aiming their rifles straight at us, ready to shoot. I was ready to spread out the wings of Pegasus and disappear; to see but not be seen.

Iron shutters grated hard on hinges. Knocking on walls and cypress trees, they threw long shadows like javelins in stormy winter nights. And the bells in the Shneller military camp were always tolling while soldiers in the cold wrapped themselves in their greatcoats. Yet, I didn't fear all this. My fear was of Arabs only, hiding behind the walls near the shooting holes, aiming at me in order to kill me.

My parents never uttered a word against Arabs. They were longing to return to the special places of their childhood— especially to the Wailing Wall—and the fear in me came only from the border which could be seen from all corners of the town.

Particularly fearful days in my childhood were those of the Sinai War. Through one of the windows in our house I could see a jasmine shrub alongside a netted fence which divided our house from neighboring houses. In a room next to the window stood a big radio set and in the evenings we listened to the daily news. During the war, when my father was mobilized and sent to the Sinai desert, my mother covered this window with a grey army blanket. I followed her movements to make sure that not even a tiny crack was left uncovered that would let out light, letting the enemy know where we were. This enemy was very tangible, and if the blanket moved a little and I thought that a tiny ray of light might be seen outside, I was filled with fear that a mighty fighter plane would fly over our house and drop a bomb. I shivered with fear and held on to the edge of the blanket covering the window.

Today I am inclined to hope for a better future. Still, I have to remember that in my box of lilacs, pressed close to my heart, I still carry deep fears of the Arabs.

REUVEN MIRAN

An introduction to Reuven Miran's work appears along with another story on page 37, and there is a photograph of him in the photo insert.

This story, "Tzipori," recounts young Reuven's complex feelings just before and during the Sinai War, when he was in the sixth grade. It needs a bit of explanation, perhaps, for non-Israeli readers. As Miran explains it, "To understand my desire to kill Yaakov Eizner, one has to understand what Israel was like in those days. Emigration was considered treason. The story is fully autobiographical, and I still remember looking up at the sky, wondering exactly where his plane was, hoping it would crash."

"The death of my agriculture teacher in the story is related to my desire to kill Eizner because Eizner expressed satisfaction and pleasure when our army attacked Kalkilya, while my teacher expressed pacifist views and paid for them with his life. My desire to kill Yaakov Eizner is the desire for revenge."

Tzipori

Translated by Dalya Bilu

Yaakov Eizner stood alone in the square. The sun was over his head and there was no one around. The neighborhood houses were white. All the shutters were closed. The streets were empty. I wanted to kill him. I took my sling gun down from my shoulder and cocked it carefully. The back of Yaakov Eizner's neck darkened inside the sight of the gun. Gray clouds suddenly closed in on the sun. The sides of the sight closed in on the nape of Yaakov Eizner's neck. He stood alone in the square. There was no one else there and I wanted to kill him. It was summer, but suddenly gray clouds closed in on the sun and a warm rain started falling. Yaakov Eizner moved and I stood still under the heavy drops of warm rain which had started coming down so unexpectedly. He ran home.

"Coward," I whispered. "I'll kill you."

The warm rain came down harder. The drops were big and heavy. The clouds shifted restlessly from place to place. There was a high wind in the sky. On the ground it was hot and stifling in spite of everything.

"Rain," cried Michael.

"Maxie, Maxie, come home," a woman's voice called from behind one of the closed shutters. She was talking German. She always spoke to her husband and children so loudly that her voice broke through the shutters and traveled around the neighborhood.

"She's calling her fatso again," said Tzipori.

A round figure emerged from a distant stairwell and ran towards the woman's voice, which abruptly fell silent.

"Stinking Germans," hissed Yoram.

"Hitler," said Sammy the Iraqi, "and now all of a sudden it's raining in the middle of summer." His eyes were reflective.

"It's because there's a storm in Europe," said Michael.

"Aha," said Sammy.

And only I was silent. I was thinking about Yaakov Eizner. I wanted to kill him.

The next morning Tzipori's father knocked at our door. My big brother opened the door a crack and said that our mother and father had gone to work. But Tzipori's father wasn't looking for our mother and father. He was looking for me. I was wearing my summer pajamas, but Tzipori's father didn't care. He came into the room with a heavy and determined tread. With one hand he dragged Tzipori, who was as red as a pimento, the kind that were always hanging up to dry on Michael's grandfather's balcony. In the other hand he held a big brown packet which he waved in front of me and asked, "Do you know what this is?"

"Me?" I asked.

"Yes you, you," cried Tzipori's father angrily. "Don't you be smart with me."

Tzipori looked at me sadly. My big brother, as usual, kept aloof.

"Yes," I said, swallowing hard, "I know what it is. So what if I know what it is?" Suddenly I knew that I had nothing to lose. I would kill Yaakov Eizner in any case. But I had made a mistake when I entrusted the packet of dynamite to Tzipori. He looked to me now like a stupid little chicken.

"Where did you take it from?" demanded Tzipori's father.

I was in no hurry to reply. Suddenly I realized there was no need to hurry. In any case Tzipori's father hadn't gone to work, and I asked myself if it was all in honor of me. I looked at Tzipori and I pitied him. He looked at the whitewashed wall as if he had never seen a whitewashed wall before. His little brown eyes stared straight ahead. It seemed to me that he was trying to bore a hole in the wall and disappear inside.

"It's a strong wall, Tzipori. There isn't a crack in it and you'll never get out that way," I said loudly, but to myself.

"Answer my question," yelled his father. His face was flushed and beads of sweat began dripping from his nose.

I looked at my big brother. He was tall and thin, an outstanding student in the tenth grade. And he was silent.

"We didn't take it, Mr. Tzipori. And your son had nothing to do with it anyway." I thought, in my innocence, that Tzipori would be insulted. But he heaved a sigh of relief. For the first time he took his eyes from the wall and looked at me.

Tzipori's father advanced on me. I was wearing my yellow summer pajamas that were at least two sizes too big. It wouldn't be easy to escape in them. I inched toward the door. My big brother kept aloof and said nothing.

"It's from the ruined posts on the hill," I suddenly blurted out. Tzipori's father stopped.

"From the posts on the hill?" he repeated with disbelief. "And the detonators? Are the detonators from there too?"

"No," I replied unwillingly. "There aren't any more. We found them in the woods."

Tzipori listened curiously. My feeling of fear was replaced by a violent desire to laugh.

"Tell me," said Tzipori's father (as if I hadn't told him up to now), "why did you give it all to Yerucham?"

I laughed.

"Yerucham?" I asked. "Who's Yerucham?"

For the first time a slight smile appeared briefly on my

brother's long face. But he went on standing aside, saying nothing, and the smile too disappeared.

"Ah," I said as if it had just occurred to me, "you mean Tzipori. I asked him to look after it for me."

"You little fools," sighed Yerucham's father (I started getting a kick out of the name), "it's a miracle you weren't killed."

It wasn't quite clear to me what he meant by "miracle," but I didn't say anything.

"But Yerucham didn't look after it," I said quietly, without taking my eyes off Tzipori. His eyes escaped to the wall again. Tzipori's father said nothing. He took a few measured paces about the room. He seemed to have calmed down.

My big brother asked, "Won't you have something to drink, Mr. Tzipori?"—and these were the first words I had heard from him in quite a while.

But Tzipori senior didn't even bother to reply. He stroked Tzipori junior's head and asked me in as gentle a tone as possible, "What for? What did you want all that stuff for?"

I couldn't tell him that I wanted to kill Yaakov Eizner and nothing else came into my head. I looked into Tzipori senior's gray eyes and saw how much he resembled his son.

"*Ntt,*" he said in the same gentle voice, "the main thing is that nothing happened."

And with these words he departed, dragging Tzipori junior behind.

"It really is dangerous," said my big brother, my big brother who had never laughed in his life.

"Yes," I said, "I know." I didn't look at him. My big brother.

That night I had a dream. I was in the big eucalyptus

glade. It was daytime, perhaps late afternoon or early evening. But all at once it was night. I was strolling alone among the trees. If I meet Yaakov Eizner now, I thought, I'll kill him on the spot. I was sure that I would. I knew that I had to kill him. And as soon as I was quite ready, he appeared. He stood there in the middle of the path and smiled. In one hand he was holding a big brown paper packet. Yaakov Eizner. How long I had been waiting for him. He approached and without a word he held out the packet. I recognized it immediately. It was the packet of dynamite and detonators that I had given Tzipori and he had handed over to his father.

Yaakov Eizner said nothing. He held out his hand and offered me the packet.

"Take it," he whispered.

I took the heavy packet from him.

"You want to blow me up, don't you?" whispered Yaakov Eizner.

"I don't like you," I said.

He shrugged his shoulders. The darkness separated us, although we were standing very close together.

"Good," he whispered. And as I had once seen someone do in a movie, he glided towards the ground and fell flat on it.

"Scatter it over me," he whispered.

I scattered the dynamite over him, especially in the region of his head and chest. The strong sharp smell filled the close darkness, and out of the darkness Yaakov Eizner offered me a detonator attached to a fuse.

"Have you got any matches?" he asked in a whisper.

And suddenly I understood everything. He was giving the orders, and I was obeying them.

"No," I said. "I haven't got any matches."

"Here," whispered Yaakov Eizner in what was almost a scream. "Here, take them." He offered me a box of matches. I didn't take it.

"You won't get away with it," I said. "You won't get away with it, Yaakov Eizner. I'll kill you."

He started writhing on the ground at my feet.

"Light it," he begged.

But I left the detonator, fuse, and box of matches in his hand.

"Goodbye," I said. "Goodbye, Yaakov Eizner."

"Come back," he cried. "Don't leave me like this."

"I'll come back later," I said and went away.

And then I woke up. I knew that it was a dream. Yaakov Eizner was a new immigrant and he didn't know Hebrew. So how could he have spoken to me?

After that I stopped speaking to Tzipori. At home no one said anything to me about the packet. But my big brother, who was a student at the high school and read a lot of books, didn't forget. Every now and then he looked at me with eyes that seemed full of suffering, and this look gave me a very unpleasant feeling. Since I wasn't on speaking terms with Tzipori junior, I exempted myself from greeting Tzipori senior too. In the evenings I would slip away to the hill, crawling about and looking for things in the ruined army posts. Our agriculture teacher had told us that this hill had always been an important strategic place. Even under the Turks, he said, bloody battles had been fought on the hill, until the last autumn of the war when the British had gained the upper hand and driven their enemies from the whole of the Sharon [Valley]. Our agriculture teacher was as well up on all the wars that had been fought in our country as if he had taken part in them himself.

He told us about the War of Independence, too, but when I crawled into the ruined posts which were full of pieces of broken, faded green ammunition boxes and tatters of army capes eaten up by rot, I only remembered the red sky of the last autumn from which the agriculture teacher never returned. Everyone was sure that the war would break out in Kalkilya, where the murderers came from. Some even spoke of the need to chop down all the orange groves next to the border, in order to help the border police in their patrols and manhunts. And one day we heard the headmaster of our school shouting at recess that he had never heard such rubbish in his life. "An eye for an eye!" yelled the headmaster furiously. "We have to destroy them in their homes!" In his excitement he spilt his tea and added a new stain to his trousers.

The orange groves were not chopped down and war didn't break out against our neighbor Kalkilya. The white village clustering on the bare mountain slopes to the east was not destroyed. The only one who knew this beforehand was our agriculture teacher. "There's no need to destroy anyone," he said, "let alone an entire village."

He said that the war would break out in the south, and I remember how they laughed at him. "Look at all the soldiers dug in on the hill," they said to him. "You think they've brought them here just for Esterika the whore?" The agriculture teacher didn't even bother to reply. And I knew that he was cleverer than the rest put together.

One night, in the middle of autumn, we were sitting on the balcony of our flat, drinking raspberry juice with soda water. It was still hot, although the High Holidays [Rosh Hashanah and Yom Kippur] had already come and gone. Suddenly I heard muffled noises and then the eastern sky was lit up and turned as red as blood. We sat on the balcony with our faces frozen like photographs in an album. My father looked at us and then my mother. My big brother retreated into himself and muttered something incomprehensible. I looked at the half empty glasses. The soda water was clear. The red raspberry juice had sunk to the bottom of the glasses.

The whole neighborhood was gathered in the street. They were counting the shells falling in the east and smiling. I thought about our agriculture teacher. Had he made a mistake? I felt a burning in my throat. In the street they were roaring with joy.

"Sixty-five!" someone cried. "Sixty-six, whaaam!"

"They're only shooting at the police station," shouted Michael's big brother. "You can see everything from the water tower!" He raced down the sandy street on his bike and as the narrow beam of light from his lamp jumped over the houses I wanted to go out after him, but my father told me to go to bed. I didn't go. Had the agriculture teacher made a mistake? I forgot about Yaakov Eizner. All I could think about was the agriculture teacher. Had he made a mistake? And what had all the soldiers really been doing over the hill? Amusing themselves with red-lipped Esterika? Yaakov Eizner had stammered that soldiers always amused themselves with girls. He knew. His parents had told him and he himself remembered. They were in the big war, far away from all our little wars.

"After Yaakov learns Hebrew we'll ask him to tell us about the big war he was in," the agriculture teacher had said one day.

Now Yaakov Eizner stood in the street counting the shells in a loud voice and another language. The sight of the crowd below drew me like a magnet, but my father said if the neighbors wanted to stand as if they were watching a football match or basketball game, that was their business. I stood still on the balcony and hated them. With every exploding shell my heart shuddered. I saw the agriculture teacher's face and the faces of other people I knew and did not know, and I wanted it to be over.

The next morning we went to school as usual. I waited for Tzipori and Yoram. They laughed as they did every morning when the woman cried from behind the closed shutters, "Hurry Maxie, hurry!" We didn't like Maxie the fatso, and Yoram never forgot to add, "Dirty German." On the way we were joined by Sammy. Michael was sick. I didn't see Yaakov Eizner until we were already sitting at our desks. His eyes were sunken and circled with black rings. He spoke to his neighbor in a hoarse whisper. Straight after the bell the teacher Bilha came into the class and we fell silent. Her eyes were red. She said, "Good morning," and her voice shook. She couldn't go on. She was crying. The tears poured down her cheeks and she didn't stop them.

"What happened, teacher?" asked Pnina, who was on the class committee and the first to recover.

Bilha sank into her chair and cried onto the table until it was all wet with her tears.

"Your agriculture teacher," she stammered, the words coming out all broken and strangled. "Your agriculture teacher was killed in the fighting last night."

The floor started shifting underneath me and so did the walls and ceiling. Everything spun around and around. Only Josef the janitor's arm was steady, strong, and sure as it carried me outside. In the infirmary I lay next to the teacher Bilha. She was lying flat on her back with her eyes closed and a damp white towel folded on her forehead. I raised myself and sat on the edge of the bed. We were alone in the room. Then I stole out on tiptoe and ran home.

The next day I stayed at home. I lay in bed reading my only agriculture notebook again and again.

There wasn't much in it. He didn't make us write down everything he said. "Write it down in your hearts and minds," he would say, although none of us, I think, understood how it was possible to write down agriculture in our hearts and minds. My notebook was nothing to be proud of. I didn't know how to draw or write fancy letters. With every page I turned, new tears flooded my eyes. My beloved agriculture teacher had made a mistake.

After the tears were over I felt calmer and I knew what I had to do.

After Tzipori's father had confiscated the bag of dynamite which I had collected with so much effort, I looked for another way to kill Yaakov Eizner. In the evening I would steal out to the hill and prowl among the dugouts. The soldiers were gone and all that was left were some empty cans and a lot of olive pits and cigarette stubs. Two weeks after my agriculture teacher was killed in the attack on the Kalkilya police station, the real war broke out, and it was exactly as he had told us it would be. Although I remembered very well that he had known about it even before he died, I told him all about it, and also about everything else that was happening in the country as I wandered about the deserted hill. Sometimes I asked his advice, but only in insignificant matters. I didn't tell him that I was going to kill Yaakov Eizner. I knew he would never have agreed to that.

The only way left was to kill him with my gun. So I took my gun to the hill, stood one crate on top of another, and drew a little circle with chalk on the top. Inside the dugouts I found some lead pellets and I shot them into the little circle. To this day I don't know how those pellets got there. I would go on shooting until the sun set. Then I would take a long look at the parched bare hills in the east. They were bathed in a very clear, bright light. I could make out every bush, every rock, every dry creek. The agriculture teacher had gone there and never come back.

One morning, at the beginning of vacation, I was awakened by the noise of a big truck engine. My big brother had gone to study French in Herzlia. An old truck was parked in the street under the balcony and two porters were dragging furniture out of the apartment opposite. Yaakov Eizner's apartment. His parents were supervising the porters while Yaakov himself was scrambling about on the truck and arranging things on top of one another. I looked at my watch. It was half past nine. Tzipori suddenly crossed the road. He dragged his feet slowly through the sand, warming up in the morning sun. I hadn't spoken to him since he had given his father the dynamite I had scraped together with so much effort.

But now he called out to me. "They're moving! They're going to America!"

I said nothing, but Yaakov Eizner paused for a moment and raised his curly black head to me. I think our eyes met. I went into the room and took my gun from the wardrobe. When I returned to the window sill there were bright stars shining in my eyes, and among them I saw the face of my beloved agriculture teacher.

I selected a particularly smooth lead pellet and cocked my gun. The rubber sling reddened in the light of the sun. On the ground below, the porters had almost finished loading the truck, and Yaakov Eizner's parents had vanished into the driver's cabin. Yaakov Eizner stood on his parents' dining room table, tightening the leather straps that held it to the wooden ladders which were the sides of the truck. I aimed my gun at his head. The black nape of his neck filled the sight. I heard him counting the shells exploding in the eastern sky. The red sky covered the whole neighborhood. I saw my agriculture teacher's lips whispering, "There's no need to destroy anyone, let alone an entire village." The floor slipped from under my feet. I let go of the trigger and felt myself ascending into the sky.

By the time I recovered, at the beginning of the second half of the vacation, my big brother was already registered for a course in English. I myself went on wandering among the deserted dugouts on the hill. The warm summer rain had stopped falling. Every morning I climbed the hill. I broke the gun and scattered the pieces in the trenches. The grass covered everything.

A number of picture postcards arrived from Yaakov Eizner. His parents sent them to the people who lived downstairs. They showed high buildings, big parks, and long lines of motor cars. Michael showed them to me, but I wasn't interested.

In the afternoons I would come back from the hill. I spoke to nobody and nobody spoke to me. Once my mother said that I had apparently not fully recovered from my illness, and she was probably right. I would go into the bathroom and lock the door. There was a big mirror there and I would stand in front of it with my head lowered but my eyes raised. I would look straight into my own eyes and my gaze would pass between my father's shaving gear and my mother's toilet bottles and come back to me.

"You're in America now," I would whisper, "but nothing, nothing is over."

There was a hard look in my eyes and sometimes it even frightened me.

After the long vacation I moved up to the seventh grade.

Ibtisam S. Barakat

A thirty-four-year-old Palestinian woman who lived under Israeli occupation in the West Bank until she was twenty-two, Ibtisam Barakat graduated from Birzeit University, went on to get a master's degree in journalism at the University of Missouri, and is now a writer in Columbia, Missouri. She is the author of numerous articles focusing on the needs of young people.

Although she is far from her homeland, Barakat is involved with the international struggle for human rights and has given a great deal of thought as to how Palestinians and Israelis can achieve the justice necessary for lasting peace. "It is of utmost importance to me," she says, "that I work with others toward a vision of justice and dignity for all, and toward transcending all hurts of racism, oppression of females, and injustices affecting young people."

Barakat's intensely emotional story of her family's forced flight to Jordan when she was three and a half years old is emblematic of the story of many, many Palestinian families who were abruptly displaced by the 1967 war and lost everything they had—even, sometimes, each other.

(See photo insert.)

Marked for Destruction

*T*he war came to us at sundown. My mother had just announced that our lentil-and-rice dinner would be ready as soon as Dad arrived. She picked up my infant sister, held out a plump breast, and began to rock and feed her. I knew I wanted to be the one rocking in my mother's arms.

My two brothers, the noisy inseparables, were chasing one another around my mother's jasmine garden, and I stood at the door awaiting my father's emergence from the evening shadows on the long gravel road that led to our home. Like every evening, I was preparing to run toward him with all the vigor of my three and a half years of life. But because I had only one pair of shoes and was only allowed to wear them on important occasions lest I wear them out, I often hopped my way along the gravel as I swung my eyes between the ground and the shadow of the man I loved.

My dad was my giant ally, and before the war I had an unwavering sense that all was well as long as he came home at the end of the day. Each time I met him, he embraced me with a splendid smile that made his right eye fade into the shape of a crescent moon. He reached out to me with his loofah-like hand, and I half hung in the air as I grasped two of his fingers and walked.

My dad often gave me five tries at guessing what the treat he had in his pocket for me and my two brothers was. When I could not guess by the fifth time, he gave me the first letter of the word, and then I guessed for certain unless it was a new treat he had brought.

But on the evening of June 5th, 1967, my dad was the one who was rushing toward me. He was in an urgent hurry, and I could see his face had no smile. His speed spelled hazard from a distance, and although he was saying something, it was only when he was closer that I could hear his wretched words: "Run back and tell your mother the war has started!" he said. I did not fully comprehend the command, but everything in me sensed the danger in those words.

As I ran home, I fell on the gravel and scraped my knees, but I didn't feel the pain except for a moment. I had sensed that my dad did not need to be bothered by a crying child. Somehow I made myself stop feeling my pain.

My mom seemed to know exactly what dad's words meant. Her shocked response was so frightening that it would forever stick in my mind as the symbol of the gravest lamentation and loss. She struck her face with both her hands and dug her nails into her terror-stricken cheeks. And then she scraped. She said not a word, and her eyes gazed into the distance. I could tell that her soul had momentarily departed the space of our kitchen where we all stood paralyzed.

Many years later, I learned that in those lines mother scraped on her face was the story of a woman whose heart had been torn by war once before. My mother was a child during the war of 1948—the war that took place after Jews self-declared Palestinian land as their national home and named it Israel. When the war started in 1948, my mother was asleep, and in the cruelty of an inexplicable moment, her mother left her behind.

Now, standing in the kitchen as my father's words hung in the air like a brandished sword, my mother was reminded that her family, her people, and everything Palestinian were bound for mass destruction once again.

My dad held my mother's arm tenderly. He spoke to her in the manner he spoke to me about the importance of closing my eyes and falling asleep when he turned off the light at night. He told her that he had heard that the planes had been targeting homes in particular and that the safest thing would be to turn off all the lights, leave our home immediately, and sit in the garden in the trench he had been digging for a water culvert while we decided what to do.

He also said he wanted to listen to the radio to find out which specific areas were being attacked, but the only radio we owned was an enormous, oven-like set that he thought would be unsafe to carry into the trench.

Before we left the house, my mother snatched my infant sister and held on to her tightly. My two brothers and I held on to my mother's dress and we all marched outside.

Inside the trench I glued my body to my brothers' and my heart surrendered to the rhythm of our vigilant breaths, all rising and falling in anxious unison. With the tip of my head, I reached to touch my father's arm that was surrounding us. His other arm enclosed my mother who was attempting to quiet our infant sister whose siren cries threatened to draw fatal attention to our hiding place, and as there was no room for love and lullabies in the tight trench, my mother sharply howled at my sister who quickly abandoned all noise.

My father and mother exchanged a few whispers and then my dad announced that there was no escape for a

EHUD BEN-EZER

REUVEN MIRAN

GUNTER DAVID

WADAD SABA
(left) and a
kindergarten
friend

YITZHAK BAR-YOSSEF

Ibtisam S. Barakat

Ahmed Younis (left) with one of his younger brothers

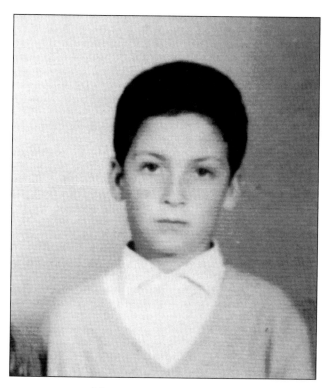

MOHAMMAD ZAHAYKEH

Marina N. Riadi

Victoria Kay-Feinerman

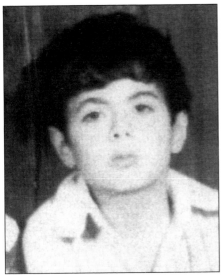

RAMZY BAROUD

REDROSE

RACHELI TAL

LIRAN ZVIBEL

human from destiny. "What is written on the forehead, the eye must see," he said. Then he prayed for gentleness in what the few coming hours or days held for us.

My dad's pained voice was bitter with the disillusionment of a captured wild bird. My brothers and I understood that something beyond what we'd ever learned or would ever understand was about to happen to our father. We reached for his clothes and held on to him firmly. I remember feeling that I would do anything at all that would make my father feel happy one more time.

As darkness came and shut off our senses, I could neither see my body nor the faces of my father, mother, and brothers except in memory. Then suddenly my mother whispered to my father that she could hear footsteps coming. My father ordered us to freeze. I stopped myself from breathing.

It quickly became apparent that the footsteps were those of a string of people from neighboring villages who were fleeing their homes.

Raising his voice only loud enough that they could hear him, my father questioned the crowd about the news.

A man's voice answered. "After their planes attack, they will be combing the area house by house. The word is that they will butcher every living thing that they find."

My parents exchanged a few whispers and then quickly agreed that it was time for us to join all the fleeing people. "Death in a group is mercy," my dad said.

"I want to get into the house and bring out some food. The children are famished," my mother said.

"But hurry, and don't light even a match," my dad warned.

My mother tucked our silent sister into his arms, murmured to us that she would be back in no time, and disentangled her body from the trench with the vigilance of a leopard prudently moving toward its prey.

Before we could settle into the thought that food was within reach, a violently pulsing noise sliced through our dread. Bullets were being fired at my mom. She let out a shrill scream and then sunk into calm.

My brothers and I screamed but we quickly stopped when my father told us that we were being "targeted" and he commanded us to remain silent and still.

The giant bullets seemed to have originated from a plane that zoomed above our heads and trailed off into the distance. It set monstrous nearby patches of the darkness afire. We could hear the piercing noises everywhere and couldn't tell what side of the sky would be the next to blaze.

After he'd secured our one-year-old sister in our arms, my father stretched his body out to my mother's and grabbed her foot. He pulled her into the center of the trench.

Seeming to have lost awareness of her body, Mother frantically searched herself for a fatal injury as she said, "I want to see my children one last time before I die."

After realizing that Mom had miraculously escaped injury, my dad held her to his chest and reassured her that all was well. "They missed," he whispered. And the warmth in his voice allowed my blood to flow anew through my veins. My mother, shocked by the astounding events, had nothing to say. Then suddenly in a harsh voice she demanded that we immediately leave.

It seemed very unwise, but mother picked up our one-year-old sister and began walking toward the house. My two brothers and I leapt after her as my father prayed hysterically that we come to no harm.

Inside the house my mother snatched the pot of lentil-and-rice from the kitchen and wrapped it in a rag. Then she dashed into the darkness and searched for a bundle of golden bracelets that were her dowry when she married my dad. I could hear her sigh of relief when she found the gold.

Then she commanded that we put on our shoes immediately. But I did not know where my shoes were and the house was entirely consumed in darkness. "I don't know where my shoes are," I muttered.

"Just find them," she said. And I and my two brothers obediently searched until we found our shoes and went outside.

My mother and father were whispering urgently in the dark. My father said that if we didn't die that night, we'd have to sleep in the wilderness. He and my mother agreed that he must get some clothes and blankets to sleep in. When he came out of the house with a mound in his arms, my parents argued whether or not to lock the door. They finally agreed to lock it and take the key with us.

Fleeing people continued to pass by our house, spreading words of impending terror. A breathless man told my father that there were no people left in the village from which he and his group had fled. He also said that they were fleeing to the caves first, and then to Jordan— our neighboring country—which might take a few days to reach.

"What caves?" my dad asked.

"Run with us," the man said before merging into the darkness.

My father announced that we were to move immediately

with the crowd for that seemed to be our last chance of being with people and escaping an isolated fate.

My inseparable brothers had already put on their shoes and held each other's hands tightly. My mother had secured my sister between her arms. My father strained to see the road from behind the mound of clothes and blankets in his arms. But I, in spite of all my desperate attempts to comply with my parents' commands, was unable to put my shoes on. They were lace-up shoes that my three-and-a-half-year-old hands were unable to lace in the dark.

"I can't put them on," I cried in a hushed voice, lest I attract attention and we all die. "Help me." But no one answered.

At that moment, a new wave of fleeing people rushed by our door. As they hurriedly disappeared, everything faded into stillness. And my family was gone. I could not grasp that they had walked away with the crowd and left me behind.

I wanted to cry aloud, but my voice had drowned in my dread. Then I could see that the only hope for me was to leave my shoes aside, storm through all that I felt, and run in the direction the fleeing people ran. As I began to move, sounds of distant gunshots, screeching noises unexpectedly swelled and then subsided.

When I looked behind I could no longer see the giant shadow of our home. And the world within and around me seemed to fade into the ghastly unknown.

The gravel grated sharply at my feet. Once again, I commanded myself not to feel. When my wary ears detected voices, I awaited them cautiously, and when they approached, I attached myself to the end of their caravan. Settling into the rhythm of this rapidly-moving crowd, I could hear men talking about what I understood was a smaller group of their townspeople who had left early and who would await them near the road to the caves.

The mention of the caves filled my heart with a hope that my family would perhaps be with the group we would eventually join. But my hopes were pierced by the flares that lit up the darkness and formed a dome in the sky. People in the caravan began to pray aloud. They said that God is one.

The lights in the sky blinded us and then there was a barrage of bombs. The feeling was that the moment of definitive destruction had arrived. But as the lights and sounds of bombardment continued and no one in my crowd was hit, it became apparent that neighboring areas were the immediate targets of attack.

Our group continued to move on, although all voices had sunk into a solemn calm. As we went, I noticed that we were joining other clusters of people, as ghostly and stunned as we were. Among those ahead of us, I thought I saw my mother holding my sister, her thick, dark braid wagging on her back.

Our group sped up to meet the group in front of us and my numbed feet flew forward. The lights in the sky came and went, but I kept my eyes on my mother's braid. I dashed through the big silent parade to survival. I pushed and threw myself through the hurrying legs of people who cursed in muted voices, lest we all die. And I moved to where I thought I saw my mom.

When I was only a few steps behind the dark braid that now wagged frantically, life meant nothing but reaching a step closer. And when my fingers touched her dress, the war seemed to halt.

Thinking that I was with my mother again, I began to feel

the feverish fire in my feet, and I could no longer ignore the pain. I tightened my grip on her dress. I let myself weep a little and let her dear dress take my weight. That respite lasted only a few seconds however. As new war flares blinked and widened their predator eyes, a disturbed face turned to scold me.

"Who are you?" she asked as she sternly shook her dress free from my hand. I could see that the woman was not my mother.

I dropped my hands to my sides, gripped my own dress, and could feel neither terror nor pain. My eyes searched for no one, and it mattered not whether I walked alone or had others around.

When we approached the caves, voices deliberated as to whether we should hide in them or continue to walk. A few of the people settled for the caves, but I found myself walking with those who chose to continue on the road.

As we arrived at a road, dawn lit up the world and announced yet another day of war. I could see more people around me than I'd ever seen before. They were gazing into the horizon where a long line of unanswered prayers hung from the sky. They were cursing. They were struggling to swallow the bitter news. They were begging one another for a drink of water. And some were still praying. And all awaited a miracle to transport us away from the war, away from our home.

I wandered among the faces and somehow saw my father, my mother, and my two brothers. I could neither cry nor smile. And although I walked up to them, and they to me, we had become a heartful of fright estranged.

Ibtisam S. Barakat

* * *

My family and I arrived in Jordan. We awaited a chance to return, and that came to us under the protection of the International Red Cross. After four months and thirteen days, there was a narrow window of opportunity for us to make up our minds about staying in Jordan or returning home. Many families worried that they might be harmed if they went back, and when the window closed quickly they remained permanently outside. But our family was among the first to return.

My mother insisted, "If they live, I want my children to know who they are!"

Upon our return home, there were soldiers everywhere. They marched with their guns in long lines on the gravel road leading to our home. My brothers and I stopped playing outside for a long time.

And over the years I understood that the war was only the start, and that our lives, and all things Palestinian, were marked for destruction by a fire that would not be put out.

AHMED YOUNIS

Now a forty-year-old university lecturer, Academic Director of Rehabilitation at Al-Quds University, and the president of the Palestine Physiotherapy Association, Ahmed Younis, Ph.D., spent his entire childhood in the Gaza Strip's Rafah refugee camp, where his family continues to live. With seventeen brothers and sisters, he and his family had to continually struggle for survival.

Today Ahmed Younis works to help those who have suffered severe physical injuries, particularly spinal cord injuries. He has authored (and coauthored with his wife, Jo Simister) many articles about community care for the disabled and has written for the Save the Children Fund in London.

(See photo insert.)

A Child in Rafah Camp
Edited by Jo Simister

I remember listening to my grandmother's stories as she told us about our land and the names of the places in our village in the South called Barbara. These were stories about her life and wonderful tales about our tradition. But when she came to speak about the poverty she would begin to weep sadly, and I, the eldest, asked her, "Why are you weeping now if your life was poor and difficult?"

Very simply she would say, "We were comfortable in our land—free, quiet, and happy inside. We could cultivate our land and eat. No one with land is poor."

Of course as a child I did not realize what she meant by these words—freedom, quietness, happiness.

At that time we were living in a refugee camp in Rafah called Shabourah. I was born there and so I had no memory of the time my grandmother was talking about. We had no land or any possessions and our houses were—and still are—made of one level of cinder block. There was no running water in the houses until I was about ten years old, just public taps in the streets. None of the shelters had a toilet, so we had to queue for a long time sometimes. We had no electricity until I was sixteen, so we used kerosene for cooking and for light in the evenings. We couldn't afford anything for heating. If it was very cold we would light the kerosene stove or go to bed.

Needless to say, there were no places to play and we had no toys. But we were creative and made toys from bottle tops and thread spools and kites from the paper from our old school notebooks. We played several competitive games needing good general knowledge. And we played football with a ball made from an old sock stuffed with rags or a balloon covered with cloth and string to protect it. Of course we also played games re-enacting our situation— soldiers attacking people or coming in the night to arrest someone.

* * *

I went to the school provided by UNRWA (the UN agency responsible for all Palestinian refugees). My father was a teacher of Arabic and he was in charge of the library in his school. In my second year of primary school he asked if I could use the library during my vacation instead of hanging around the house or out on the streets doing nothing. That was my beginning with books. I started reading all kinds of children's stories, and then Arabic novels by Egyptian writers.

As I grew up, every day I heard something about our homeland of Occupied Palestine and the universal hope that we would go back to it one day. We would build new houses instead of these shelters which leaked so badly in winter that we would have to get up in the night to change our position and which offered us no protection from the heat of summer. I spent all my childhood hearing of these dreams from my parents, my grandmother, and many other relatives . . . and from President Gamal Nasser's speeches on Egyptian Broadcasting insisting on the liberation of Palestine.

On June 5, 1967, when I was ten years old, I heard that war had begun and that we would soon be returned to our homeland, but I could not grasp this. After two more days, the older people said that we were occupied now by the Israeli Army, and they began to talk about the invasion of Gaza by the French and British during the Suez Crisis of 1956 and how badly the Israeli soldiers had treated the people then, and how many had been killed.

As soon as they arrived, the Israelis imposed a curfew. There was a lot of shooting in the streets and some people were killed the first day. After that, they mostly shot into the air. The first day, I was in the house watching one of my brothers in his cradle. Our neighbors, a woman and her several children, decided to visit her mother in another part of the camp. As soon as they left their house, it was blown up. I was so shocked I could not move, and other women from the neighborhood came running to see if we were still alive and carried us out of the house. My brother still has a small scar above his eye from flying debris.

During the year that I was fifteen, the Israeli authorities permitted the people of Gaza to go into the occupied areas, and my father promised my second brother and me that we would visit our village. We went, and it was the first time we saw our father cry. I was deeply impressed, but I could not understand.

My father asked us to dig in the ground to try to find my grandmother's flour grinding stone and all the treasures she had hidden when they fled from the village. But we did not find anything. Citrus fruits had replaced the village and all the stone houses had been destroyed. It is still possible to see where the village was from the piles of stones and the cactus growing there. My father described the boundaries of our fields, the garden around our house, and told us the names of the places and the people who had lived there. We believed one day we would go back there.

Towards the end of secondary school, I asked my father if I could go to work like my friends to save money to go to university in Egypt. I remember him saying, "Look, son, I am concerned for your studies more than anything else in the world—and not only yours but your brothers' and sisters' also —because we have lost our land and our way of survival. In the past we were not concerned about such things as education, but now we have no other resource. Your certificate will be your means to survive in life. But I do not want you to go to work because it will spoil you for your studies. And then we will lose everything twice over— once by being turned out of our homes and again by the ruin of our children."

At the time I could not follow his reasoning, but I did not go to work. I spent the whole year in our house, only going out briefly between the time my friends returned from work and the start of the evening curfew at eight P.M. Even if there were no curfew, it was not safe to be out on the streets.

In the evening I would talk a little with my father about our life and hopes for building a future. There are twenty-one in our family: eighteen brothers and sisters and then my parents and my grandmother. We were all living in the same house with no possibility of finding another place because we had very little money. You cannot imagine the life in that camp . . . the streets, the houses, everything very dirty, very awful . . . but we had to live somehow. We would talk about marriage and family and community matters, and how to build up enough resources to make a proper home for ourselves.

Cairo was my first enormous step into the world outside. I was nineteen and had never been out of the Gaza Strip except once to the village and once to pray in Jerusalem. Everything was so strange, everything overwhelmed me—the high buildings, the traffic, the way of living, the women's dresses. I was shaken to the core, but I kept one thing only in front of my eyes—my studies. I had to finish school and be able to help my father.

Cairo means many things to me, but I can say it in one word: Freedom. I began to know life, to determine what I needed to achieve my aims, and to modify those aims. In the first two years in Cairo I advanced more than in the whole of my life before. I began to read freely, not only in my chosen subject, but in all the matters that interested me—psychology, philosophy, politics, everything. Imagine! I could select the book I wanted to read! In all the camps—and even in the whole of the Occupied Territories—you cannot find the book you want to read.

I was free to walk in the streets without carrying my ID card and to go when and where I wanted, even at night, which had been forbidden in the camps. I could eat what I wanted.

I forgot the domination of the occupation and the previous restrictions of my life. I learned how to deal with many different people on different levels. I felt as if my life in Cairo was the strong foundation on which I was constructing one of those huge buildings that had at first overwhelmed me so much.

After graduation I worked in Cairo for several years. In fact, I was there fourteen years and then I felt I should return to my roots. Now at age forty, I think I understand the words of my grandmother. I think I am beginning to know about the yearning for quietness and happiness. I realize why she was weeping when telling us stories about the land. And I have discovered why my father cried when he showed us our village. More and more I have learned what it means to desire the land and self-determination. And to be free.

SHULI DICHTER

Shuli Dichter grew up in Kibbutz Ma'anit and has resided there all his adult life. He and his wife, Avital, have three children. A teacher for many years, he has taught everything from Bible studies to Arabic, history, and geography. Currently, in partnership with Jalal Hassan, he is the director of Children Teaching Children, an educational program of civic studies for Jewish and Arab students and teachers based in the Jewish-Arab Center for Peace at Givat Haviva, Israel.

Asked about what he thinks the prospects are for Israeli-Palestinian peace, he said, "I have no illusions. I think that it is most important to maintain a true and honest dialogue at an eye-to-eye level between the two peoples. Both sides of the conflict should continually reexamine their myths about themselves and about the other."

In this short autobiographical story, he conveys a very young child's point of view of the Palestinians' loss of their homes in the upheaval of 1948 to 1950.

In the Courtyard of the Children's House of the Kibbutz

"*M*oishe, what are you doing?"

"I'm building houses for the Arabs because they don't have anywhere to live now."

Moishe hammered the earth without lifting his eyes as he forcefully tamped down the foundation. He was busy at work. Moishe was always busy building or dismantling something or other. His head would lean forward in a determined fashion, and he wouldn't bother to straighten the sleeves of his shirt that had fallen from his shoulders.

"What do you mean, they don't have houses?" I asked.

"Yes, I was overhearing my father talking with Tzvi L. And he said that the Arabs were expelled and now they don't have anywhere to live. Move that branch away!"

I moved the branch immediately and went to the children's storage facility to find another hammer. I joined Moishe and began to dig at the earth according to his instructions. We met in the middle and together we created the courtyard of the dwelling units for the homeless Arabs.

It was noon, the time between lunch and our afternoon naps. We saw Sarah, our kindergarten teacher, coming towards us across the field. She stopped next to us and, moving the hem of her skirt so that it would not cover my shoulder, she asked us what we were doing.

"We are building a house for the Arabs. They do not have anywhere to live because they were expelled," I volunteered.

"Well, is that really how you build a house — digging with a hammer?" she asked.

Moishe, in a position to defend the planning and execution of whatever he was doing, answered, "Sure. Tzvi told my father that if they don't have anywhere to live, they should be under the ground. So, I am preparing the house for them under the ground."

Moishe turned to me. "Why did you stop working? Continue to dig."

Sarah giggled to herself and announced that this was certainly not the way to build houses. And, furthermore, this was naptime, not housebuilding time.

In bed, while I was staring up at the white ceiling, I imagined the Arab family who would come to live in the house that Moishe and I were building for them under the ground. Slowly, the images of the Arabs evolved into the familiar drawings in the book about the city mouse and the country mouse who also lived in houses under the ground.

As soon as our naptime was finished, I went back to our construction site and I saw that people had trampled the foundation created by Moishe's diligent hammer. I called him and he hardly lifted his head from his new project—sleeping—and said, "That place wasn't good for a house anyway."

That evening I asked my father to once again read me the story of the city mouse and the country mouse. In my bed, I pictured their families on the white ceiling with many, many mice —children, many, many children— coming to visit each other and bringing food from the upper world, multiplying and multiplying, over and over . . .

MOHAMMAD ZAHAYKEH

Mohammad Zahaykeh calls Jabal-Al Moukaber, Palestine, his home. Married and expecting his first child, he is an author, journalist, and TV reporter in Jerusalem.

In perhaps one of the saddest stories in this anthology, he tells of the childhood loss of his father and his family's home. "In spite of my difficult upbringing," he says, "I grew fond of life and I have a good sense of humor. I have managed to overcome personal hatred and to be open-minded and willing to learn about other people's cultures."

Zahaykeh's first book, The Uprising of Journalism, *was published by Rawan Press in 1992. (See photo insert)*

A Child's Misgivings
About the War

*T*he sun slipped into the horizon. I stood in front of our house on the main road that connects Jerusalem and Bethlehem. My hands were behind my back as I gazed into the distance, enthusiastically anticipating the appearance of my father's figure from behind the curve. He would bring us candy and tasty things. I angrily scolded my younger brother, who stood to my side, because father was late, and we stared into nothingness.

Suddenly I heard screaming voices in the courtyard. They kept saying that war had started and that we had to run to a safe place. They said that our house, especially, was in the zone of fire.

All of a sudden, I was picked up by one of my family's relatives—a strong, wide-shouldered young man—who put me on his shoulders and swiftly evacuated me and the rest of my family while bullets glittered and screamed in the air and fell on the ground near our feet.

I started screaming, "Where is my father? I want my father! Why don't we wait for him?"

My mother's voice, sharp as a knife, said, "Be quiet. Don't be afraid, miserable kid. Your father will join us later."

Fear filled my young heart as we crawled on all fours like animals to avoid gunshots. We looked for and found a cave to hide from the flying bullets that seemed like scattering straw in the middle of a tempest.

In the big dark cave crowds of people hid and listened to the radio speak of war, military assaults, and movements of armies and soldiers. My mother's voice grew louder as the passing time filled her heart with more and more worries about my father's end.

Those were long and fearful hours of waiting and watching my mother, her eyes full of tears. Neighbors and relatives tried to console her and lend her strength, assuring her that my father would arrive soon. But he never did.

Darkness cast its shadow and the night arrived full of a fearful loneliness. Suddenly people started whispering to each other as they slipped out under cover of darkness, heading to an unknown location. Horror and fear of death took hold of them as they thrust forward. I saw some tread on thorns, others on pointed rocks. Still they crawled on to avoid flying bullets that came from all over while women wailed, children cried, and dogs barked.

It was midnight when we squeezed into a small cave. There I witnessed something that scared me and will continue to haunt me as long as I live. My mother was rending her clothes and tearing her hair as the tears ran down her cheeks. She cried bitterly, surrounded by women who futilely tried to calm her down. I knew then that my father had died, and that we would never see him and his smiling, joyful face again. Never again would we see my father in the midst of our small family in the evenings, telling us wonderful stories. We would never again wait for him to bring us candy in the evening or to hug us before we went to bed. The bloody war had taken away my father.

That gloomy summer, my family decided to spend some time in the wilderness of Sawahreh—a remote desert that extends to the shores of the Dead Sea. We'd stay there until the situation settled down, we thought. Afterwards, we would return to our house where my father had died.

"The orphans are here; the orphans are gone." That is how people referred to my siblings and me. My broken heart was filled with sorrow for the loss of my father and the void he had left behind.

In the evening, when I was all alone herding my uncles' sheep, my imagination carried me back to our home where my father was buried. Tears flowed from my eyes as I saw the knolls and hillocks where I used to run and play. I lamented those days and wondered if they could ever return now that I had lost my father.

In the passes, plains, and knolls of the wilderness, I frequently saw the Israeli army patrols stop youths and men and hold them for long hours under the burning heat of the sun. The soldiers hit and tortured them severely before they led them to detention. Anger filled my breast and blood boiled in my veins. I felt as if embers flamed in my heart and I silently wondered where is my giant of a father to teach those ruffians a lesson?

The situation remained unstable and my family had to stay in that distant, remote area. Living in the wilderness took away an entire school year as I was five years old when the war broke out. The following year, my family elders hastened to move us to a village in the Palestinian countryside so that I could go to school. For an entire year in the new area we had a tremendously difficult life. I was bothered and embarrassed by the fact that everybody considered us underage orphans who required compassion and pity.

During that year my family survived on aid from well-to-do people in our area. They gave us the means to meet our basic needs.

When the school year was over, and as calm partially returned, my family decided to return to our house in Jabal Almukaber, which overlooks Jerusalem from the southeast. When I took my first steps into the courtyard I felt, for the first time, as if I were a stranger to our house. Signs of heavy shelling were apparent; the walls and doors contained the remains of bullets, shrapnel, and shells. And the house had been looted after its doors and windows had been removed.

Nothing was spared except for the remains of old, worn-out furniture.

One afternoon, seven of our relatives wearing Palestinian keffiyas [scarves] around their necks came to our house. They talked briefly with my mother and then they got up to go, their faces dark and frowning. They stepped out to the yard behind the house and started digging.

I screamed at my mother, "What are they doing, Mother?"

She stepped aside and began to wail and cry. The men were unearthing my father's body to move it to the village graveyard. I couldn't stand the sight. I secluded myself behind a nearby mound and cried.

After several days had passed, I heard my mother proclaim, "Your father is a martyr, Mohammad. Did you see how perfect and healthy-looking his body seemed when the men took him away? The worms seem not to have touched it."

Over the next few months my mother frequently recounted strange stories of how my father was martyred. She told us of her visions of him in her dreams:

"The day following the beginning of the 1967 war," Mother said, "some of our men took the risk of coming to our house in the middle of the shelling to find out about your father's end. When they reached the courtyard, they lay on the ground and called to him in low, rattling voices. They were hoping he'd come out of one of the rooms or one of the neighboring caverns. As the shelling was getting heavier, one of them decided, in a final attempt, to enter a cavern on the western side of the house. There he witnessed a terrifying scene. Your father was squatting and leaning on his right

193

shoulder. Next to him was a jug of water. For an instant, the man thought your father was still alive and started trying to wake him up, thinking that he was only sleeping. He realized the bitter truth quickly though."

We held our breaths as my mother spoke the next terrible words. "Your father had been dead for hours, and his soul had flowed to God's mercy. The man, tears drowning his face, rejoined his company. The men instantly realized the truth of the matter and wept. They had no time to waste, though, and ran quickly to where the body was. In a rare courageous stand, and under gunfire, they carried your father's body and buried it in our yard because they felt that it must not remain unburied. Later they withdrew to the nearby valleys."

Sometimes my mother would wake us in the middle of the night and say, "Did you hear soldiers calling for your father and ask him for help?" Fear would fill our hearts. We'd have nightmares when we went to sleep.

The window of the room where we slept overlooked the yard where my father was buried:

> *It is about sunset. Suddenly I see my father carrying something that looks like a knife. When I call to him, he disappears into an alley. I run after him, against my will, and scream: "Father, Father, do you hear me?" But he doesn't respond and continues to run. I follow, and when I catch up with him he turns around to face me but he has turned into an Israeli soldier. He stares at me with sparkly eyes and lifts his weapon and points it at my face.*

I would wake up from such nightmares horrified and perspiring profusely. Fear would lock the breath in my throat.

When I recounted the nightmares to elders, they explained that my desire to see my father was connected to my fear of the Israeli soldier who had caused his death. Terrible dreams and nightmares accompanied me for long nights, especially because my mother never stopped telling her stories about my father. She told of his heroic deeds and his manly stands. She told us of how a hyena attacked him once when he came back from the wilderness on his white horse. My father, smart and courageous, got rid of the hyena by lighting a match and throwing it at the beast.

My mother said, "Your father was killed because he refused to leave our house and to believe that we could be defeated. When he heard the Israeli soldiers' footsteps, he came out to welcome them, thinking it was the Iraqi army. (Many people were saying that units of the Iraqi army had arrived to fight against the Israelis.) He was greeted by a shower of gunfire, though, and fell dead. Later, Jordanian soldiers came and tried to help him. They put him in the cavern where he was found dead. Your father was killed as he was defending our home — our little homeland. You must never forget that."

I used to play not far from the earth pit that housed my father's body. I saw swollen mounds which hid the corpses of Jordanian and Iraqi soldiers who were killed in the war. Those were, then, the souls of soldiers who called for my father at night, I thought, as my mother had told us. A few months later, Israeli bulldozers arrived and removed those human piles. I stood on a big rock, awestruck, and stared at the machines as they pounded the bones of the dead. Somehow, I thought my father's bones were among them, and tears filled my eyes.

The same bulldozers came back later and removed the well that my family drank from and tore down the caves near our house. They also confiscated a good part of our land and others' on which they built a huge settlement to house thousands of Ethiopian and Russian newcomers.

One incident sticks in my memories of those days. While the Israeli bulldozers were tearing up our land and removing the well, a cousin of mine, who was in his twenties, threw himself on the floor of a cave that the drivers were trying to fill with dirt. The driver stood astonished and undecided as to what to do. The slightest movement of the machine would have meant that my cousin would have been buried alive.

People gathered and much clamor ensued, but my cousin refused to leave the cave. Several people tried to convince him to leave, but he decided to die instead, clinging to and loving the land where he grew up. I knew I was about to witness a hot confrontation between the people and the settlers, but a great number of Israeli security and police forces arrived and instantly threw tear gas inside the cave. They forcefully removed my cousin and took him to prison.

Today, as I pass by the knoll that has my father's grave and that overlooks Jerusalem—the glowing dome of the Rock and the great Aqsa mosque which embraces the eternal Holy Sepulcher Church—I recall the remains of the memories of the beautiful times we had with my father and those sad events that we survived in his absence. Feelings flow within me—springs of sorrow for my father's departure. Yearning for him fills me and I feel as if the knolls and hills echo my cry: I am proud of you, Father . . . despite the pain and suffering your departure has caused us, you remain a lively image among us. Here the people who knew you still describe you with love and admiration and tell people about your attributes and virtues.

This cub is this lion's son. I ask God to have mercy on your soul. And we want you to pray for us while you are in the other world so we won't be victims to more wars, and our children won't face a similar tragedy.

TANYA GARDINER-SCOTT

Tanya Gardiner-Scott was cross-culturally adopted in Israel by her Scottish father and Serbian-American mother at the age of six months. She grew up in the Highlands of Scotland, but lived with her parents in Jerusalem from 1959 to 1960 and 1966 to 1972. After being educated in Great Britain and Canada, she emigrated to the United States in 1986. Now a thirty-nine-year-old professor of English at Mount Ida College, she often publishes essays about the work of author Mervyn Peake and medieval literature. She also is a contributing author for several science fiction/fantasy biographical dictionaries and encyclopedias.

"Shards," her account of her experiences as an eight-year-old living in West Jerusalem during the Six-Day War, traces the echoes of that war into the present.

Shards

"Where were you in 1967?" you asked. My parents and I lived in West Jerusalem, at St. Andrews Hospice, where my father was the Church of Scotland minister and ran the thirty-bed hostel for guests. It overlooked the Old City and Mount Zion, with only the Hinnom Valley separating us from what was then mostly Jordanian territory. So when the firing began on June 5, we were right on the front line. In fact, the Israelis had asked my father if they could use the church as a lookout post, but he had refused, reminding them that it was a holy place.

"What was it like for you? You must have been scared," you said. I started to answer—and suddenly, to my horror, I was back in Jerusalem in my eight-year-old body, hearing that funny click and then the air raid sirens, running to the room with no windows to which my father had told me to go, clutching the first-aid box with its cold metal edges as if it were my mother's hand.

There were others at the hospice, but my father was at the supermarket, my mother at language school, and I was alone inside, determined not to show my fear and clutching that damned box for dear life.

I hope nobody will be hurt—I don't know what I'll do if there's blood. I wonder how we'll all fit in here. What will we eat?

And then reloading—suddenly—where's the noise? The silence yawned like a bottomless pit. The minutes were eternity.

This noise HURTS! It doesn't matter that I couldn't see—I could hear. The bullets whining, shells bursting, the tinkle and sudden crash of broken glass falling a hundred feet and the shudder of the building as a mortar penetrated half of its outer wall. The older girl cried a bit—she was fine—her mother, our housekeeper, was with her. We had been at school together that morning, and my father had brought us home and then gone shopping for food, just in case.

Suddenly my father came bursting in, shopping bags, un-believably, still in hand, with a story about forcing the manager to let him leave the supermarket, driving as far as he could before the Israeli Army stopped him, and then using his training in the Black Watch (an elite Scottish regiment) to dash from door to door on his way through the bullets. He says he was in one doorway and decided that if a clergyman died with beer bottles in his bags it wouldn't look good . . . He left his beer. Hope *somebody* had a free drink!

"Any word of your mother?" he asked. My guts clenched with icy passion. Mother—I need you—and I bulldozed that thought as it started to erect itself in my heart.

All right, Father—and we went into the small room with no windows next door, while the others stayed in the room he'd secured with mattresses over the windows and a protective cliff outside.

We were crouching by the phone and calling the number of the language school. When there was an answer my father started to shout, and I wished I could shut up the shooting so he could hear. The noise was deafening. I'll just sit here and maybe—"HERE, honey, say hello to your mother."

"I love you." BANG. CRASH . . . RAT-TAT-TAT—faster than the words of love could blot out, my mother's voice drowned by the cacophony outside. My father, trying not to cry, me trying not to cry, knowing that she was under a table talking to us while the phone line held. BANG. CRASH. "That was your end this time. I love you. See you soon." And the line went dead. Shot down.

My father opened the door to the next room and said, "I'm going to feed you all now." Then he ducked and dodged to the kitchen and boiled a chicken he'd bought so we had fresh food between the now ten of us in there. Oh, we had things to do. We had a fiddle, and a recorder, and, most important of all, a radio. Blankets. Candles—candles that I'd made him buy even when he didn't think we'd have a war. And I STILL can't keep down sardines in tomato sauce to this day.

BANG. CRASH. Twenty minutes later by someone's watch. BANG. CRASH. Time had stopped and the only sounds were silence and the barrage. How long? Well, we still had water and food, and we sat there grimly trying to talk and sing and listen to the radio. Mustn't let the side down. Must support my father. Mustn't think of mother. Sleep. And then suddenly I sat bolt upright on the mattress the other girl and I were sharing—the glass was crashing. The old Armenian caretaker was shaking my father saying, "Make it STOP! Make it STOP! MAKE IT STOP!"

Bleary. Unrested. Time's tracers streaking the sky, time exploding all around us. MAKE IT STOP! The days went by.

The morning of June 7 there was suddenly silence. Even my mother came back, and we watched the surrender of the city through binoculars, the raising of the flag on the battlements of the Old City, the celebrating in the streets. And there was a soldier who shooed me away from his tank when I wanted to see like all the other curious kids.

Well, yes, I can talk about it. I'm here, two decades and more later, a college professor continents away. Not the ghosts my mother's family in Serbia thought we were when we showed up four years later unannounced. Solid. Flesh and unspilt blood.

So why, when you asked me so gently if I was scared, did I run to my room clutching the congealed fear like a metal box, close the door and go into MY windowless room and not be able to stop crying? The medicines I had used then were useless now; the wounds were open, bleeding, the tears un-sobbed back then, and I rocked and cried, wept and cried, screamed and cried. CRIED. CRIED. CRIED, and finally slept.

Six years later, at boarding school in Scotland, I got the letter from my mother. "IF there's war, dear, you know where we are and we'll be all right."

The Yom Kippur war had begun. There was the agitated voice of a friend on the phone. "The firing's started. What are you going to do? I'm going to try and volunteer."

"I can't—I'm in school. What can I do? Good luck."

The receiver clicked, and I rushed off to my dorm.

God, what's that awful noise? Sounds like an animal howling at the moon. Guts clenching with melting ice. Breath screaming through constricting paths. And with every breath my wailing, dry-eyed, gut-drying, body screaming O NO NOT THERE NOT NOW O NOOOOO!

Days later, hearing that my parents were all right. Long days, helpless days.

The 1980s. With the Intifadah [Palestinian uprising] raging, and ordinary people being stabbed to death by Palestinian activists, every time I read or hear "stabbed," "in the street," "at the cafe," "just looking," "killing," "revenge," "stabbed," my guts clench. It could be them, walking to the post office, going to pay the rent. And the child inside starts to scream, high and piercing. And I say to her, Honey, I'm here to be with you, to love you, to comfort you if the worst which could be the worst goes on. People make choices. They know the risks. And part of me thinks the world in my head would shatter like the glass shards falling a long way down. SILENCE. THEN NOISE AGAIN.

But I know I can weep and cry—and do go on.

1990. SCUD. SCUD ALERT. MISSILE INCOMING TO ISRAEL. When I am not in the classroom, I am glued to the Gulf War TV reports in my Boston suburb. I pick up the phone with shaking hands. "Are you safe in the room? Have you your masks? Are you OK? I love you no matter what."

"Yes, yes, we're fine. Our neighbors are there for us."

I'M THERE FOR YOU. I LOVE YOU. YOU'RE WHERE YOU WANT TO BE—STILL IN JERUSALEM. I accept your choice. Something in me would be lost if you were killed, but something, born of that choice, in that land, from that SILENCE BANG CRASH would survive.

MOHAMMAD MASAD

Currently writing his doctoral dissertation in history and teaching Middle Eastern and Islamic History and Civilization at Washington University in St. Louis, Mohammad Masad was born in the West Bank in 1958, where he lived until he left for graduate school in the United States in 1984.

Masad's story takes place a week after the end of the 1967 Six-Day War—he is nine years old. On this day he and his father undertake a very sad venture—a visit to their village of Zeita, which they've been told the Israeli Army has almost completely destroyed. The little boy registers one shock after another as he discovers that only four houses in his part of the village have been left standing.

Borderland

*M*y father turned to the taxi driver and asked him to drop us at the second dirt road. Then, with his hand on my head, he said, "So my boy doesn't get hurt walking in the rubble. And, in any case, this is the right way home."

I couldn't help feeling more curious than ever. I pondered what my father had said. I thought I understood what rubble he was referring to but tried in vain to visualize it. It seemed this trip was becoming an enigma. It was supposed to be a quick visit to our house in the village to bring some salted goat cheese and olive oil. These were to replenish my family's supplies at the house we rented in the nearby town. I had to plead tearfully, over my mother's objections, before my father agreed to take me with him.

Perhaps he needed company or thought he might use my help somehow. But taking this road? And at this time when the war had barely ended? I had never before come to Zeita from this direction. Nobody ever did except the fancy-looking officers of the Liaison Committee and the corpses or runaway soldiers and infiltrators shot dead by Jewish guards on this side of the border.

The driver hesitated for a moment; then he agreed with a little grumble. "By God, uncle, I only do this because of the little boy. I swear I never wanted to go past the right turn at the Birkeh," he said, referring to the large depression at the right and the natural dirt path snaking out of its northern rim. "You know it's still a risky business, uncle, but I will do it for God's sake."

My father thanked him and then added with a mild reproach, "By God, brother, the whole trip was a gamble! This road you took, all the way from Shweikeh to here, has been closed to us for twenty years . . . I mean this whole time you've been driving inside the '48 lands, inside Israel. A hundred meters more will not change anything."

The driver didn't answer but shifted gears and climbed down the hill just before the Birkeh. As the village came into view, he looked quickly, shook his head and said in a low, sad voice, "There is no strength or power except through God." Then, turning to my father, he said, "You people of

Zeita, may God help you in your calamity. May God grant you patience."

I was sitting next to my father half-listening as I looked outside the window, anxiously studying the unfamiliar surroundings. I was nine years old but felt like I had grown up a whole year for each day of the past two weeks. The war had lasted six days and ended a week ago, but the air was still rife with fear and apprehension. I was still recovering from my family's flight to Kufr al-Labad on the first day of the war and the trek back through the mountains to our house at the western fringes of Tulkarm.

The Arabs lost the war, and the signs of our defeat were everywhere. The most indelible sign for me was the sight of my older brother's friend, Mustafa, realizing the disastrous crumbling of the Arab armies, smashing his radio to the ground, and crying like a child.

Nobody could tell with certainty what to expect, what would become of us, how long this defeat would last. The same night we returned to Tulkarm, my mother started ranting about seeing the tormented ghosts of the four neighbors who got killed in the bombardment. She told my father that as soon as life returned to normal, she would not stay in that house one more moment.

Life was not quite yet back to normal. The white flags of surrender fluttered on rooftops and dangled from balconies. They looked like pieces of cloth torn out of the same death shroud. People ventured out only to buy necessities, and a night-long curfew was still in effect. My family spent the days swapping war stories with the neighbors, gathering news, and silently watching the military jeeps and armored carriers of the victorious enemies roaming the streets from behind window curtains or slightly opened doors. Fear reigned everywhere, as long and heavy as the days of that summer.

The soldiers shouted orders in broken Arabic over the loudspeakers. Occasionally their Arabic became semi-fluent as they shouted obscenities. The most-repeated phrase in all of these announcements was the name, "The Israeli Defense Force." A name which prompted my mother to murmur things like, "May God defend us against your evil," or "May God render you defenseless and send you back to where you came from."

At nightfall, however, we would huddle in the living room, lights off and only a candle burning, to talk in whispers and listen to the incessant shooting ripping the quietness of the night. There were tense moments of anxiety and fear every time a military vehicle stopped by our house. Our whispers would gradually come to a halt as we sat there listening to the sound of the strange crackling radio messages relayed between the soldiers and their headquarters. What were they saying? None of us understood Hebrew.

Within a few days of our return, some of the rumors that flew mindlessly in the first days of the war were discredited, while other ones proved to be more credible. There were no mass rapes and no mass indiscriminate killings of civilians. But many people were indeed expelled to the east of the River Jordan, and those who, after having fled or been deported, tried to return were shot at and forced back. Also, there were villages that suffered deliberate destruction. Zeita, our village, was one of them.

My father first learned of this the day we started back from the village in the mountains where we'd been hiding. He met a man from Baqa al-Sharqiyyeh, a village close to ours, who told him that Zeita was razed to the ground. The man didn't see it himself but heard it from a number of sources. My father was in a grave mood for the rest of the day. He vented his frustration mainly on my mother who, upon learning of the disaster, walked aimlessly around the house, slapping her hands together and announcing mournfully, "Oh my father, oh my beloved mother, what an awful calamity! Where was this evil hidden for us? Now we are done for forever, and the rag of a house that we had is gone."

My father's shouts of, "That's enough, woman! For God's sake, cut it out!" did little to stop my mother's lamentations nor did it change my father's temperament.

The next morning my father decided to go and check things himself. The few taxi drivers he found refused to drive outside town. So he went on foot all the way to the village. He returned just before dusk and told us in a weary voice that the whole western half of the village was dynamited. Only the Zawiyeh of the Dervishes and four houses, including ours, were left standing. He also found out that the shop he owned in the central part of the village was broken into and looted by people stockpiling food supplies. There was a little sense of relief regarding our house, but the grim reality of the enormous destruction, reflected on my father's face, drowned out everything else. I could sense the gravity of what happened when my father, who normally didn't smoke, lit up a cigarette and walked around the house aimlessly, repeating to himself, "God Almighty, strike them down . . . God Almighty, God Almighty . . ."

* * *

The taxi was speeding down the slope before the first dirt road. To the right was the Birkeh, now dry and covered with wild plants of all sorts. Two white concrete structures indicated the dividing line between two mutually hostile worlds. Two border posts, standing there like two headless statues, two mysterious tombstones.

A little farther to the east I could see the periphery of the village fields where people grew okra, green beans, muluk-hiyyeh [mallow plant], and cauliflower. There was the spot where the Abdulrazzaq brothers were shot dead by a Jewish sniper some years ago. They were working in the field when their donkey was startled and began running toward the border. The first brother was shot as he approached the forbidden zone trying to rein in his donkey. The second brother was shot as he tried to drag his fallen sibling away from the death trap. As the news spread, the people flocked to the cemetery overlooking the field and watched helplessly, until the fancy-looking liaison officers arrived and arranged for the removal of the bodies.

Suddenly I became aware of the scene beyond the fields and the cemetery. The houses which lined the outskirts of the village were not to be seen. Instead, I could only make out heaps of rubble and concrete, one next to the other. The new landscape was hard to grasp. The tall, white stone buildings with their painted doors and balconies and barred windows had disappeared. The elegant two-story house of the Awwads, right across from the Zawiyeh, where they had the elaborate wedding of Fawzi last summer, was reduced to a pile of mutilated concrete and iron. It was mystifying and confusing, this sudden demise of houses—big and strong houses which to me looked like they could last forever. Even the remaining unchanged elements—the Dervishes' residence, the cemetery and the two old cedar trees on its top, and the border posts—were now equally bewildering, looking more like lost and solitary figures against the scarred horizon.

The taxi dropped us at the second dirt road and turned back. I stood there and watched my father surveying the area. The almond and peach groves stretched along the other side of the main street and up the rocky slopes of the small hill that hides the village of Jett. I knew my father had relatives there whom he had not seen since the border divided Jett from Zeita, not long after the end of the 1948 War, the Catastrophe.

In front of us was a little path, running in the middle of the grazing area that connects the Birkeh to the sloping wide stretches of land known as al-Qat'at. The air was thick with the sweltering heat and the aroma of overgrown plants. As we walked eastward, I could see other border posts between the edge of the pasture and the most western village groves.

I had a strange feeling walking on this side of the border. This was the other world, infinitely forbidding and alien, that I normally watched from a safe distance on the other side of the border, sometimes curiously waving to oblique figures of shepherds who might wave back or simply wave their guns threateningly. This was the side I saw every day, but always as a distant, silent show; so clear in the open space, yet concealing beyond its ridges a world unknown; so innocent-looking, yet something sinister loomed behind its surface. Here I was walking in the very place which I have always thought would devour the wretched souls who strayed into it.

My father walked slowly, looking around him with a faint smile on his face. Suddenly, he stopped and said, "It is the breeze from the sea. . . ."

I did feel a gentle rush of cool air, and the plants swayed slightly. He then continued as if talking to himself, "The sea is not that far from here. Some silent summer nights I think I can hear the waves from the roof of the house."

He was quiet for a moment. I was thinking how much bigger than the Birkeh the sea was. I knew the name "Mediterranean" from my geography classes, but I had never seen a sea before, though this Mediterranean was said to be really close. Most of the land the village lost in 1948 was part of a huge collectively-owned plot known as Raml Zeita which stretched all the way to the sea.

My father continued, "Before the Catastrophe, I always went to the Raml and came back this way. How many times I did that!" I followed his gaze, softly caressing the stretch of borderland, before he added with a shake of his head, "By God it is amazing that it took another war, another catastrophe, that we had once again to taste the bitterness . . ." And he fell silent, took my hand, and walked away.

Trying to keep up with his steps, I suddenly realized I wasn't anxious anymore; that this was not a forbidden territory. I felt as if I had walked that way hundreds of times—as if this path was not any different from the clearing behind our house in the village.

We left the border posts behind us and entered a path lined with cacti. The bunker on the right led through a deep trench to a building with a watchtower. This was the front line where Jordanian soldiers would take turns guarding the border. The place was deserted, and there were no signs of fighting. I thought about Hamid, the soldier from Irbid, who would let me play with his binoculars as he practiced target shooting with my brother-in-law. They would do this near the clearing separating our house from the road, often shooting dum-dums at small coins. I found myself wondering if he was alive or dead.

During our flight, I heard heart-breaking stories about retreating Jordanian units wiped out by Jewish planes; about the burned tanks and charred bodies near Jenin and Nablus; about dogs running around with human limbs.

Pointing to the bunker, I asked my father if he knew what had become of Hamid.

My father sighed and said, "Only God knows, my son. I know for sure there was no fighting here. The handful of soldiers they had here were ordered to leave as soon as the war broke out."

He walked faster as we approached the bend in the path where the road curved to the left and the cacti grew thicker and taller. I listened to the familiar rustle of his yellow *qumbaz* (traditional long dress) and felt content. Sheltered from the hot sun by the shade of the cacti I walked almost in a state of bliss.

If only I could make sense of those piles of rubble, of the scarred horizon. Were they destroyed during the fighting? But my father said no fighting took place here! I asked him, "Father, why did the Jews destroy the houses?"

He waited a moment before he answered. "After the Jordanians left the village, the people put their faith in God and waited, not knowing what would happen. Only a few people from the Civil Defense Unit were armed with old rifles. One of them, Abu Saleem al-Qutt, may God curse him, hid by the cedar trees and opened fire at some Jewish cars on the other side. He never hit anything, but he boasted that he destroyed a tank and beat up a whole Jewish unit by the Birkeh . . . the accursed liar and his rotten rifle . . . Soon after that, the Jewish army entered the village without a fight, and the people hoisted the white flags on the roofs. The army ordered the people to gather on the clearing at the eastern edge of the village. They had to sit there under guard, burning in the June sun with no food or water for a good part of the day. The soldiers told the people they were searching for weapons when, in fact, they were busy blowing up their houses.

The people heard the explosions but were not sure what was going on. Some thought the army might be blowing up bunkers and trenches. Hours later, as the explosions got closer and clouds of dust and smoke filled the sky, some people became more suspicious. But from their vantage point on the eastern clearing, they could see none of the actual destruction. So, when the army finally told the people to go home, they went home only to find that half of them had become homeless."

My father paused, as if unable to continue. He sighed deeply and repeated, "There is no strength or power except by God" several times. We reached the end of the path and emerged from between the cacti to the wider road. The bunkers on the right were still there as well as the trenches dissecting the clearing on the left.

Not far from the bunkers were the houses that survived the carnage. Al-Masri's room by the road, the Balbisis' house behind it. Then a little farther north, our house of two separate rooms flanked by a kitchen and a bathroom. Two more houses to the east of al-Masri's room were also standing. Farther east and south was only destruction. All I could see were enormous heaps of building material, jagged and twisted concrete blocks and metal beams, and splintered roofs sitting in the dust. How could they do this? Why did they do this?

As we were leaving our house, a jar of cheese between my arms and a tin container of olive oil carried by my father, I suddenly remembered my mother's constant complaint about having to live so close to the border. I wondered if she would change her mind now that our house escaped demolition.

I asked my father if he knew why they left these houses standing.

He shook his head. "How should I know, my son? Then, pointing to the sad ruins, he said, "First let someone explain why they did that . . . destroying people's lives like this. But there is a God. There is God . . ."

We reached the road and he turned right. I asked him, "Are we going back the same way?"

He entered the cactus path and went west without looking behind or answering. I remembered his pause and faint smile on our way home, his soft caressing gaze and what he had said about the sea and the breeze. I hurried up and turned and followed him.

Glancing behind, I took one last look at the houses and only saw the bright reflection of the sun. The sun was shining right into my eyes. I was already feeling the weight of the jar of cheese, and I was doing my best trying to keep up with my father. The sweat was pouring into my eyes, and I could hardly make out his figure ahead of me. His tin container of olive oil was bursting with light, and the rustle of his yellow *qumbaz* echoed in the solitary silence of the cactus path.

MARINA N. RIADI

Marina Riadi's family lived in Jerusalem until they were forced out in May 1948. Now living in Atlanta, Georgia, she has worked for peace organizations in the Middle East, Europe, and the United States for twenty-five years and has had several books and articles published about the Palestinian-Israeli peace process.

In this poignant story of her twelve-year-old yearning to understand the children and the adults caught up in the Israeli-Palestinian conflict, one can see the roots of Riadi's lifelong interest in peace work.

(See photo insert.)

Born in Bethlehem

*M*y first experience of the war in 1967 brought many questions to my young mind, some of which still are unanswered. I was twelve years old and very eager to know how Israeli children my age felt during the war. Were they as frightened as I was? Did they worry that they might lose their parents or other family members as I did?

Naturally, after the Israeli army occupied our little town of Bethlehem and the rest of our lands on the West Bank and the Gaza Strip, we were not allowed to travel freely within those lands. We were not allowed into Israel proper either. We became captives in our own homes, forced to stay in our small towns. I wanted so much to travel into Israel and see the Israeli people, their families, and their children.

On some gray and lonesome summer afternoons, when Bethlehem became very quiet, I would gaze at the horizon and the yonder hills and imagine what it would be like to cross the "borders," thereafter known as the "Green Line," and discover how children lived in Israel. I wanted to find out about their lives, their hopes, their fears, and their dreams.

My father, observing the extent of my curiosity, decided to take me on a short venture into Israel. My mother and the rest of our family became very anxious as my father announced that he and I were going to West Jerusalem to explore and talk to Israelis.

My mother gasped and with half a breath said, "You'll be arrested for going into Israel without a permit. Then what will I do? Where will I find you? Plus, you're taking the child with you, which makes two of you to worry about. No, you're not going!"

But, my father, being as determined and stubborn as always, decided not to heed my mother's warnings, and off we went to Jerusalem.

I will never forget the elation and excitement that I experienced as soon as we got into the taxi that drove us to the border beyond which we would have to walk. Neither my father nor I thought about how long the walk would be. We were both ready to go and full of the energy and stamina needed for such a venture. I walked up Jaffa Road, then Ben Yehuda Street, and over to King George Street. I observed and scrutinized every passerby, while trying to keep a low profile and blend in with the rest of the pedestrians.

My father was cautious not to attract any particular attention, but at the same time he was totally relaxed and confided that we were going to be perfectly safe and undisturbed. He was right. The more we walked and looked in store windows to check out Israeli merchandise and compare it to what we had in our Bethlehem stores, the more I felt relaxed and happy to be walking along with my father in a city which he loved dearly and to which he belonged until he was forced out in 1948.

I felt so proud to see that my father knew his way around West Jerusalem and could show me the new construction that had taken place since he had last seen it. Occasionally he would wonder about the location of a certain cafe or a restaurant where he and his friends had met. So, we would stop by at one of the stores and he would ask the owner about the place. Most of the time we found out that the store owners were new Jewish immigrants who did not know the sites or the city as well as my father. I felt very proud to realize that my father, who had not lived in West Jerusalem for the past twenty years, knew the city better than its present inhabitants.

But this fact brought a dilemma to my mind. I started wondering about how someone like my father can know a city which is not his anymore better than those who now live in it. Why did he have to leave it if he knew it and loved it so dearly? What were the circumstances that extracted him so abruptly from his roots? Did he have to go in order for the new immigrants to come. And, if so, why? Why couldn't he stay while the new immigrants came in and settled? He could have helped them get acquainted, oriented them to Jerusalem, and given them his knowledge and love for the city.

All these questions were racing in my mind as we crossed from one street to another. Occasionally I would look up at my father to see how he was feeling and if he still had the strength for more exploration. But, having been the strong athlete that he had been for years, my father was tireless and gathered more vigor as we walked on.

We arrived at the YMCA. He pointed out its high tower to me and described how he used to go there directly after school to work out, play racket ball, and practice boxing. He also showed me the local radio broadcast station where he played his music and performed on the air. He told me how on many occasions he would play along with Jewish musicians who were new immigrants from Europe—mostly from Germany and Poland. He told me how much he enjoyed learning from them about European musical instruments and teaching them about Middle Eastern instruments. I watched him yearn for those days and for those people with whom he developed strong friendships.

I watched him become sad and disillusioned as he described his life prior to 1948. He spoke fondly of his Jewish friends and even told me of a Jewish family whose daughter he used to take out. He said that her mother often told him that she prayed fervently that her daughter and my father would one day marry each other.

I listened carefully to his stories, absorbed every event and minute detail, as if it were an important milestone in the journey of my own life. I sensed my father's pain as he described the separation and the forced parting from his home, his city, his friends, and—most of all—his fond memories.

I was getting a little hungry, even though my mother had fed us a good and substantial lunch, in case we did not make it back home in time for the next meal. My father suggested we go for a snack of coffee and cake and chose the Kapulski pastry shop, a small cafe which was in business in 1948 and was one of the few that continued to operate. We walked in and, once more to my amazement, my father seemed familiar with the family who owned the place. He inquired about the welfare of the owners he had known, but, to his disappointment, he was told that even though the present owners were familiar with the names of the past owners, the place had been sold to new owners who decided to keep the old name.

We sat down, had a beverage and a pastry, and observed passersby and walk-ins. My father told me that Kapulski was the best pastry shop in West Jerusalem and that his family would order platters from there for parties, receptions, birthdays, and other social events. It was another landmark of my father's years in Jerusalem.

Eventually we both realized that we were getting tired. In addition, the emotional and sentimental feelings that surfaced with all the recollections of Jerusalem started to weigh on us, with the heavier burden laying on my father's shoulders.

On our way back towards the border, I stopped to look in the window of a music store. I loved music and I bought and collected all the latest hits and musicals from movies as soon as they were available in the market. My eye caught the album of the movie *The Sound of Music.* I was astonished to see that the album had arrived and was available for sale. I gasped and looked up at my father. Without saying a word, he understood what I wanted. He looked at me and said, "Alas! I'm out of Israeli money. This has to wait for the next time we come up here."

Upon hearing that, I was so disappointed that I was at the point of crying over the album. One more look at me and my father decided to walk into the store. I lingered behind, a little apprehensive of what my father was up to. This was only a few days after the 1967 war, Israeli currency had not gotten distributed in our markets, and our Jordanian currency was no longer good in Israeli markets. Moreover, I was well aware that my father and I needed to remain incognito on our venture lest we end up being stopped, asked for a permit, and arrested for going into Israel.

But my father was fearless as usual. He walked up to the music store owner and, stretching out his hand to greet him, introduced himself to the Israeli man. I was still standing halfway between the entrance to the store and my father. The store owner responded in a friendly, welcoming manner to my father's greeting and shook hands with him. I was bewildered. I asked myself if my father knew that man before 1948. Was he a friend, a neighbor, an acquaintance? I thought my father and I had agreed not to bring any attention to ourselves—not to reveal our identity—and especially not to tell anyone where we were from.

I started wondering if my father was making a big mistake and one that would jeopardize our safety. But, at the same time, I knew my father very well and believed strongly in his good judgment and common sense. I decided to let go of all fears and give my full attention to the situation as it developed. I also knew deep down in my heart that my father would only do the right thing and that we were safe.

The next thing I heard was my father asking the store owner if he would accept Jordanian currency. The man responded that not only would he accept Jordanian currency, but that he would also honor it. I became completely confused. I thought we were enemies meeting in the aftermath of the war, and now we were about to make a commercial transaction with Jordanian currency in an Israeli store where the owner is paying homage to Jordanian money. I started doubting my own capacity for understanding reality.

The music store owner proceeded to explain to us that he was a new immigrant from Iraq and that he, himself, was new to Jerusalem. In fact, as soon as he spoke to us in Arabic I could hear a different accent and dialect from ours.

My father divulged our tightly held secret and told him that he was from Jerusalem and that he grew up in the vicinity. He also explained to him that we were now living in Bethlehem and he was bringing me to visit his city and share with me his past history and memories. I could tell the man was moved. With tearful and very expressive and compassionate eyes, he looked at my father indicating that he fully understood the tragedy.

I, still a spectator watching every move and interaction between the two men, was still worried about our safety and return home. I was also getting anxious and wondered if and when the transaction would take place so that I could take my album and run home to listen to it.

When all was said about the two men's lives and histories—the Israeli man's experience in Iraq and my father's life in Jerusalem—my father explained the reason for our going into his store. The man seemed to understand my father's wish to please me and buy me the album with Jordanian money. He said that he, himself, had children and knew what it meant when a child wanted something.

I wished I could meet his children, especially those who were close to my age. I wanted to ask them about the war and what happened to them. I wanted to find out about their experience as victors and winners of that war. I simply wanted to know them.

The music store owner walked over to one of the shelves behind the counter, pulled out a brand new album, put it in a paper bag, and handed it over to me. I was delighted and ready to go before anyone else, who might be less friendly and understanding, discovered who we were. My father handed the man the Jordanian money, but, to my amazement, the man would not take it. Instead, he told my father that we could pay him the next time we came to Jerusalem. He said that because of the exchange rate the album would cost my father much more if he paid in Jordanian money rather than in Israeli money.

My father did not care the least about the price and insisted that he take the money, placing it in his hand. The man took the money and handed it over to me saying, "You have a wonderful father. I hope you know that. There aren't many people in this world as honest and straightforward as your father. Do appreciate him and learn all you can from him."

I was in total agreement with what he said, for I already knew the value of my father. I was very surprised to see that the man had come to know and value my father as well as I did in such a short time. He insisted on not taking the money and waiting for us to come back on another occasion. My father felt obliged to leave him our name, address, and phone number. But the man refused to take that information, assuring my father that there was no need for that since he was sure we would come back to pay him with Israeli money.

I was totally amazed. I could not understand how that store owner came to know and understand my father in the first place, much less trust us to walk out with his merchandise and go to an area which he could not access easily and safely because of the state of war.

At that point I thought I had to rise to the occasion and prove worthy of such a father. So I offered with some regret to give back the album that I was holding in my hand, close to my heart, and to buy it on our next trip to Jerusalem. I put the album on the counter and sadly walked back toward the door of the store.

The Israeli man followed me with the album and put it in my hand saying, "You see, I want you to come back, I want to see you again." Looking at my father he added, "I hope next time you come you will bring the rest of your family. I would love to meet them all."

I looked up at him and said, "Sir, I'm just curious, how would you know people whom you can trust from those whom you cannot trust?"

He answered without hesitation. "You look at them straight in the eye and you can easily tell those you can trust from those you cannot. Your father, young lady, is beyond all doubt. One look in his eyes, and I could tell that he was a trustworthy man. You are very lucky to have him."

I held the album even closer to my heart, and my father and I thanked him and reassured him that we would be back to pay him in Israeli money as soon as we could.

OMAR MAHDAWI

In this painfully revealing story of the Israeli occupation of his village in the West Bank during the Six-Day War when he was sixteen years old, Omar Mahdawi records both the details of the death and dismemberment that he witnessed and also the frightening thoughts and feelings that these horrors evoked in him.

Now living in New York with his wife and two daughters, aged twelve and fifteen, Mahdawi works as a cameraman, director, and producer of films.

Although this story depicts, perhaps, some of the worst violence against Palestinians of any of the stories in this book, Mahdawi says, "I have no hatred whatsoever against the Israelis, Jews, or anyone else. I do feel sorry for them because they are also the victims of their own power and abuse of power."

He believes that peace can come only when the Palestinians have their own independent state in the West Bank and Gaza, with East Jerusalem as its capital.

Childhood/Manhood

I was born and grew up in Shwaika, a small village in the West Bank, along the borders with Israel. Life was very simple in the fifties; there was no television and the village didn't even have electricity or running water. There was not much to do but wait till the time came when you finished secondary school and left, first to go to university and then to work in Kuwait. That is what I did in my sixteen years in Shwaika—just waited to leave.

I was very lucky though because my best friend had lots of books accumulated by his brothers who went to universities in Cairo. And books were not my only window to the outside world. At the age of ten I discovered the movies in Tulkarm, the neighboring town with two cinemas and both of them always showed a double bill. My mother never knew about it. She was busy running the household as my father, like most of the men in the village, was working in Kuwait.

Apart from books and movies, my small world was limited to endless walks on the west side of the village to watch and admire the activities across the border on the Israeli side. Observing the water sprinklers of the irrigation system, the train on its way from Haifa to Natania, the ruins of Qakun, a small Palestinian village destroyed by the Jews in 1948, I speculated on how many days it would take Nasser to liberate Palestine from the Jews.

My friends were more enthusiastic in this matter than I was, as most of their lands happened to lie on the wrong side of the Armistice line. In summer and autumn we took the risk of crossing the borders to collect the olives and almonds before the Israelis did. It was not really stealing because we knew the land belonged to the village before the creation of the borders.

The danger never came from the Israelis but from the over-zealous Jordanian soldiers who patrolled the borders and would beat up anyone caught anywhere near them.

Most of the victims were the people of Qakun who lived in the nearby Tulkarm refugee camp and who had the peculiar habit of coming to cry at the borders while staring at the ruins of their village and seeing what the Jews were growing on the land.

I was beaten only once, at the age of eleven, when I was caught with four friends while gathering wild fennel. We were imprisoned, beaten up, and forced to sing loudly: "Long live King Hussein."

On summer nights we slept on the roofs and watched the lights of the Israeli kibbutz while listening to Egyptian radio. Above us, the sky was full of bright stars. Then the Big Bang came, and, like the rest of the Arab world, I was unprepared.

When I woke up on 5th June 1967, the war had already started and the Egyptian military communiqué claimed the shooting down of twenty-three Israeli planes. I rushed to join the crowd near the only cafe in the village. Suddenly a shell exploded nearby, followed by a second and a third and then many more. People ran in every direction and I ran with them. I hid for a while in the olive groves on the eastern side of the village and, after a while, I went home, against the advice of the people leaving the village.

My mother refused my requests to leave the village like everybody else. She said that when they had left Haifa in 1948 they had been expecting to go back in a few days, but they never did, and they lost everything. She would not make the same mistake again. I had no alternative but to stay with her and my three sisters and two brothers.

By the end of the day the village was deserted. Apart from the Israeli war planes on their way to and from the east, there was no other sound. Even the shelling was infrequent. It was an eerie atmosphere.

Joined by an old couple who were half deaf, we crowded ourselves in a storeroom under the verandah and spent our first night of the war there. Every now and then my mother or I went up on the roof to spy on the noises of the night. For the first time, there were no lights on the Israeli side.

The next morning was very quiet and many people came back to fetch supplies. An old man called Musleh, passing by on his way to his house, ignored my mother's warning of gun bursts. Women carrying loads of supplies were urging my mother to leave. Suddenly the shelling resumed and everyone was fleeing again.

Someone said a lot of people had been killed and injured, and that many of them were lying in the street in front of the mosque. Zeyad, the name of a boy who was in my class at school, was mentioned. Without thinking, I grabbed a piece of cotton wool and ran to the village center to help Zeyad.

The village center has a few shops grouped strategically around the main entrance of the mosque to catch the men after prayers. When I arrived there, our neighbor Haj Ismael was sitting on the terrace of one of the shops. One side of his face, from his mouth to his ear, was split open, and he was holding it in his hands. His eyes were asking for help, but I told him to go home because first I had to help Zeyad, who was lying nearby in a pool of blood.

The shelling was intense and I had to get Zeyad inside somewhere. He was a little heavy for me, but I managed to get him to stand up and walk the few steps to a small vegetable shop. In front of the shop stood the owner, Abu Zebda, an old man in his sixties. He refused to give any help or even to say anything.

Once inside the room, Zeyad threw himself on the floor and called for his mother. His arms and body were shaking violently. I tried to restrain him and look for his injury. On the top part of his left shoulder there was a big chunk of flesh missing, and I could see the bone and a lot of thick blood. I stuck in the piece of cotton I had with me, but it was too small to fill the hole. I kept telling Zeyad not to worry and that his mother was on her way.

Abu Zebda came inside and sat on the floor, leaning against the wall opposite the door. The shelling intensified, and at one point the room was filled with dust. I jumped into the corner. The next shell must have hit the shop directly because the door was half blown in. I was sure the room and the minaret of the mosque would collapse on top of us.

When the dust had settled I saw that Zeyad was very quiet and I thought he must be asleep, although his eyes were open. Abu Zebda, who had been quiet until then, started making strange noises and calling for his mother. I was very frightened, but I called him a coward for refusing to help. He said he was injured and wanted to unbuckle his long robe to show me, but I said I did not want to see it. He started rising slowly against the wall, groaning in agony and calling for his mother. Then he slid down again as he looked at me. I was very frightened and thought he was going to attack me.

Outside it was raining shells and I was afraid to venture out. I barricaded myself behind some empty boxes and got ready to defend myself. Abu Zebda kept trying to stand up and sliding down again for some time before he collapsed and never moved again. I don't know how many millions of hours passed while I was in the corner of that tiny shop waiting for any movement from Abu Zebda.

Zeyad was lying still. His face was yellow and his eyes were open. He was not looking at me or at anything in particular. Slowly I started to realize that he could be dead because he did not move or even breathe. But then how would I know if he were dead? I had never seen a dead person before even though I was sixteen years old.

Well that is not exactly true—I had seen many people dying in the movies and their friends usually closed their eyes. I do not know why they do that, but they do, and I thought maybe I should do the same. Zeyad was not exactly a good friend but he was a classmate and he had no one to help him. His mother did not come, and his father had died a long time ago in Kuwait.

I thought I should close his eyes. I knew how to do it. In the films the hero usually looks very sad, leans down and looks at his dead beloved and gently closes the eyes. I thought I definitely could do that. Now I became the hero, my sad face filling the screen, my hand stretching out gently and closing the eyes, and everyone in the cinema was crying.

The next moment filled me with terror. I must have tried to move towards Zeyad when all the boxes I had barricaded myself with fell down, shattering the stillness of the room. I folded myself in the corner, closing my eyes and covering my ears. I didn't want to see Abu Zebda attacking me. I didn't want to hear him screaming. I didn't want to be here. I wanted my mother. I wanted God. Where was God?

But God was not there. Abu Zebda and Zeyad were not there. I was not there myself. The tiny room became a desert and my head was speeding aimlessly in it. Every time it stopped, my eyes wandered between the two bodies and I just wanted to masturbate.

I had this overwhelming urge to masturbate. Surely this is not the right time or the right place to do it. No, no I should not do it. Anyway, it could make me blind and then everyone in the village would know what I'd been up to.

Oh how much I hate this place! Well, maybe I should masturbate. No, no, I should not.

Millions of hours passed. Most of the time I was not in that tiny room with these still, quiet bodies. I was watching a movie, talking to my friend Subhi, and reading *Robinson Crusoe* again and again. Then my head would come back and the urge to masturbate would begin again.

But then there was no time to do it. I could hear movement and talking outside. I crawled to the door. There were two women outside. They asked me if Abu Zebda was there. I nodded yes and crawled back to my corner. They came in.

"He is dead," said the older woman. They went through his pockets and removed some papers, notes, and change and ran lamenting and howling. They were his wife and daughter-in-law.

It was some time before I realized the shelling had stopped. Then my legs were racing each other. When I arrived home, I threw myself on the floor and went to sleep immediately.

I must have slept hours and hours because when I woke up it was already dark. At first I could not remember anything or explain the blood on my clothes. Everything seemed unreal and I thought it was just a dream. But I remembered the split face of Haj Ismael and I told my mother, who rushed to his house and found him still alive. She helped him to tie his face together and advised him to try to make it to the hospital in Tulkarm while he still had the strength to walk. He had no one to help him. His wife had died a long time ago and his only son was living in Kuwait.

That night was quiet with no shelling, but there was a big fire eating the bales of wheat left to dry at the edge of the village. We left the storage room under the verandah and slept inside the house. The Israeli radio was telling people to raise a white flag and not to resist the Israeli defense forces while the Egyptian and Jordanian radios talked about the shooting down of more Israeli planes. It was confusing.

My mother seemed alarmed by noises coming from the top of the hill. At first she thought it was Iraqi forces sent to help, as the radio had claimed. Then she became suspicious when she recognized the language.

In the morning we realized the town had been taken by the Jews. It was too late to leave. We had no alternative but to sit there and wait and think of the massacre of Deir Yassin [see 1948 in the chronology on page 352]. I decided I should die first. I didn't want to see my sisters raped and shot before me.

We all sat quiet in one room. I still remember the expression on the yellow face of my two-year-old sister who sat quiet like the rest of us, listening to the approach of the soldiers. We could hear them breaking down the doors of our neighbors' deserted houses.

Then our turn came. They started banging on the iron gate. I shouted that we were inside. My mother hit me with her elbow, but it was too late. They wanted us to open the door. I said it was open. They entered the verandah. There

were a lot of them and they looked at us through the window; they seemed astonished to find us.

One soldier who spoke broken Arabic asked if there were
other people in the village and told us to stay inside and not
go out. A friendly young blond soldier started chatting with
me in English. I managed to understand that they had already taken Jerusalem and Sinai. It was comforting to talk to
him. He was nice and I did not think of him as an enemy. I
felt safe.

They left us in the house and carried on with breaking
into houses and emerging with transistor radios. Some time
later they came back and asked for me. I was inside but my
mother denied my existence. One of the soldiers came in and
found me in the courtyard and took me. He said I had to go
with them. My mother started begging and pleading with
him to spare me, saying I was young and had nothing to do
with this war. Everyone else started crying. I thought they
were going to kill me. There was nothing I could do. I could
not resist. I could not run away. And I should not cry.

I found a comb in my pocket and kept combing my hair.
I managed to understand from the friendly young blond soldier that I had to go with them to bury someone not far away
and that then I could come back. I explained that to my
mother who became more suspicious and insisted on accom-
panying me. I walked near the friendly soldier as the others
seemed angry with us.

It was only a few minutes walk until we reached the swollen body of Musleh, lying face down in the middle of the
street in front of his house. The soldiers asked us to dig a
grave and bury the body. We said we didn't know how to do

it. One of them got angry and pointed his gun at us. Another soldier found a spade and handed it to me.

We chose a spot under the fig tree in front of the house and I started digging. I never knew before how hard it is to dig a grave. My mother helped a little but I did most of the work. I didn't want to see her humiliated in front of the soldiers. The blond soldier offered us cigarettes. I refused but my mother took one and started smoking.

After a while I ran out of energy and said I had dug enough. They asked us to bring the body and we said no. My mother made signs that meant they should do it themselves because they were the ones who killed him, and that made them angry. We took a ladder, slid it under the body, and carried it to the edge of the grave. My mother decided not to do anything else even if they shot her, claiming that Islam forbids a woman to bury a man. I lifted the edge of the ladder and the body fell into the grave making a noise like a drum. The right arm was stiff and stuck out of the grave. Each time I pressed it down, it sprang up again. I pleaded to Musleh to keep his arm down, but he never listened. I found a big stone and placed in on top of the arm, shifted the soil to cover the body, and then jumped up and down to make sure the arm would not spring out again.

We were allowed back home and told to stay inside. There were lots of soldiers in the village. Around midday the loudspeaker in the mosque announced that everyone in the village should come to the mosque or risk being shot. We went there, and many people started arriving, but the number was still less than a hundred. We sat waiting for at least two hours. The children started crying and asking for food. Some women pleaded with the soldiers to let them go home to bring some food. They were given an hour. My mum went with them and got some bread and cheese and a sackful of clothes.

At about three in the afternoon, we were marched out and taken to the main road on the east side of the village and told to wait there for the buses which the soldiers said would take us to the River Jordan, to King Hussein.

We sat under the almond trees surrounded by soldiers. One of them was talking into a wireless device. After a while they said the buses were not coming and we would have to walk to Jordan as fast as we could. It was absurd as we were at least forty miles from the River Jordan. The soldiers seemed in a hurry to leave and they were ordering us to move. An old man suggested a shortcut and we started our march. As it happened the route was taking us in the opposite direction of the road to the River Jordan.

The baker was carrying his crippled mother on his back and the woman kept farting. It was difficult to stop laughing. At sunset we arrived at Deir Al-ghusun, the next village to us. The people there gave us food and shelter for the night. They could not believe what had happened.

The next day seemed the longest day on earth. We were all waiting for the arrival of the Jews, and the people of Deir Al-ghusun were preparing themselves to be deported. I learned from my mother that she left her jewelry and money buried under the lemon tree in the courtyard as she was afraid the soldiers would take it if they searched us. Some women from our village decided to go back to Shwaika at night to retrieve what they had left hidden there. My mother was planning to go with them, but they went without her as she was not as fast as they were.

I had two dinars in my pocket. Now I was the man of the family. I had to look after all of us. What should I do?

In the morning there was a discussion. Someone said we should not go anywhere because, if we survived the journey, we should expect nothing in Jordan but hunger and humiliation. It was not long before we decided to go back to Shwaika and let the Jews shoot us. At least we would die in our village.

It was an emotional departure. Some of the people of Deir Al-ghusun walked with us some of the way. We approached our village in silence, expecting the bullets at any moment. But there was no movement and no sign of Jewish soldiers at all. Each family went to their home. In the evening, I was devastated when I listened to Nasser's speech on the radio. He was resigning. It was the ultimate defeat.

In the next few days a lot of people came back, but many were unfortunate. They were picked up by the Israeli buses and taken to Jordan where they still live till this day.

Three months after the occupation I started getting restless. The schools and cinemas remained closed. My best friend Subhi never made it back from Jordan and I could not get the new issues of *Almukhtar*, the Arabic *Reader's Digest*. I felt like I was being suffocated. I told my mother I wanted to go to Jordan to finish my education. She didn't mind. My wait to liberate myself from the village life was suddenly over, thanks to the Israeli occupation.

The car that took me to Jordan was a pickup truck owned by Jamil Al-Hamdan from my village. He was making money transporting the belongings of the people who had become refugees. From that journey three images have stuck in my mind. The first is of an Israeli bus traveling in front of us, full of people singing in Hebrew; the second is of an Is-raeli soldier at the last checkpoint asking me to sign a form which I could not read because it was written in Hebrew. I learned later that I had signed away my right to return. And the third image was of our vehicle crossing the river and going deeper and deeper in the water, not far from the de-stroyed bridge which used to link the West Bank and the rest of the Kingdom.

When I was saying goodbye to my family, one of the neighbors noticed the threat of tears in my eyes. She told me men don't cry. So I did not cry. My eyes were burning but I refused to cry.

It is not easy to be sixteen. One is not exactly a boy and not exactly a man. The boy in me was full of fear and curios-ity, while the man in me was full of desires and shame. Later on in life, I did a lot of foolish things to prove to myself that I was a man and not a useless coward. I was so ashamed of myself that, for many, many years, the story of what hap-pened when I was trapped with Zeyad and Abu Zebda was a secret. I did not want anyone to know the thoughts that had gone on in my mind. I blamed myself for their deaths. I thought I was completely useless. I could have helped Haj Ismael, but I was not interested in him, and left the eyes of Zeyad open to be pecked at and eaten by the chickens. If I had looked at the wounds of Abu Zebda maybe I could have saved him.

But the worst thing was the shame of my crazy desire to masturbate in that situation. That shame was driving me mad. I was afraid people would look at me and know. I bur-ied it deep inside me and succeeded in forgetting it. But it didn't go away. Sometimes it just explodes and I find myself struggling against waves of guilt and shame.

The waves of shame and guilt are trying to drown me and I have to struggle to float free of them. I have to struggle not to cry. One day I might be able to free myself from this guilt and shame. Until that day comes, all I can do is to forget and to keep pretending I am somebody else.

NIHAYA QAWASMI

Twenty-seven-year-old Nihaya Qawasmi was one of eight children in her family—six girls and two boys—all born in Jerusalem where she still lives today. For the last four years she has worked as a journalist and has published many stories about the life of Jerusalemites in the daily paper An-Nahar *and many feminist and political articles in the daily* Al-Itihad. *She also assists foreign journalists in covering the Palestinian cause—all despite the fact that she received no formal higher education. "I came out of scratch," she says. "I didn't study at a university. I studied English through reading the dictionary and watching American movies."*

Qawasmi says that the most important things in her life are Jerusalem, her career, her husband, David, and her mother. For her, the future of Jerusalem is the future of the Israeli/Palestinian peace process. "I don't think that peace will ever come," she says, "because, since the time Israel occupied the east side of Jerusalem in 1967, every Israeli government has declared that it will never give back East Jerusalem to the Palestinians. . . . I don't see any hope of establishing a real peace all over the region as long as Israel keeps Jerusalem under occupation."

Qawasmi's strong statements in this story about the relationship between the Holocaust and the occupation of Palestinian lands reflect the feelings of many Palestinians who ask why they must pay for what European Nazis did to the Jews more than half a century ago.

Children of a Tenth-Class God?

*T*he Intifada [Palestinian uprising] started in my last year at school. The Israeli government shut down most of the schools, including mine, because they knew that most of the demonstrators were boys and girls.

Demonstrations broke out all over the Gaza Strip, news reached the other Palestinian cities, and the demonstrations spread. There were daily clashes with the Israelis and daily martyrs fell on the road to freedom. The world started hearing about a people suffering in Palestine. International TV crews came to witness what was happening here and we managed to gain the sympathy of citizens all over the world—but not the governments!

From the underground leadership of the Intifada we received leaflets telling us what to do—how to demonstrate, throw stones, make Molotov cocktails, and burn the land under the feet of the occupier. We were ready. We had nothing to lose.

One day when I was at school, a group of young men broke into the school to force us to go out and demonstrate with them. I didn't want to go. A young man came and forcibly opened the door and my friends got scared. I wasn't afraid because I had enough experience at my previous school. So I went and closed the door. I didn't want the girls to join the boys—not for religious reasons—but because I knew that if those girls were arrested by the Israeli soldiers they wouldn't be able to face the Israeli interrogators threatening to rape them if they didn't cooperate. It was my duty to keep them out of it because they were inexperienced and were not ready. I asked the girls to stay away from the window in case the boys threw stones at us to make us leave.

Our teacher was from a Palestinian village inside Israel. She had not the slightest experience and was the most scared of all of us. So I took charge of the class. A few minutes later we heard shooting. Then we started smelling tear gas. So I told the girls to get down on their knees because tear gas is light and would go up. That's how we would escape suffocation.

Sometimes I think that the Palestinians are children of a tenth-class God; we don't deserve to live and breathe, we are the scapegoat of the world, we had to leave our country to make space for the Jews who decided to establish their homeland and state on our land, and erase Palestine from all the maps of every atlas, just like that.

Well, I didn't give the orders to those Nazis to gas the Jews. It wasn't me. Why do I have to pay for it? Why do I have to pay for the crime of Europe and the world for what they did to the Jews? They let them down, expelled them, and the USA refused to receive them on its land. And in order for the world to escape from feeling guilty, they gave the Jews our land—so who's going to feel guilty for what happened to me? Which nation is going to pay the price?

Well, I'm a flower and when you cut me and put me in a vase I won't survive because I need my homeland.

The Jews say that they lived in Palestine three thousand

years ago. That is true, I can't deny it. I studied the history of our land, but that fact doesn't mean that they have the right to come back and expel me. My family came from Iraq hundreds of years ago. Would it be fair if I go back to Iraq, enter any house, and say to the owner, "My family lived here hundreds of years ago, and you have to leave because I'm moving back home"? Would anybody justify that?

Late at night when everything is quiet I think about how I will ever forgive the Israelis for what they did to me. I don't mean stealing my homeland, killing my people, turning me into a refugee, or depriving me from having a Palestinian state. I'm talking about myself—what they did to my personality.

I wish I had a normal life: no tension, no rage, no hatred, no hard feelings towards anybody. Even if they leave my country and give me back my rights, how will I overcome these feelings inside me? How will I raise my children in a peaceful environment when I don't have peace inside me. How will I avoid telling them about the tragic life I've had, the pain I've suffered, the humiliation I've been through.

I don't know what to do. I'm helpless. I've seen painful scenes in my life that I can't erase from my mind. These pictures will always stay with me. I think it would take an extraordinary human being to forget about my past.

VICTORIA KAY-FEINERMAN

A twenty-three-year-old writer, wife, and mother of a one-year-old boy, Victoria Kay-Feinerman is earning her masters degree in literature at Bar-Ilan University in Ramat Gan. Several of her poems have been published in the university's literary magazine and she has also had her work published in ARC 11, *the journal of the Israel Association of Writers in English.*

Born in Manhattan, Kansas, Kay-Feinerman didn't live full-time in Israel until she was thirteen. One of very few Jews in Kansas, and one who considered herself religious, she felt isolated until her family moved to Israel. "I was always the Jew, the outsider," she says, "and I knew I belonged with my people."

Now a permanent resident of what she calls her homeland, Kay-Feinerman says she fears for the future of her country: "One of the reasons I decided to have a baby in the middle of my studies is that I was worried what might happen if war broke out and my husband was called to duty. I figured that I'd at least have something left of him in the case that, G-d forbid . . ."

The Yiddish alti zachen, *"old things," that echoes throughout this story is a moving counterpoint to the new life Victoria Kay-Feinerman protected within her body just as she protected herself within a sealed room during the Gulf War.*

(See photo insert.)

Alti Zachen

"*Alti zachen, alti zachen!*" old things, old things. The tinny-sounding Yiddish phrase is barked over a megaphone propped in the passenger side window of a faded old yellow truck which rolls slowly down the street in the afternoon heat. My nap-time repose disturbed, I get up off the bed and open the window onto the street. A rush of steamy stickiness invades my air-conditioned flat as I look at the ragged orange couch, scratched wooden chairs, small crib, and battered gray refrigerator piled in the back of the truck. The driver would buy or sell.

"*Alti zachen, alti zachen!*"

The dry Arabic accent gives the cry a funny ring, one that never ceases to amaze me. Who would have thought it? An Arab speaking Yiddish! Even I, a Jew, don't know Yiddish. The German-Jewish language is a dead one, killed in the Holocaust, a language which universities must tempt students to learn with the offer of a five-hundred-dollar reward for receiving a decent mark in the course. So why should Arabs, of all people, wish to revive it?

"*Alti zachen, alti zachen!*"

The wail rises and falls. I remember wondering at the start of the Gulf War whether the "*alti zachen*" trucks would continue to sell their wares while the Jews huddled in attics, or whether they would stay shamefacedly at home, reluctant to see the persecution of the original Yiddish speakers—the

Yids, the Jews—by their Iraqi cousins. I was seventeen at the time, and I thought that the Arab peddlers' use of the Holocaust language was a touching and sensitive attempt at communication. They felt for us, and I knew that we and they were unified by the fear and hatred of the common enemy of the time. They probably stayed at home rather than drive their trucks around so as to be close to their own sealed rooms when a siren went off, warning of the approach of a Scud missile.

I'll never forget the night the first siren went off! The sharp wailing rose and fell repeatedly, and I groggily opened my eyes. . . . Realization struck, and my heart rose with the siren and stayed high in my throat. The door of my room flew open, and my Dad tersely ushered me upstairs to the sealed room where my mother and two sisters were hurriedly opening their gas mask kits and pulling on coats and pants.

The windows of my parents' room were covered with shiny brown masking tape and large sheets of plastic. The plastic protected us against possible biological or chemical warfare, and the tape kept the windows from shattering. My dad shoved a wet towel under the door and was starting to cover the cracks with tape when we heard someone rapping on the other side. It was the cat. He somehow knew. After a short argument with my mom, my father quickly reopened the door while turning his face from the incoming air. The large white cat dashed under the bed, and the door was sealed. We would watch him to see if the air was clean.

The thick rubber gas mask covered my face and stuck there. It was a steam room inside the mask, and as the eye-windows began to fog up, I began to panic. I couldn't see, I couldn't breathe, and I wanted out. I could hear the distant booms over the soothing words of the radio announcer and my constant Darth Vader–like breathing. What if they had sent poisonous gas? If I took my mask off to clean the lenses, would I be gassed to death like my great-grandparents in Auschwitz? I lay somewhere in the gray fog world, my hands and feet covered in plastic bags, gasping—gasssssping.

We spent many other nights silently crouching upstairs in the sealed room, eventually moving into the closet for further safety, all five of us crushed into the hot little coffin, and I felt like Anne Frank. The cat continued to rush upstairs at the sound of a siren, even after we followed the radio announcer's latest advice and made the basement bomb shelter our sealed room. The cat remembered that the siren meant he must run upstairs and was unable to learn a new meaning for it. As we could not risk our own lives to drag him out from under the third-floor bed, clawing and hissing in sheer wide-eyed fear, we gave in to his inevitable death.

One Friday night, a missile hit too close to my city, Petach Tikva. The lights went out, and the house shook, and the windows rattled. I looked at my parents, wanting to see their expressions. Were we going to die? But the masks confined us each to our separate universe. Like astronauts floating in space, there was a gaping vacuum between us, and I started to pray, "Hear, oh, Israel, the Lord is God, the Lord is One."

The next morning I went for a walk downtown with my gas mask slung in its box over my shoulder. The results of the Kristallnacht crunched under my Sabbath shoes and glittered sharply in the window panes. Apartment owners peered furtively out of open living rooms at the shattered plastic shutters that littered the streets. *Alti zachen.* Old things.

I look outside my window and watch a neighbor buy a worn yellow lampshade from the Arab dealer of old things.

It was only later that I heard rumor of what the *"alti zachen"* people had done during the missile attacks. They had danced on their rooftops, fiddling and cheering the Scuds on. Probably laughing in Yiddish.

I think of buying a used crib from the *"alti zachen"* man, but the outdoor heat clings to my face in a sweaty mask, and I close the window.

"Alti zachen, alti zachen!"

The truck drives slowly off, and the voice fades away. Perhaps I'll take the course in Yiddish next year. Would it revive the bones of my great-grandparents to do so?

I lay back down on the bed and breathe deeply of the cool air, one hand resting on my ripened belly, the other on the large white cat.

Rivka Rosen (pseud.)

Born and raised in Jerusalem, Rivka Rosen moved to the United States when she was thirty years old. She and her husband lived in Manhattan, where the first of her two sons was born. After long years of study and training, she completed her Ph.D. and became a clinical psychologist. She is now in private practice in the eastern United States.

Having grown up as a secular Jew in Israel, she says she is now reconnecting to Judaism through a Jewish feminist group, a Jewish meditation group, and a Reconstructionist congregation.

When asked what her thoughts are about a Palestinian/Israeli peace agreement, she said that "the solution is for both sides to compromise on their dreams since both people claim the same area as their own. . . . There should be two countries: a strong Israel as well as a Palestinian state."

In this very moving account of emotional and physical losses resulting from the Arab-Israeli conflict, Rivka Rosen explains why the move to the United States was the right one for her. Still, she says, "Israel is my homeland, and a big part of who I am, what I think, and care about."

Caught in Conflict

I bear the marks of our conflict with the Arabs in my body.
I bear them in my soul.

*I*n the spring of 1970 I was a nineteen-year-old soldier in the Israeli army, stationed in an army-settlement in southern Israel, in the Negev desert. I felt we were partaking in the Zionist renewal dream: we were making the desert bloom. With irrigation we were creating a habitat in a previously unsettled place. We were cultivating a vegetable garden in this arid, hot spot and sending our produce to nourish the nation.

I didn't mind getting up before dawn in order to finish work before noon, when the blistering sun would force us into the shade. I didn't mind living in tents until we could move into the houses that the army was building for us, or the duty of guarding the settlement with a fellow soldier—a male. In basic training the army had taught us girls to shoot, although we did not really believe we would engage in active combat. When our commander decided it was inappropriate to let girls and boys guard together at night, we did not mind too much. Although, there was some loss of pride. Our commander reduced the girls' roles from warrior-farmer-service providers to farmer-service providers only.

I believed that I should do as much as possible for my country. My parents had parted with a comfortable life in the United States and all their family and friends when they migrated to this country in 1946. They believed that there could be no safety for Jews other than in their own homeland. A generation earlier my maternal grandmother had fled Russia following a pogrom in which Cossacks murdered her firstborn, a male baby. She boarded a boat to cross the Atlantic. My mother was born on that boat, en route to America.

There were no pogroms in America, but my parents encountered anti-Semitism. They became Zionists; World War Two and the Holocaust further convinced them of the need for a Jewish homeland. After the war they boarded the first civilian ship to cross the Atlantic. Their ship was sailing in the opposite direction of the boats that their parents had traveled on when seeking safety in America.

Although Israel was created to be a safe haven for the Jewish people, we were in ongoing violent conflict with our Arab neighbors. I grew up in Jerusalem, a mile away from the tall wall that divided the city into two parts. On one side were us Israelis. On the other side was our enemy, the Arabs, who occasionally shot at us from behind the wall. I learned to take these shooting episodes for granted, as a background to my life.

Growing up in Israel, I took it for granted that I was to serve several years in the army. I joined a unit that combined the ideal of actively defending the country with the ideal of building agricultural settlements in uncultivated areas of Israel. I opposed, however, settling in the territories that Israel had conquered in the 1967 war. I believed that Israel should be ready to exchange the occupied territories for a peace agreement with the Arabs.

When my unit was stationed in the Negev desert I was pleased, although we were on the border with the Arabs. Occasionally they shot at us, but these shootings were infrequent. They reminded me of the shooting episodes from across the wall in Jerusalem. I experienced my life in the Negev desert as meaningful; I took pride in growing tomatoes and onions. I also enjoyed hiking around the spectacular rock formations surrounding our army-settlement as well as the lively social life we had as teenagers away from home.

When we received the order that our unit should relocate to the Golan Heights, I was distraught. I did not wish to move to another army-settlement and certainly not on the Golan Heights that Israel had conquered in the 1967 war. I did not want to build a settlement in the occupied territory.

It was with grave misgivings that I obeyed the order and relocated to the army-settlement on the Golan Heights. I hated everything I saw. Burnt army vehicles from the 1967 war lay scattered along the roads, although almost three years had passed. The fields were black and the houses in the deserted Arab villages were reduced to rubble. The area was scarred by massive marks of war, death, and destruction. Our army was blowing up the deserted Arab villages which made me sad, guilty, and angry.

I perceived the destruction that I was witnessing in the Golan Heights as part of the ongoing cycle of violence that Jews and Arabs were inflicting on each other. The Arabs rejected the Jews and fought us, and the Jews won the battles and destroyed Arab houses and villages. Both peoples suffered from this cycle of violence.

Our new army-settlement itself was hard to reckon with. The houses, at the foot of a cliff, were black, probably from the smoke from their chimneys. There was no vegetation within the bounds of the settlement. The ground was bare. Whereas in the first army-settlement the bare desert formed beautiful shapes, here the barrenness was ugly. Our commander did not allow the girls to cultivate the vegetable garden outside the fence because he considered it too dangerous. Now we were neither warriors nor farmers; our sole role was service providers.

At the time, my relationship with my high-school boyfriend was fading out. He was serving in the Air Force and we had difficulty maintaining our long-distance relationship. I began to take an interest in our handsome commander. I decided that at the next Sabbath evening party I would indulge in some "saloon dancing"—Rock'n Roll and the Twist. I had previously refrained from such foreign dances, faithful to my beloved Israeli folk dancing.

But that was not to be.

I never made it to that party.

The day began as usual in our settlement. Some guys came in from their night shift of guarding the settlement; other guys were leaving for work in the vegetable garden. The girls were busy cooking and working in the dining room. I was setting tables. We were unaware that it was the third anniversary of the 1967 war.

And then the shelling began.

No warning.

Just bombs exploding around us.

We ran toward the shelters. I didn't know where they were. We had lived in the settlement only a few weeks and had not yet had a drill for a shelling. I ran behind the others.

And then I couldn't run anymore.

I was on the ground, hit in my legs by a bomb exploding behind me.

The shelling continued.

Four of us lay on the ground. Yoram, who was a veteran and was only moderately wounded, took command. He told us, three young women on the ground, to try to crawl to the wall of the closest building, to move away from the open space where we lay so vulnerably exposed. My friend, Galia, who was wounded in her hand and abdomen, was howling behind me. I was able to crawl to the wall and Yoram helped Galia, behind me. Dorit, the third wounded girl, made no movement. She was making strange, gurgling sounds. Yoram tried to talk with her. She did not respond.

The shelling continued for what felt like an eternity. Shells were pounding into the settlement all around us. I thought I might die. My mind went to my mother. I had become very protective of her after my father died in a car accident when I was sixteen. I prayed silently in my heart. I prayed despite my disbelief in any God. Lying on the ground, feeling close to death, I asked that God—if there was one—would tell my mother that I loved her.

Oddly, I did not pray to God to stop the shelling. I did not consider the end of my life as tragic for me, probably because of my depression following my father's death, and because of my belief in self-sacrifice for the country.

While on the ground, I kept thinking about our Air Force. Why were our planes not coming? They are so swift; they led us to victory in the 1967 war. I had been angry at them for striking civilians in refugee camps in Lebanon. I had argued the issue heatedly with my boyfriend. Now, I thought, when our planes are really needed to fend off an attack, why aren't they coming? What's taking them so long?

In a lull in the shelling, some of our guys came out of the shelter with a stretcher to carry the wounded to safety. Yoram instructed them to take Dorit, and they did. Later I learned that all efforts to resuscitate her were in vain.

Our guys tried to come out with the stretcher again but retreated under renewed heavy shelling. When they reached us again they rescued Galia. They came once more, for me. In the dark shelter, protected from the shelling, I began to have physical sensations. The pain began to register. A medic was bandaging my legs. I was thirsty but the medic didn't allow me to drink, only to suck on a wet cloth. There was a lot of commotion around me.

Our commander called for a helicopter that flew the wounded to a hospital. The medic on the helicopter injected me with morphine. I recall asking for more doses, but he refused.

Once in the hospital, it seemed to me that people kept asking me the same questions over and over. I was dazed. I underwent extensive surgery. For days a team of surgeons tinkered to remove shrapnel and soil and to patch bones, blood vessels, and flesh together on my legs and to graft skin on top. They transplanted blood vessels using a pressure chamber that the navy utilizes for deep-sea divers. The surgeons repeatedly put me into the chamber that was like a coffin—body-sized and dark—isolating me from my surroundings. The chamber enabled them to regulate my blood pressure in the transplanted vessels. I did not want to enter this chamber; I was frightened by the isolation from the world.

My sister tried to maintain contact with me while I was in the chamber. She played a tape recorder and I heard the sounds vaguely. Later she told me that she had argued with a surgeon. She believed that the surgeons should be honest and tell me the length of time they would keep me in the chamber, as I requested. The surgeon thought I should be led to believe that I would be out "shortly." When my sister confronted her, the surgeon replied that if she would have known beforehand how long she would suffer in the Holocaust she would not have survived. Later I learned that a patient who went into this chamber had become psychotic.

The surgery was successful; the surgeons saved my leg from being amputated. They published their accomplishment, and the hospital raised funds to purchase a medical pressure-chamber with communication channels between the patient in the chamber and the outside.

I was a "good patient," not complaining about my ordeal, and the medical staff loved me for that. Although my attitude won me lots of approval, it didn't help me to process my loss. It was uncommon for girls to be caught in the battlefield and that made our incident sensational. Politicians and high-ranking army officers visited the injured soldiers along with the press. Friends flocked to the hospital from all over the country. The army arranged for an escorted limousine to bring my mother from Jerusalem all the way to the hospital and accommodated her and my sister in a nearby hotel from which they could visit me daily. I had an inspiring visit from singers in the military band. They were a large choir and filled up my small hospital room. They invited me to request my favorite song. It was the "Song of Peace." Some say this song was later unofficially banned on Israeli radio because the lyrics were considered unpatriotic.

I was unable to grasp clearly what had happened to me and to foresee the consequences to my life. From now on I was limited in many things I loved: I was unable to dance, hike, or engage in rigorous athletic activity. My body was deformed and I suffered chronic pain. I lived my next years in denial, although I was visited by my trauma in recurring nightmares of war, death, and dismemberment. I required repeated hospitalizations because I neglected to take care of my injured leg. The denial enabled me to function, but blocked me from processing my loss and anger.

I continued to oppose settling of Israelis in the occupied territories. I identified with the Palestinians—the victims of the Jewish state—but also with the Israelis—those inflicting atrocities in the occupation. I was overwhelmed by guilt. It seemed that we had lost all moral ground. My unresolved anger fueled my despair. I felt hopeless about a peaceful solution to our conflict with the Arabs. Our violence against them would only breed violence against us, and the cycle would never end.

I did not want to participate in this cycle, and I left my beloved country. I crossed the Atlantic, as my parents had done a generation earlier, but in the opposite direction. I went to study and then settled down in the USA with my own family. Thus, I was the third generation in my family to split their lives between two countries on either side of the Atlantic.

After several years of living abroad, I ceased having nightmares. This was a surprise and a relief. It was an indication that, despite the heartbreak and the longing that I experienced due to the separation from my homeland, my move was necessary for my recovery. The safe haven that my parents believed in became perilous for me physically and mentally. I felt I was consumed by the conflict. I needed the distance in order to feel safe from the continuing wars between Israelis and Arabs.

The distance also afforded me a perspective within which I try to understand and heal my body as well as my soul.

NAHLA MARY BEIER

This story by Nahla Mary Beier depicts the frustration and humiliation she and many Palestinians have endured while attempting to visit relatives in Israel. Seventeen at the time of the story, Beier was born in Jerusalem, where she lived until she was sixteen. Subsequently, she has lived in Beirut, Lebanon, and various American cities, where she has taught college English. She is married with three children and now lives in Natchitoches, Louisiana, where she teaches English at a high school for gifted students.

When asked about her hopes for Israeli/Palestinian peace, she said, "I don't see any solution in the near future. There might come a time (for my children's children?) when Palestinians and Israelis will have finally learned to relate to one another as essentially people who share a common humanity. Until that happens, I try to keep Palestine alive as an idea in my children's minds."

One More River to Cross

*I*t's hard to breathe in the rusty, over-crowded bus. My hair, expertly cut and tinted in Lebanon to give me a sophisticated look—older than my seventeen years—now hangs limp and clammy against my neck. I wish I had pulled it up into a ponytail. My knees feel shaky with fatigue although it's only eight in the morning and we left Amman, the Jordanian capital, just a few hours ago.

My brother Maher and his best friend, Kamal, hang desperately to the rails in the aisle as the heavy, loud-mouthed peasant they've sandwiched between them yells at her wailing toddler, threatening to throw him out of the window to the soldiers below.

I catch a glimpse of Ziyyad scrunched in a corner of the back seat. His glazed eyes ask no questions, hold no grudges; he comes fully fortified against the harrowing of Allenby hell with good quality Lebanese hash. Rami, another friend of my brother's who habitually crosses the Allenby Bridge with us, finds this a fortuitous occasion for one of his patriotic sermons.

"Take it easy, sister," he admonishes the woman, who turns to give him a dirty look. "We shouldn't take it out on one another when we're sorely tried. To become a nation, we need plenty of patience, good will, and cooperation." He pats the child she has with her on the head. "Here, sister, let me help you with this lovely boy. Just give him to me."

The woman doesn't buy Rami's exhibitionistic display of civic spirit, but seems too hot and depressed to care. She gives him another knowing glance, then passes a bundle of squirming dirty rags and tangled curls over the heads of passengers and into Rami's open arms.

"There, there, little guy," Rami croons loudly as he rocks the screaming child against his shoulder, stopping every now and then to smile sweetly at anybody whose eye he can catch.

Overwhelmed by the heat, the flies, Rami's hypocrisy, and the pungent smell of perspiring flesh, my attention wanders. How many times since I began college have we made this soul-deadening, two-day trip from Beirut, through Syria, Jordan, and across the bridge to Jericho and then Jerusalem—a trip that would take only a few hours if we could simply enter Israel across the Lebanese border? Christmases, Easters, and summer holidays. Six times in two years. I feel faint at the thought of two more years of Allenby trips before I graduate.

Apart from the summer heat, though, the trip has gone somewhat smoothly so far. We were detained only two hours at the Syrian border yesterday and, despite their undisguised hostility to westernized, long-haired, bell-bottomed college students, the Jordanian border guards didn't confiscate our Lebanese sweets and edibles, so we had at least a little something to offer our relatives in Amman in gratitude for putting us up for the night.

A loud expletive disrupts my line of thought.

"Damn it, woman!" Rami roars, holding the child at arm's length and looking down disgustedly at his freshly soiled bell-bottoms. "Why didn't you tell me he leaks? Here, take him. Take the brat!"

Maher and Kamal make ridiculous, hooting noises and slap each other's open palms, and Ziyyad surfaces from his trance long enough to grin and make a thumbs-up sign. I laugh till the tears stream down my cheeks, retriggered by the man sitting next to me, who writhes in his seat in helpless convulsions of mirth. As the bus approaches the wooden bridge and pulls off to the side for the last Jordanian inspection, I'm still laughing as if my very life depended on it.

The Jordanian soldier who surveys us from where he stands near the driver's seat has one hand on a revolver hanging from his hip; the other hand adjusts the emblem of the royal Hashemite dynasty, a golden brooch in the shape of a crown which holds together his checkered, red and white headdress. His accent as he addresses us betrays his Bedouin origins—hence his deep suspicion of any behavior or manner of dress that deviates in the least from the purely Islamic and Arabic.

"Everybody without a Jordanian passport, get off the bus at once," he orders.

The few, unfortunate residents of the Gaza Strip struggle to cut a path through the crowded aisle to the back door. Having not been ceded to Jordan—as we West Bankers were—or to any other Arabic country after Israel wiped Palestine off the map in 1948, Gaza people remain without any legal identity, the most wretched among the wretched. Now they have to undergo special interrogations as their multiple semi-official documents are scrutinized one last time before they will be allowed back on the bus.

The Jordanian soldier moves slowly down the aisle, inspecting the passports we hold up to him, glancing at each face to make sure it matches the picture. His eyes rest on me for a while, taking in with obvious disapproval my hairstyle and bare arms. Then he takes a few steps back to the seat in which Maher is now sitting.

"That girl your sister?" he demands.

"Yes, she is."

"You're certain?"

"Can't you see we have the same nose and jawline," Maher responds in exasperation, "not to mention the same family name on our passports?"

The soldier's anger explodes with an excessiveness that

reminds me of our now almost forgotten, exaggerated laughter.

"Think you're smart, college boy!" he sputters, thrusting his face to within an inch of Maher's. "Getting a degree in insolence? Huh? When I ask you a question, I expect a straightforward answer, you understand?"

I can't see Maher's face, but Kamal, who's sitting next to him, raises both hands up in a surrendering, placating gesture.

"He didn't mean to be insolent, sir," Kamal purrs. "And you're quite right, we really don't learn anything worthwhile in college these days. Oh, and if you don't mind my saying so, sir, I happen to know that the girl really is his sister. I swear."

The soldier eyes him suspiciously, glances back at me a couple of times, seems ready to ask another question, then suddenly changes his mind and moves on to inspect more passports, muttering something about the "Goddamn college boys."

"What was that all about?" I ask Kamal as we're waiting for the Gaza people's release.

"He was turned on by your arms," he grins. "Maybe he wanted to ask your hand in marriage from big brother here."

"Very funny," I humor him, then confess more seriously: "I don't think I could stand it if I had to face this alone."

"Relax, kid. And remember that we shall overcome some day, just like the Americans say."

The bus finally starts inching its way across the narrow wooden bridge. Below us meanders a pathetic, muddy stream that once was a legitimate river. A refrain from a song the nuns taught me at my high school in Jerusalem echoes in my head:

> *One more river,*
> *And that's the River of Jordan.*
> *One more river,*
> *And that's the river to cross.*

Most of the river's water has now been diverted by Israel to irrigate acres of arid land around its settlements. I think of all the half-truths that have shaped the image of Israel in the West like their much-admired "miracle" of making the desert bloom. Impressive, like Israel itself, if you don't ask what damage it inflicted on non-Israelis. The Jordanians on the other side of the river whose rich, arable lands were turned into desert in the process understandably fail to appreciate the "miracle."

We come to a halting screech at the end of the bridge. The doors fly open and two very young soldiers in camouflage fatigues peer in, Uzi submachine guns held firmly with both hands. Now we're an occupied people.

"*Boker Tov* [Good morning]," says one of them in Hebrew. Then he repeats his greeting in Arabic: "*Sabah alkhair.*"

A couple of people snicker, but most of us look straight ahead with blank faces, wary of offending another round of testy soldiers.

"Let's go," the Israeli soldier orders the bus driver in broken Arabic. "Pull up over there, and everybody stay seated till all the luggage is off the bus."

"Oh, boy!" exclaims Ziyyad, momentarily roused. "We get to see our bags explode!"

I smile with a certain smugness, secure in the hard-earned

knowledge that guides the actions of Allenby veterans like ourselves. Once, before I knew better, I brought some "L'air Du Temps" for Mother for Christmas and a black-label bottle of Johnnie Walker for Father. I never could quite get the smell of perfumed whiskey out of my clothes that summer.

"Don't look just now," Maher interrupts my reminiscing, "but the woman behind you must have packed some breakables."

The poor woman, elegantly dressed in an expensive suit, knotted silk scarf, and matching purse and shoes, watches in horror as her genuine leather suitcase comes flying off the roof of the bus to quickly disappear under the pile of suitcases, cardboard boxes, rugs and bundles of cloth being tossed unceremoniously on the ground.

"Must be her first trip," I say. "She'll learn."

"Look—tourists." Kamal points to the luxurious Pullman bus passing us by. Elderly women with blue-tinted hair, big straw hats, and pearl beads lean back against the well-cushioned headrests, smiling in air-conditioned contentment. Their Israeli guide points in our direction while talking into his microphone, and many peer out of their windows cheerfully waving.

"I wonder what he's telling them," says Maher as he retrieves his bags. "Maybe he's saying this is an ancient Arab custom, to hurl personal belongings from high places to placate Allah or something. They probably think we're having the time of our lives."

"Well, if they came looking for dirty Arabs, this is certainly a good place to find them," mutters Ziyyad, catching a whiff of the smell wafting from his sweaty armpits and pretending to gag. "Good God, what I would give for a bubble bath! Goddamn tourists! Their last stop in Jerusalem was probably to take pictures of the only donkey in the Old City. Now they can show their nieces and nephews our favorite means of transportation."

We stack our luggage onto huge wooden shelves and run to beat everyone else to the first inspection station, where we have to reclaim our Israeli identity cards. Hundreds of people are already lined up between metal bars, facing four or five windows with open shutters. Inside, uniformed Israeli officials, seated under huge ceiling fans, sip soft drinks from glass bottles while mechanically signing documents and calling out names in a thick guttural accent.

"Take a deep breath, everyone," counsels Rami. "It's going to be at least a couple of hours before the luggage search."

The IDs we now await do not guarantee us any real rights in Israel, but merely a temporary residence on our own land, provided we do nothing to endanger the safety of the State of Israel. By contrast, any foreign Jew who comes to Israel is granted a permanent citizenship within a week, although neither he nor his ancestors have ever seen the place, except perhaps in illustrated brochures. Nevertheless, our cards are essential to our safety and mobility in Israel. They keep us from getting thrown off buses and cabs at the countless surprise checkpoints erected daily on the West Bank. Occasionally they ensure that we'll be questioned before we're beaten if we happen to be within the vicinity of an explosion in Tel Aviv or West Jerusalem. In short, life under occupation is unimaginable without an ID in one's pocket.

I squeeze in line behind Maher and Kamal and survey the ugly cement buildings we still have to negotiate, following maze-like, narrow paths marked by metal railings. I think of Dante's City of Dis, into whose ever-deepening circles Virgil showed the way.

" 'Abandon hope all ye who enter here,' " I mutter to myself in English.

"What?" Kamal fixes me with intelligent, slightly protruding eyes. He has often looked out for me. Of all my brother's friends, I like him the best.

"Did I tell you I aced the political science exam last week?" I ask, self-consciously changing the subject.

"Good for you!" He looks genuinely pleased.

"Couldn't have done it without you. Your extra coaching paid off. I mean I really finally understand those 'crucial ideological differences' between the National Democratic Front, the Popular Front for the Liberation of Palestine, and Fatah—as well as what the Trotskyists and the Maoists on campus really want. Not that we got questioned on those!"

We laugh a little, managing to forget our thirst and the oppressive heat, but not for long.

At two in the afternoon, we all finally have our ID cards in hand. Now we tug at our heavy luggage and are herded into a huge cement enclosure dominated at the far end by long metal tables with benches on two sides. Since there are no metal partitions here, it's everyone for themselves. Heavy-set peasant women with strong arms and short tempers are not easy to compete with for space, so the old and the puny can find themselves on a Sisyphean quest, repeatedly edging their way towards a table and almost perching on a bench, only to be shoved to the back of the enclosure. Since it's Arab against Arab, the Israeli guards don't interfere, except to yell at anyone who gets too close to the official tables.

The boys help me push my suitcase along and pull on my arms to stop me from drifting backwards. At some point, we come to rest behind the first two human waves threatening to break upon the tables. Beside me an old man with a burgundy fez tries to remove his drenched jacket with one hand, fails, and drops the box in his other hand on another man's foot. A peasant woman two rows behind keeps accidentally whacking people around her with a rolled rush mat that she's balancing on her shoulder. Why would anyone want to bring a rush mat to the West Bank? Since weaving mats is one of the few things we're still allowed to do without competition, they're plentiful and very cheap. The woman holds on to that mat as if it were spun of gold, however, staring defiantly at anyone who objects.

Ahead of me, a woman in a heavy, shapeless, grey coat and a white scarf tied under her chin loosens the wrappings around her baby, who's screaming so loudly he's turning blue. The stack of gold bracelets jingling against her plump wrist suggests she must have been visiting a husband who has left his family on the West Bank to make money in one of the Arab Gulf states. A practical custom, converting assets to gold. The price doesn't fall when the value of the shekel drops again, and one doesn't have to use Israeli banks.

The elegant lady from the bus who had foolishly packed some breakables finds herself pressed too close to a swarthy man in peasant dress who keeps clearing his throat and spitting noisily into his handkerchief. She holds her body stiffly at an odd angle, her aristocratic face registering profound revulsion. I lose myself for a while, fleshing out in my imagination the lives and futures of the people who pass the Allenby Bridge.

"Pull your bag up on the table, then sit on that bench," the young soldier orders, his square jaw moving in a regular motion as he chews a wad of gum. It bothers me that I can't see his eyes behind the dark sunglasses. He dumps my belongings on the table and hands the suitcase to another man in civilian clothes who takes it to be x-rayed.

"Medication," he announced, rummaging through the heap. "Not allowed. Pens not allowed either." He throws the offending items in a trash can by his side.

Oh, well. Last time they let the medicine through, but they keep changing the rules. I try to look completely uninterested in his decisions.

"What's all this?" he asks, flipping through a thick notebook.

"Notes I take at school."

"Damn it, they're going to delay us at least a couple of hours while they read all this stuff," Maher, standing behind me, mutters angrily. "Why did you have to bring notes? You're on a holiday."

"What do you study at school?" the soldiers asks more casually, handing the notes to the civilian.

"English literature."

"Where?"

"In Beirut."

"Beautiful city, is it?" His voice sounds almost wistful.

"Oh, absolutely wonderful. Pity you can't see it."

His hands run expertly along the edges of a black skirt he has picked from the heap, then tear the hem out where the material feels thicker.

"Got yourself a boyfriend in Beirut?" he inquires softly, sorting through and caressing my underwear.

I pretend I didn't hear him. It feels good to know I'm managing to stay quite calm, even now as he's ripping the brass button off my favorite handbag. He finally unzips the plastic bag containing my makeup.

"Makeup not allowed."

My anger gradually gains the upper hand, especially when I notice that the makeup bag, instead of being dumped into the trash can, has been placed discreetly on the ground underneath the table. I react without thinking.

"Got yourself a girlfriend in Tel Aviv?" I ask with feigned innocence.

His sunglasses slip down an inch, and the look in his dark brown eyes assesses me in a fashion that seems more curious than hostile.

"Sit on the other bench until your suitcase comes back."

He pushes his glasses up and motions Maher to take my place.

A few hours later, we find ourselves straddling yet another bench in the middle of a courtyard lined on two sides with small, windowless rooms. It's time to be strip-searched. Our bravado has completely vanished by now; nobody feels like quoting the classics or tries to sound in any way smart or witty.

I mess with my ponytail, having discovered a rubber band in my purse. It's eerily quiet for a place this crowded. Only the children whimper occasionally. The adults, fanning themselves mechanically with open hands or bits of cardboard, generally withdraw into their private worlds, their rather vacant eyes focusing with a mixture of dread and anticipation whenever a door to one of the rooms flies open.

An elderly Moslem woman on the bench in front of me is

motioned into a vacated room. I watch her adjust the many layers of black cloth that cover her from head to toe—except for her face—then check around her feet for her handbag. It will take a while to remove all those layers of clothing and put them on again. The two young women after her are wearing short, sleeveless summer dresses. They'll go fast. In half an hour to forty-five minutes it will be my turn.

The wail that suddenly escapes out of the windowless room is piercing it its desperation. "No! No! May Allah bless you, please don't!"

"Wider. Open your legs more, I said. Wider." The Israeli soldier's disembodied voice echoes eerily in the enclosure.

Not even the children are whimpering now. My thigh muscles tighten involuntarily. I pull on my skirt but it won't go down my legs as far as I want it to. The people around me blur into huddled masses, their dread-filled, knowing faces no longer visible.

I hope Mother didn't throw out my old comforter when she got my room ready this morning. I rub my freezing bare arms and undo my ponytail to cover the back of my suddenly sensitive neck. Oh, God. I can't bear to hear her scream. The very first thing I'll do when I get home is take a bath. Or just a warm shower. With my clothes on, like Victorian women used to do. Maybe I'll ask for a hot cup of minted tea with lots of sugar like Mother makes it, and hunt for a good, old book to reread.

How can they do this to her, a shy old woman, probably some child's harmless grandmother? How can we just sit here and listen to this? Mother must be getting anxious for us to get there by now. I wonder what she made for dinner. What are Maher and Kamal thinking as they hear the woman pleading? What happens to them every trip behind those closed doors? Will we ever talk about it to each other or to anyone else?

Enid Blyton! I think I'll reread her series of children's adventure books this summer—engaging stories about four children and their dog romping about the lush English countryside, solving mysteries while nibbling on hot, buttered scones and cucumber sandwiches. Please, please, make the poor woman stop sobbing. Just let her put her layers back on.

The soldier who strip-searches me is in her mid-twenties. Her military beige miniskirt clings to her slim thighs; her shapely tanned legs taper into pretty sandaled feet with red toenails. Her sun-bleached hair is pulled into an elegant bun, pinned low against her slightly freckled neck. As I slip into my skirt and button up my blouse, I sense that she's discreetly looking the other way. I'm finally dressed and ready to face her. The hazel eyes returning my gaze are long-lashed, intelligent, and do not seem unkind. Can she possibly enjoy her work? She probably likes to go see *The Sound of Music* again and again, probably purrs to the kittens at some pet shop, and cooks sweet and sour shrimp for her boyfriend. But, then, how can she steel herself to look up the vaginas of old women who would be mortified at having their ankles exposed? Does she will herself to believe they might be hiding explosives in there?

I put my hand out to reclaim my ID. Is she hesitating for a minute, while considering some explanation? Is there some hint of regret—or even an apology in those hazel eyes? Maybe under different circumstances we could have become friends, I catch myself thinking. But the pleas of the Moslem woman in black still echo in my aching head. We never could have been friends.

"Good to see you, kid," Maher smiles, exhaustion stamped on his face. "I was afraid I'd never run into any of you again. Have you seen the others?"

This is our final stop. We call it "The Shoe Station." During the strip-search, our shoes are removed and carried to a separate room to be x-rayed. Now about fifty or so of us sit in a hot room in our sweaty, bare feet, awaiting their return. The smell of unwashed flesh is stunning. Periodically, the door opens, and an official throws a cartonful of shoes into the center of the room. We all scramble to the floor, tossing the wrong pairs out of the way, then, failing to find ours, settle back to wait some more. On the third throw, I locate only a single sandal. Maher's shoes have finally surfaced, and he's slipping them on.

"'Should I just give up?" I ask, feeling that I will start throwing shoes against the walls if I have to wait any longer. "I can probably hop on one foot to the taxi station if you'll help with the luggage."

"Don't be silly. It can't take much longer now," he says reassuringly.

I wonder to myself what crime Dante would have designed to fit this infernal punishment. It doesn't violate my sense of this unending phantasmagoria today to suppose this place fictitious and our experiences in it a result of an overactive imagination. We could be pampered aristocrats, for instance, who have had hundreds of servants to bathe and anoint us and disguise our body odors. Now we are deservedly thrown in this pit so we can experience what feet really smell like.

Dressed, shod, carrying what's left of our stuff in what's left of our luggage, we head towards the exit gate, through which we can already glimpse a fleet of cabs, their drivers loudly announcing their various preordained destinations—Hebron, Ramallah, East Jerusalem. The soldier at the exit gate sits at a small, wooden table covered with pamphlets and brochures. I don't recall the table from previous trips. Kamal and the rest of the gang are now visible on the other side of the gate where they must have been waiting for us for some time. They wave with relief and point to the taxi they've already secured.

The soldier glances at my brother's face, comparing it to the ID picture, then places the ID and a brochure in his hand. Glancing over his shoulder, I notice first a detailed map of Palestine in a corner of the front page, then the phrase "Welcome to Israel" in Hebrew, repeated in English, then in Arabic, announcing the content of the brochure.

Maher grows pale and his hand starts shaking. He lays his suitcase on the ground, carefully sticks his ID in his back pocket, readjusts his glasses on his nose, then draws a step closer to the soldier.

"I was born and raised here," he says in a low voice that trembles with suppressed emotion. "So was my father, my grandfather, and my great-great-grandfather. I don't need your stupid brochure to teach me how to get around this place."

With that, he rips the brochure into tiny pieces and flings them dramatically in the air over the Israeli's head. The soldier jumps up, lunges for the Uzi leaning against his chair, and points it straight at us.

"That was a BAD thing to do," he says, carefully articulating every word. "Now you have to go all the way back to Amman."

Still pointing his gun at us, he picks up his walkie-talkie and calls for someone to escort us back to the last bus to Jordan.

"Call my folks when you get home," I yell at Kamal, who's watching the scene in utter dismay. "Tell them we'll try again tomorrow."

On the bus, my captive anger hurls itself against the bars. I cry uncontrollably, kick the seats, bite my nails till I draw blood, and sputter accusations at poor Maher, who absorbs them with stoical resignation. Finally spent, I touch his arm in a conciliatory gesture. "At least they won't find anything in the luggage to throw out or confiscate tomorrow."

Unless they change the rules.

RAMZY BAROUD

Twenty-six-year-old Ramzy Baroud did not leave the occupied territory of the Gaza Strip until he was twenty-two years old. He currently lives with his wife, Suzy, in Seattle and attends the University of Washington full-time. After he graduates, he says he wants to return to Palestine to help his people.

Although his story clearly depicts his and his family's suffering under Israeli occupation, Baroud says, "that suffering has never caused me to hate another person because of their religion."

A book of Ramzy Baroud's poetry, The Letters of Decision, *was published in Gaza in 1991.*

(See photo insert.)

My Mother Palestine

Written with the assistance of Suzy Baroud

As I look back on my mother's life, I have to think that the only benevolence she experienced in her forty years was death. She came into this world in the peaceful and green village of Beit Daras. Her first five years there were happy. Hers was a small village adorned with lush green fields, olive groves, and acres of fragrant lemon and orange trees. The landscape was beautiful and the atmosphere was permeated with a sense of simplicity and stillness.

Then the Zionists came. They invaded her village and drove everyone out at gunpoint. My grandmother recalls how the villagers gathered together and fearfully plotted their retaliation against the invaders. The Zionists were armed with weapons provided by the departing British, while the people of my mother's village had only simple farming and kitchen tools to fight with.

So many of them were killed, trying to protect Beit Daras. Others fled to life as refugees in the crowded refugee camps in the Gaza Strip. I remember my mother weeping as she recalled their journey to Gaza. Her mother held her hand and carried her younger sister. My mother was only five, but this journey changed her into an adult. Children grow up fast in war.

On the journey to Gaza her father died. The family was unable to stop, for there was no shelter, food, or water. They couldn't lose the crowd. So they had to bury him on the side of the road.

Now my mother was a refugee. For the rest of her life she would live in a lowly camp, riddled with disease, surrounded by barbed wire, filled with despair. Here she would grow up, marry, become a mother. In this camp she would be known for her sweet disposition and her generosity to the poor, even though she was so poor herself. And here in this camp her children would watch her die.

I think that my mother's and father's story is so honest and beautiful. Both of them were terribly poor. Their families were neighbors in our camp, called Nuseirat. When they married, they had nothing but each other. For years they survived on soup my mother created from discarded garlic skins, grass, and salt. They suffered so much and yet their suffering gave them incomprehensible strength. The daily hardships produced in them a blazing vibrance in the midst of the turmoil of occupation.

Soon after they were married they had a son, Anwar. He was their shining pride. They adored him. He was their only son and he brought a rare joy to their lives. Anwar was two years old when he became very sick. My mother and father tried to take him to a hospital, but the refugee hospitals had little or no resources to provide for the masses of people. My mother carried Anwar on her back for miles to a makeshift clinic established by the United Nations. Her hope was lost when all they had to offer her was two aspirin tablets. Quietly, she took them and walked home with her dying son on her back. She did everything she could to make him comfortable. And she wept and sat beside him as he died. My father was completely filled with despair and rage. Even today he is overcome with grief at the mention of Anwar's name.

Time passed and they started to rebuild their family. They had six children. I was the fourth. I was a sensitive child. Often, while my brothers played with the other kids, I stayed near my mother. I have beautiful memories of lying under the fig tree in our house reading *Treasure Island* while my mother sat beside me making bread. The smell of the fresh bread, the warmth of the sun, and her presence always filled me with calm, even while there was a war outside our door.

We never had money. We lived on bread and canned tomatoes provided by the United Nations. But whenever I wanted a book, my mother somehow found a few lira [small coin like a penny] to buy one for me. She couldn't even write her own name. And yet she was the wisest creature I have ever known. My mother's name was Zarefah, which in Arabic means "unequaled." Her name personified her absolutely.

My mother and father, though they had few resources, really worked as a team to provide for their children. I remember as a young boy when my father had just ten lira in his pocket—not enough to buy bread. He took the money and traveled into Israel to see if he could find anything. He walked along the streets and soon found that his ten lira would buy him nothing. In despair, he flagged down a taxi to return home, not knowing what to tell his family. As he walked towards the taxi he noticed a man in an alley. The man was throwing boxes into a large dumpster. My father approached him and, in his broken Hebrew, asked him what he was throwing away. The man opened one of the boxes and showed my father hundreds of thousands of rusty razor blades. Cases and cases of them had been exposed to moisture and were, this man thought, no good.

My father offered the man his ten lira. The man laughed and took the money. For more than three months my mother and father scrubbed each blade with olive oil and lemon juice. They dried them in the sun and wrapped each one in tissue paper. Their hands were covered with hundreds of tiny scars, a reminder of one of our many valiant fights for survival. The money my father made on this venture lasted for months. He truly had the spirit of an entrepreneur. With some of the money my father bought my brothers a bicycle.

* * *

It was not just my family but all families in the camp that suffered. The government made it illegal to start any kind of industry in Gaza. If a man tried, along with his friends, to build a factory, it was destroyed with dynamite and the men were arrested. If a man tried to secretly work in Israel, he would be punished. Once while I was traveling into Israel with my father I remember seeing a horrifying scene at the main checkpoint at the border between the Gaza Strip and Israel. It was the body of a young man, perhaps eighteen years old, who had tried to sneak over the border to work. The soldiers killed him as a "security measure" and threw his body on the ground for everyone to see. It was to be an example to any "subversive" who tried to sneak across to find work on the other side without permission.

One of the most valuable contributions refugees received from the United Nations was the flour they provided for bread. Each family was rationed a twenty-five pound sack of flour each month. I remember standing in lines that went on for miles, waiting with my mother. She stood in the hot sun, talking with the other women in line, and listening to them lament of their problems. She was always consoling someone, even as she humbly stood in line to receive her charity ration.

The flour came in white cotton sacks. Across the sacks was bold blue and white lettering. Of course most of us couldn't understand what was written on them. One summer the U.N. realized that they had an overwhelming surplus of these white cotton bags. So they brought together dozens of women from the camps and set them to work making pants and shorts out of the leftover bags.

I vividly remember that summer playing football and being so excited that the United Nations provided very reasonably priced uniforms. Everywhere in the camps, kids paraded around in this new item that had hit the local markets. And across every young boy and young girl's backside large white and blue letters screamed "not for sale or trade."

As people reflect on their childhood, perhaps they remember their first music concert, the first football game they attended, or their first kiss. My most vivid memory is the first time I picked up a stone. I was ten years old. I was with my best friend, Mohammed. Mohammed and I were in the same class in a boys' school run by the United Nations. Across the street there was a girls' school.

One day while we were walking home from school we heard the sound of screaming. Someone said that the Israelis had surrounded the girls' school. Mohammed ran in the direction of the school. Although I was terrified, I followed him. Tanks surrounded the school and soldiers were throwing tear gas grenades over the walls into the school. I was numbed with horror for I knew that this tear gas, in an enclosed area, was deadly.

Mohammed turned to me and yelled, "Ramzy, we must do something!"

My first reaction was to turn around and run home. Mohammed and I were not daring boys. We were the "smart kids" who spent our lunch breaks reading or doing homework rather than playing football with the rest of the boys.

I couldn't believe I was watching my friend Mohammed pick up a stone and start charging the tanks. I found myself running behind him. My hands clutched the stone so hard that my knuckles turned white. I felt like I was in a dream as I stood just yards from the fortress of tanks. Hundreds of boys were with us, yelling and throwing stones. Some boys were climbing the walls of the school trying to help the girls on the other side.

The scene rapidly developed into a hail of bullets from the Israeli soldiers. We scattered. I was running so fast that I lost one of my sandals. In the chaos of the moment, I lost sight of Mohammed. I walked home alone. I felt a sense of manhood. I was proud that we defended our sisters. I worried that some children might have been injured or killed. I wondered if I would ever find my lost sandal. I just wanted to run home into the arms of my mother. There I would be safe.

News of the incident spread through the camp quickly. As I passed by, women beckoned me to come into their houses to drink a cup of tea and to wash. I was a mess. They must have known that I had been there. I hoped they knew. It was the first time I felt I had really done something heroic.

I heard someone say a boy had been shot. I wondered who it was. Some people said he was alive while others said he was dead. I suddenly felt an urgency to be with my mother. I ran the last mile as fast as I could. I stopped on the side of the road to collect an empty tear gas grenade. On the side of it I read "Produced in Saltsburg, Pennsylvania."

Out of breath and relieved to be home, I opened the door. My mother cried out in relief and embraced me as she wept out loud. My feelings of manhood quickly disappeared, and I was a little boy again, home safe with my mother. I told her of the events at school. I whimpered about my lost sandal. I wondered if I would have to go through the rest of the school year with just one. My mother seemed preoccupied and troubled as she heated soapy water for my bath. I didn't know what was wrong, and I was afraid to ask.

Later that evening, someone came to the door. My father briskly ushered the guest into the sitting room. I walked in. They were drinking bitter coffee. I burst into tears. It was Mohammed's father. It is our custom that bitter coffee is reserved for times of mourning. Mohammed's father put me on his knee and, with tears pouring like rain, he told me that the boy who had been shot was Mohammed. He survived the injury, but he no longer recognized me, nor his father or mother. He couldn't speak anymore. He couldn't do anything.

But for some mysterious reason he remembered one thing. He remembered how to pray. From then on, instead of spending his days laughing with me at school, he sat in the mosque. He arrived every morning at 4:00 for the dawn prayer.

Sometimes I still go to see him. But not so often. It is too bittersweet to remember him as he was and to see him now. Somehow it's like mourning his death with each encounter. He just smiles at me with an emptiness in his eyes. But he has taught me something that I will never be able to repay. He has taught me the lesson of sacrifice. To me he is a living martyr.

The world sees these boys with stones in hand and says that they are terrorists. I look at them and I see heroes. Now, as the fire rises, and the children gather in the streets with nothing but their own courage to protect them, I stand in front. I am no longer the last to pick up a stone. I must continue our struggle. Not only for myself, but for my brother Mohammed.

As I grew older and the Intifada [Palestinian uprising] erupted, these violent confrontations with soldiers became more and more frequent. They once would fill me with terror but, as I grew older and became accustomed to them, they became just another obstacle to life in a refugee camp.

At night they used to impose curfews throughout the camp. Soldiers would ride around in their jeeps and if they saw anyone outside, that person, without being questioned, was swiftly arrested or shot in the street.

One night I remember waking up to a tremendous clamor of shooting and bombing. It was so loud and alarming that I thought there must be hundreds of people outside. I lay so still on my bed, silently looking to my brothers, whispering to them, as if the soldiers might hear me in our room.

At 6:00 A.M. when the curfew was lifted, masses of people went outside to see what the fateful results were of the night. I stepped outside my door to hear a blood-chilling wail. It was our eighty-year-old neighbor, Ahmed. His sons were in prison and he had no one to take care of him. The only life companion he had was his old donkey. I pushed through the crowd, following the cries of Ahmed.

He cried over and over, "God is Great, God is Great!"

I made it to the center of the crowd to see Ahmed's faithful donkey lying in a pool of blood. He had "violated" the curfew by getting out of his pen. Ahmed was afraid to go looking for him. So the donkey wandered the streets until the army spotted him and then they tore his worn-out body to pieces with their guns. In our country every part of nature is victimized. All of God's creation is groaning with incomprehensible pain.

That night I dreamed of a funeral procession. It was a procession of children, and they were carrying the carcass of Ahmed's faithful friend. They carried it with overwhelming honor and buried it near the graveyard of the martyrs.

Once I saw a small boy killed by the soldiers just outside of our house. I was peering out the window and saw him wandering home with a handful of sweets clutched in his hand. Violence erupted nearby so suddenly that, before the little boy knew it, he was in the middle of a battlefield. I shouted at him to run towards my house and I ran to open the door. Just as I opened it, I saw the small child fly through the air from the force of the soldiers' gunfire.

His name was Saed, which means "smiling." He was six years old. Although I didn't know Saed, I felt compelled to attend his funeral. Hundreds and hundreds of people were there. They were spilling out of the graveyard onto the streets.

The air was filled with the strangest feeling of holiness. As the sheik read from the Koran and the women cried with Saed's mother, I noticed a dove on top of the minaret of the mosque. The dove flew down from the minaret and landed directly in the center of the crowd on Saed's grave.

Everyone was completely still. For what seemed like hours you could hear nothing but the awe-filled whispers of the people in the crowd, quietly proclaiming under their breath, "God is Great, God is Great." The dove didn't move.

He wasn't startled by the people. He just stood there, ever so still. At that moment I knew that God was really there with us. As he sent the dove to Noah, he sent a dove to us.

M̲y mother tried so hard to entertain us kids inside the house. She never felt settled when we were outside, vulnerable to the Israeli army. She became even more fearful when we were told of a new policy instituted in the area. This policy was referred to as "the broken bones policy." It said that Israeli soldiers were to implement corporal punishment on anyone near a confrontational incident. So, if two boys were throwing stones near the market, the army was to retrieve the boys, break their arms and the arms of anyone else near the incident. They thought that perhaps this would be a deterrent to stone throwing.

One night the whole camp was awakened by the soldiers' loudspeakers. I lay frozen and afraid to breathe, listening to their chilling cries. "Every man between the ages of fourteen to sixty is to report to the boys' high school immediately. We will be doing random searches of your houses. If we find anyone hiding at home, he will be shot on the spot."

My mother jumped from her mattress and frantically prepared our clothes as she recited verses from the Koran. "Allah is Merciful and Compassionate," she uttered as she dressed her five sons, her face ashen with terror.

With our fathers and our neighbors we made our way through the dark paths of Nuseirat camp. I walked with my friends, wondering what our destiny would be. Some of us thought it was real trouble. Shady, my next door neighbor, thought we were going to receive an award. I jokingly hit his arm and laughed nervously at the suggestion.

We arrived at the school to meet up with more than 20,000 other men. The school was surrounded with jeeps and tanks. There were soldiers everywhere. Their floodlights lit up the school grounds. We spent the entire night there while the soldiers systematically grabbed a young boy here and a man there, striking their arms with wooden clubs and pounding their legs with heavy blows. Many were chosen as examples of what happens to "terrorist stone throwers." It was the longest, most horrifying night of my life. I will never forget it. I do not want to forget it.

At dawn we were released. Of the mass assembly, at least half returned home with a fractured arm or leg.

The nightmare didn't stop that night. There were daily raids and women and men alike were struck down by the army.

It was early in the morning when they came to our house. We sat on the floor with our pajamas on. My mother had boiled tea and we were having a breakfast of tea, bread, and eggs. A thundering came from the door. It was broken down and dozens of soldiers poured into our house. As my father tried to reason with them and my mother screamed and cried, they dragged me and my four brothers out to the street. Still in our pajamas, they tied our arms and legs together. My father came and diplomatically, yet frantically, tried to convince the soldiers to let us go.

Their leader yelled, "We'll show you what happens to boys who don't follow the rules!"

As they were about to strike us with their clubs, my

mother, in a frenzy, ran at them. She cried *"Allahu Akbar"* (God is Greater) and made herself a human barricade between her sons and the soldiers.

One soldier took his gun and thrust it into my mother. It was not a bayonet, but it penetrated into her chest like a dull sword. She gasped and fell to the ground. My father screamed. My brothers began to cry. We couldn't do anything because we were tied up.

The soldiers backed away and my father ran to my mother's side, wailing. He held her head and kissed her hands as the blood trickled out of her mouth. It took fifty days until she finally died. My father did not leave her side for one moment. He sat holding her hands and kissing her feet until the last. As I remember her now, the only comfort I have is that on the fiftieth day her frail body was swiftly swept up into the arms of Allah.

My mother fought and died to defend her children. Until we are free, we will not cease in our struggle. Our mother, Palestine, will one day be liberated. This I am sure is true.

GHAREEB (PSEUD.)

Seventeen years old when he wrote his story, and one of the youngest writers in this book, Ghareeb says, "I am just a young person who wants to live his life without fear . . . [but] I fail to see any feasible solution or hope for peace." A resident of Ramallah, Ghareeb has been witness to too much brutality to have retained his childhood innocence. In his own words: "In my mind the sound of a bullet, the echo of a kick, the cries of the people, and the images of the dead will never be buried." Nevertheless, Ghareeb says that he is "lucky to be alive and out of prison."

A Look into Memory

*M*ost people mark the beginning of their lives by a birthday, wedding, or some other happy event. This forms a launching point after which they remember most of the things that happen in their lives and feel that they are beginning to grow up.

I have marked the end of my childhood with blood. My earliest memories start on December 9th, 1987. I will never forget how everything was closed down, angry soldiers were yelling everywhere, and the TV showed images of lots of dead bodies. The Intifada [Palestinian uprising]—that was the start of my grown-up life.

Schools were shut down right after the uprising started. Teaching was illegal, and to be in school was a crime. Teachers resorted to teaching illegally in their homes. If I had been caught going to my teachers' houses by the Israeli army, I would have been guilty of a crime. At that time, you would spend the night in the worst jail in the area, get beat up, and have to pay a fine.

In the summer of 1988, the schools were reopened. I will never forget one hot August day. My Mom woke me and my brother up for school. We got dressed and were about to eat our breakfast. Suddenly, I heard the sounds of Quran reading coming from all the mosques. I was scared to death.

On our way to school every mosque was lit and the Quran was being read—something that is only done when a major bad thing has happened. When I reached my school, I learned the horrible news: a ninth grade student from the school had been found dead in the mountains outside the city. He had been beaten and tortured and shot to death by the Israeli army, and then he was left for two days. I will never forget the picture of his bloody, swollen corpse.

My next clash with the Israeli army came in the summer of 1990. My brother and I were practicing karate at a local karate club which was right beside an Israeli army post. Stones were thrown at the army and in they came, pouring into the club. They rounded us all up and lined us up against the wall. They separated the older students from the younger students and began practicing their karate kicks on the older students. I stood there in horror as they beat the students up. Then they interrogated us about our names, where we lived, and the whereabouts of our coach.

The Israeli soldiers took the older students down the street and locked us younger students up in the club. They left us there for more than half an hour while we listened to the sounds of their beating the older students. Later they came and told us to "Get out right now!" An eleven-year-old and a thirteen-year-old—my brother and I—hurried away from this place of horror, but the looks on the older students' faces and the sounds of the beatings will echo in my memory forever.

In my mind the sound of a bullet, the echo of a kick, the cries of the people, and the images of the dead will never be buried. I'm carrying a deep wound, a wound that keeps getting deeper and deeper every time peace is postponed and manipulated.

The echoes, the ghosts, and the voices make me wonder: will I ever be able to forgive and forget? Will time ever bury such a tragedy and help me to start over again as a normal human being?

I have lost the innocence in my childhood to the guns and the boots and the sirens. Yet I am lucky, for I have not lost a member of my family to the dungeon or the gun. But I can't help but wonder about my Palestinian brothers who have lost someone—or who are lost themselves. I can't help but wonder, will it ever end?

AMMAR ABU ZAYYAD

Sixteen-year-old Ammar Abu Zayyad has lived in Bethany, Jerusa-
lem, all of his life. Written in 1997, this overview of the violence he
has witnessed, suffered, and, in some cases, participated in indi-
cates that there is more tension between Israelis and Palestinians
today than in any time he remembers.

"There is a great difference between my childhood and that of
other children in the world," he says. "I opened my eyes on a world
that didn't give me any rights. So, I put aside my toys and retrieved
the stone—the only thing that made me feel better."

Zayyad says that the most important thing in his life is to finish
his education and to live long enough to see the founding of the
Palestinian State.

Healing the Wounds of Childhood

*I*t was a faint knock on the door, a very gentle one that I
would never have associated with the green figure behind it.
It was 1989, and I was not yet eight, and the knock seemed
harmless enough, but when I opened the door I found a big,
vicious, angry, green soldier asking for my father. I had no

idea what to do. I froze until he was joined by two of his colleagues. They shoved me aside and came into our apartment. They thought that a stone had come from our house and they suspected that my older brother Ali had thrown it at them. They wanted to arrest him even though they could not be sure that he had thrown the rock. The thing that really struck me was the quality of the knock. It's been over eight years now and I still can't harmonize the knock with the knocker. A gentle knock is something the soldiers are not known to use. It gave me the idea that maybe that soldier's awkwardness meant that he didn't really want to do what he was doing. Just maybe.

Not long after, the soldiers turned my uncle's house next door to ours into a guard tower. The whole family was terrorized and my cousin often cried because of their presence in the house. The situation went on for months and we thought they would never leave. Then one day the soldiers decided to search the house and they found a small piece of paper with a drawing of the Palestinian flag on it. They went crazy and took my uncle for questioning. Then they brought him and his ten-year-old son, Samer, and told him that if he didn't hit Samer as hard as he could they would do it. He had no choice but to agree and do as they pleased. My cousin was unaware of how his father was forced to hit him, which made him blame his father. Not till years later did he come to understand and by then he had some pretty hard problems. All this because of a drawing done by a kid.

* * *

Ammar Abu Zayyad

Perhaps my father's arrest in 1990 was the most important event in my life because it caused me to give up Hamas [radical Islamic group] for Fatah [Palestine Liberation Organization (PLO)]. He was arrested "administratively," that is, he was taken, convicted, and sentenced without a trial. I was eight at the time and full of anger because I couldn't understand why my father was so ruthlessly taken away for a whole six months. He was taken to Nablus and put into an Israeli prison. I vomited at the end of my first visit there—the prison aroused such feelings of hatred toward all Israeli people in me that I dreamt of killing each and every one of them. That was the only way I saw to ease the sufferings of the Palestinian people. I couldn't find any weapon but the rock, and I took it to be my weapon.

I gladly added the word "enemy" to my vocabulary although I wasn't sure what it meant. But I knew who it was. I decided that I should and must be part of those fighting the "enemy." I started watching the news every day, awaiting nearby action. But it never came, so I decided I should go get it if it wouldn't come to me. I gathered a few friends and every day we would fight the enemy without our parents having any knowledge of it. Soon—just like on TV—I had learned and perfected the art of stone throwing.

[In 1993, Ammar gave up stone throwing and began investigating the possibilities for peace. He learned about the Oslo agreements and, in the summer of 1994, he attended a three-day camp where Arabs and Israelis held roundtable discussions. "I realized," he says, "that not all Israelis are killers and ruthless, immoral animals the way I had seen them from the window of my past years." Subsequently, he participated in many seminars and became an active member of Palestinian Youth for Peace.]

Today, the 1st of April, 1997, as I sit here and write, I remember the situation outside, and I laugh at myself and wonder how I still have faith in the peace process. Thirteen days ago the Knesset (the Israeli parliament) agreed to start building a new settlement near Jerusalem, which is a violation of their agreements. The whole world is against it and so are the Americans, but they must always use their veto when Israel is in danger of U.N. Security Council condemnation.

The situation is more tense than at any other time. We are back to the intifada: stones, martyrs' arrests, and attacks because of the settlement building. On my way to school, I have to pass through three checkpoints. At each I must show my birth certificate. I am often made to return the way I have come. Often the soldiers hit me like yesterday at the Ras Al-Amoud checkpoint. I was hit and then detained for about an hour. I've had worse times. I've been detained four times in severe rains.

All I ask is to be left alone to go to school and study without being harassed. Is it too much to ask? I don't know.

I have given you the events that shaped my feelings and thinking toward the occupation of our land. I wasn't telling a story, but I was telling the facts about my country and how

I'm living my life. The life of a child in Palestine is a cruel one in which one's only salvation is his/her imagination, for the reality is a very harsh one. Our future and the childhood of the next generation—is it going to be like mine? Well, it's up to you.

REDROSE (PSEUD.)

Redrose was eighteen when she wrote this story about student reaction at her secondary school to the Dizengof Square bombing, October 20, 1994. One of her main concerns was to be certain to thank her friend Nir, who typed the manuscript for her. "It's hard to find a friend who charges only my happiness for his time and efforts," she said.

Sylvia Asher, one of Redrose's teachers at the secondary school she attends in Tel Aviv, informed her about the opportunity for publication in this book and has supported her efforts throughout the lengthy editorial process. Now Redrose, known as "the genius writer" on her school's World Wide Web homepage, is already inquiring about positions in international journalism and is hereby putting out the word that she's looking for a paper in need of an Israeli correspondent.

Although she finds herself giving up in frustration about the Israeli/Palestinian situation at times, Redrose says that "even a lost cause like peace with the Arabs is worth a fight." To illustrate her point, she wants to pass on a metaphor that she learned from her chemistry teacher:

"Two frogs got trapped in a jar of cream. They couldn't jump out of the liquid and they couldn't climb because the sides of the jar were slippery. One frog said, 'By dawn I'll be dead,' and went to sleep. The second frog swam all night long and in the morning found herself floating on a pat of butter."

(See photo insert.)

Face of Peace

*T*he news will always have new things to report about: calamities, corruption, politics, crime. But here in Israel, in the last three years, calamities came much too often and they were much too sad.

Three years ago that was all it was for us—news. The assassins were killing people every day, but it was so far from us, a minor phenomenon. The uprising was something I heard about in the news—it was a concept, not a reality. Peace? Peace was a lovely word, in fact it was a fashion. If you were against the peace process, it meant you were not enlightened. I imagined that there would be hugs in the streets, harmony, and love. On the 13th of September, 1993, the first peace agreement was signed in Oslo, but for us it was still just news.

But we talked about it every day. Did I say "talked"? Shouted was more like it. You could have seen fireworks when we argued, it was such a loaded issue and everybody was so violently supportive of their own opinion. By the ninth grade those arguments came so often that just the word "Peace" became a match that could light a fire. Where else in the world would you find fourteen-year-olds so interested in politics? Here everybody is interested because here it's not a matter of which candidates' smile is more photogenic; it's a matter of life and death.

Three years ago we felt safe, and as much as the issue was

close to our hearts, it scarcely really touched us. Alas, this safe period in our lives came to an end. On the 20th of October, 1994, came fear and terror. We were in class, it was the ten o'clock break, and I was confronting a math exercise that was beyond my concentration.

"Damn! I will never get this right!" I thumped the miserable table that served as a scapegoat for my frustration.

"Are you out of your mind? You scared me to death!" Rinat jumped at me.

"Sorry, this thing is scaring me to death. I will never get it right—not before tomorrow's test anyway."

A shout from the back of the class interrupted our conversation. Lilach, Keren, and Ifat were listening to a radio.

"This isn't happening! It's not real!" Ifat said with amazement.

Then I saw a tear in Ifat's eye and Keren and Lilach looked worried.

"What's wrong?" I asked. And Rinat and I went to listen to the radio.

". . . The number of dead or injured is yet unknown. The chief of police estimates there are between ten to fifteen dead and over fifty injured. We turn this transmission over to our man in the field . . ."

We didn't know at first what this was all about, but it seemed like the world had gone suddenly darker.

"Was there an accident or something?" Rinat asked.

The radio kept on: "The police have sealed this area." (The reporter's voice was trembling.) "So I'm not exactly sure where the explosion took place."

"Explosion! What is he talking about?" Rinat asked.

"I'm standing now at the Dizengof Square—"

My heart ached and I could not believe it.

"—next to the fountain of water and fire . . . The fire of the explosion has faded away, now is the turn of the tears to fall. The situation is not clear now, but I can tell you, you wouldn't want to be where I'm standing."

He was silent for long seconds. "There is blood everywhere. It's horrible! You can see fingers on the floor, and hair covered with blood, and human flesh all over the sidewalk and the road. The bus is split in two. I guess the explosives were at the center of the bus. The chief of police will have a statement within the hour. Until then I return the transmission to the studio. It's a sad day."

Keren turned the radio off. We were stunned and speechless.

A bunch of guys entered the class, back from the break rambunctious and cheerful. Yonni was chasing Yaniv, throwing chalk at him.

Alon entered the class and came toward us. "Did somebody die, or did the math teacher add more material to the test?"

"There has been an assassination at Dizengof," Keren said.

"Dizengof?!" Alon was aghast.

I panicked. "And if it happened in Dizengof, nowhere is safe anymore. Allenby is not safe, the central station is not safe! Oh, my God, how will I get to work?"

"Can't you see that is exactly what they were aiming for—your fear?" Keren cried. "They just want to intimidate you."

"Well, they are doing a fine job intimidating me," Liron said. "And what daunts me even more is that I don't have a clue who 'they' are. It's a faceless, hateful enemy we have. There is no way to fight him."

"Liron, why do you think they picked Dizengof?" Lilach asked rhetorically. "Because for us it's a symbol of routine. Bus 5, which everybody knows. They want to take away our security. They don't care how many people died today. They are just happy they managed to get to Dizengof, to bus 5, the heart of our city. It's a psychological war."

"They are still blowing people away, no matter what their purpose," Liron said.

The history teacher came into the class. Even before she spoke, we could all see on her face that she had heard the news. We loved her lessons. She made history relevant and interesting. We admired her as a human being. She was funny and witty and such a strong woman. I wanted to see her reaction. And even if I forget her exact words, I shall never forget the spirit of those words:

"It's harder for me to teach than it is for you to study. But terror is the lowest point of no return and they have passed it. You have here a live example of what history is all about. 'Blood is the oil of the wheels of history.' When I was teaching you about the horrible losses of the pogroms, the numbers seemed meaningless. You weren't shocked to hear about hundreds of Jews dead at random, out of the blue. Dead because of politics and antisemitism.

"You were shocked about the figures of the Holocaust. SIX MILLION. That's quite a figure. Compared to that, the pogroms were nothing, minor. It didn't look real to you—just something that happened a long time ago.

"Now you have a live example of what the pogroms were all about—an unfair slaughter of people in their own street.

It's not a war; you face a faceless enemy, a nameless enemy, an enemy whose only aim is to intimidate, to horrify, to thrust his ways upon us violently. And what are his ways? The same as always, everywhere—'We don't want you here. This land is ours.' But this land is ours and nobody will take our promised land. We've fought for this home because we were homeless. But now we have to stick to our fight more than ever.

"I'm not saying fight the Arabs; I'm saying fight the terror. Terror does not equal Arabs. And I'm not saying fight their terror. I'm saying don't be influenced by it. It's frustrating to punch the air, and you might want to have a scapegoat to hate and to hit, but when your enemy is shapeless, don't shape him into what he isn't.

"I've already seen a new graffiti outside near the gate. Can anybody guess what it said?"

"Death to the Arabs," Liron said.

"If this was a test, it would be the first one you would pass," Alon said cynically.

"No," Liron said. "I've forgotten a word. 'Death to the Arabs and to the Alons.'"

"Sure, why not?" Alon scoffed. "Spray them all like cockroaches! Throw them to the sea with weights. Get real, Liron! You think the world wouldn't notice. Six million Arabs just take a walk and drown."

"What could the world care?" Liron defended her stand. "The world didn't interfere when six million Jews were slaughtered."

"But the world did interfere, or else you wouldn't be here," Alon said.

"OK, so we'll kill 'em and the world will interfere and

say, 'naughty, naughty, don't do it again.' We'll say we're sorry and send our condolences to seven Arab states, along with large checks, and in a few years everything will be forgotten and forgiven and we won't have Arabs anymore."

Liron seemed to have it all figured out. But she was right. That was the nature of the world—to forget horrors, to forgive horror makers.

"I hereby declare you Liron Adolf Hitler," Adi said.

"It's craziness, what you're saying," I said.

"Yes, well, the world is a crazy place. I'm just adjusting," Liron said, waving her hands as if to say "nothing can be done about it."

"No, I mean even your thoughts are non-human. How can you talk about murder as if you were talking of . . . of cockroaches. Haven't you any sympathy for the Arabs' condition? They are like us in the Holocaust. Germany and Poland had been our homeland. And we didn't have any place to go. We expected to be left as we were, but they hated us just as you hate the Arabs now, Liron. And they talked about killing us just as you are talking now. They are no different from what we were back then."

"Oh, yes, they are, honey!" Liron interrupted me. "We didn't throw any stones or blow up any buses. Besides, we didn't have any place to go; they have seven countries. They practically own the whole Mediterranean coast. So, save the 'poor victims of politics' theory for another sucker."

She was harsh. I hadn't the words or the enthusiasm to argue with her.

"Your hatred is plugging your ears to what is right."

"And your innocence is plugging this country from salvation."

"Now, can I continue?" the teacher asked.

"Sure, go ahead," Liron answered shamelessly, and the lesson went on amidst the continuous struggle of opinions.

That evening everybody plugged themselves into their TV sets. Some went to Dizengof to see the horrors with their own eyes, to sympathize with the pain. Radical mobs demonstrated, blaming the whole world—the Arabs, Yitzhak Rabin, Arafat, the left wing—and wishing death to them all. Twenty-two people died that day, but hatred demanded more deaths.

There was so much anger, so much pain, so much candlelight . . . so little hope.

The next bomb was Bet Lead on the twenty-first of January. The same sad story, the same anger and hatred, doubled and tripled as the number of the dead rose in the news. And me, I was just fearing things to come, very confused, but still trying to think positively—naively??

RACHELI TAL

Racheli Tal was born in Seattle, Washington, in 1982. When she was five, she and her family emigrated to Israel, where they eventually came to live in the religious settlement called Beit-El.

In the two stories that follow, written when she was fourteen, Tal gives us an eyewitness account of how deadly the Arab-Israeli conflict can be. In keeping with the Israeli settler goals that she describes in both stories, Racheli says that when she grows up she wants to establish a new settlement in the Golan Heights.

(See photo insert.)

My Life on the Firing Line

I was standing on top of the mountain looking down at the valley below. Men with guns and torches were climbing up the mountain. I tried to run away but they had me surrounded. I could see the deep hatred in their black eyes. One of them tried to catch me. I screamed, and then . . . I woke up.

I sat up in bed, sweaty and frightened, but happy to find myself safe at home. If I believed in bad omens I would have taken this as a bad sign, but I had no idea of what was going to happen.

* * *

My name is Racheli Tal. I'm fourteen and I live in the Judean religious settlement named Beit-El. I have two parents, Israel and Chana, and two younger sisters, Miriam, aged eleven, and Rikki, who just turned six. Our settlement is nineteen years old and has about eight hundred families. The settlement is very developed, with schools for children up through high school (there are separate schools for boys and girls), a post-high school yeshiva for religious studies for boys, a clothing store, a bakery, an electronics factory, and even a swimming pool.

When I was five and a half years old I came from the U.S. with my parents. We lived for a year in an absorption center and three years in Jerusalem before we moved to Beit-El. I love Beit-El because it's small and I know almost everybody, but sometimes it can be scary. When we ride the bus to Jerusalem we have to go through the Arab city of Ramallah. Sometimes the Arabs throw rocks at us; that's why we aren't allowed to open the windows in any bus or car. The windows are made out of a very strong kind of plastic-glass to keep the rocks from breaking them, but they aren't bulletproof, so if your car gets shot at it can be very dangerous.

I always thought it was kind of odd that it's our state and the Arabs are allowed to hurt us. Today I know things aren't so simple. The Arabs claim the state is theirs because, when the Jews were in exile from the Land of Israel, the Moslems were in control for a few hundred years. They are commanded to do "jihad"—holy war—against nonbelievers like Jews and Christians. On the other hand, it says ninety-seven times in the Bible that God gave the Holy Land to the Jews and later King David made Jerusalem Israel's capital. That's what all the fighting is about, and that's one of the reasons everything happened last summer.

I remember the day well. Outside the hot sun was blazing. I was sitting in the rec room by the fan, bored out of my mind and trying to think of something to do. I was just about to give up when I heard a knock on the door. "Come in," I shouted.

It was my best friend Naamah. Just then I noticed a huge smile on her face. I could tell she had some news and she was dying to tell me. "All right, spit it out!" I told her.

"Listen, Racheli, you won't believe this. You know the Artis, the mountain that's beyond the swimming pool? The whole settlement is going up there to build a new neighborhood, but the government doesn't know about it."

"Just a minute," I stopped her. "What exactly are we going to do up there? And how do you know all this?"

"We are going to start making foundations for the houses and, until caravans [trailers] are brought, people who volunteer will sleep up there in tents. The chairman of the settlement's governing council called my mother and asked her to be responsible for passing out the message. When my mother told me about it I immediately ran over here. Come on, let's go tell everybody."

But there was no need. Everybody knew about it already. That's the way it is when you live in a small place.

We started heading up the mountain. It was already four o'clock in the afternoon and it was starting to cool down so the climb wasn't too hard. The mountain is about 3,000 feet high, and from the top you can see the Jewish settlement Ofra and the Arab village Dura el-Kara. They are pretty close to Beit-El.

When we got to the top of the mountain, what we saw was total chaos. The men were putting up tents and tying wires with light bulbs to the generators. The kids and teenagers were clearing away the rocks and thorn bushes. Little kids were running around everywhere and their mothers were just standing watching. Some people were walking around with video cameras. I saw some of my friends moving rocks and making a path, so I went and helped them. I worked for about two hours. I got dirty and scratched by thorns, but I felt good. I knew how the first settlers felt when they came back to Israel after 2,000 years of exile and had to rebuild their land. I felt like I was building my land for something I believed in: the Jews living in Israel, planting and settling it.

That's when my friend Reut tapped me on the back and woke me up from my daydreaming. "Racheli, we're planning to sleep here tonight. Let's go home and ask our parents for permission. I'll meet you by the swimming pool in an hour."

"Great, let's go," I said, and we headed down the mountain.

It wasn't easy to persuade my parents to allow me to sleep on the mountain. Since Yitzhak Rabin came to power, the settlements have not been allowed to build houses, so what we were doing was illegal and the police and army might come and try to take us down forcefully. Similar things were happening in another settlement named Efrat, and the army came and violently pulled them off their mountain. My parents were afraid that the army would come to Beit-El and use violence. But in the end they let me go. My father said that usually it takes the army two to three days to come, and it was unlikely that they could come that night. I took my pajamas and sleeping bag and headed for the swimming pool. I met Reut there and we started climbing.

Halfway up the mountain we saw that my father was wrong. A few military jeeps and police cars had already come and soldiers were walking around talking to Ketsale and other members of the Beit-El governing council. Suddenly I got scared. Would the police really use violence like I saw them doing on TV? How does it happen that they use violence on the citizens of their own nation instead of using it against the real enemy?

I was still lost in thought when my friend Michal came up to me and told me to join the group. For about an hour we goofed around and snacked on sweets we had brought. Then we heard the voice of Pinchas Wallerstein, the head of the regional council, speaking to us through a megaphone. We crowded around him and listened closely. This is what he said: "Things are not going the way we expected them and the army will be here sooner than we thought. The army can't come up here tonight because the mountain is too rocky and too dark, so they will probably come tomorrow at the crack of dawn. I ask all of you, when the soldiers come don't run away—and stay calm. We are staying on this mountain. It is our land and if the Arabs ever come and capture the mountain it endangers all of us. Just look around—it's one of the tallest mountains in the area. You can see Beit-El and Ofra perfectly from the top. That is why we must protect this mountain with all our might, and if they take us down we will come back again and again and again."

"When the soldiers try to take you down, do not use violence under any circumstances! You may tie yourselves to rocks, to poles, to each other, and explain to them why we are doing this. But do not use violence. In the morning you will get more instructions."

Each of us went away to our own corner to get ready to go to sleep. But my friends and I didn't sleep a wink. We got up and built a campfire, then sat around and talked. At about four a.m., when the sun was starting to rise, we put out the campfire and joined a group of people who were sitting in a circle and singing Israeli and Jewish songs.

We sat down and joined the singing. At six a.m. the sun was already high in the sky, and all around on the nearby mountains was a blue mist of a clear sunny morning. We got up and made our morning prayers and ate some breakfast we had brought from home. At seven a.m. people started swarming up the mountain to strengthen us and to take part in resisting the evacuation. Now the number of women doubled and the number of men tripled. Altogether there were about 450 of us.

The evacuation was delayed and delayed. Finally, about nine a.m., we saw the soldiers climbing up the mountain. I went and sat down in the women's tent with my friends, and we hooked hands so we couldn't be moved. About two hundred troopers surrounded the men. Then the women soldiers came to us. They talked nicely and asked us to get up. Instead of getting up, we started to sing nationalistic songs. The soldiers stood around looking helpless, not knowing what to do. I felt sorry for them. They didn't want to be there and it wasn't part of their army duty. The men soldiers looked helpless too.

Then after about a half hour the Border Police came. They started barking orders at the soldiers and were upset that they were becoming too emotionally involved with the settlers.

The soldiers started pulling at the men who gripped each other even tighter. In the background I could hear Pinchas Wallerstein and Ketsale yelling and trying to keep everyone's spirits high.

Just then a woman soldier came up to me and asked me nicely to get up and go away. I didn't budge. She asked me again and I could see she was getting nervous. This time I told her that this was my land and her land too and she should come and sit with us. She said it was illegal and she had to fulfill her orders. I told her I was not getting up.

She called one of her friends and they tried to pick me up. I held on to my friends tightly, but they tugged and freed me from their grip. Then the first woman soldier held my arm tightly and led me down the mountain. Halfway down, she let go of me and said, "I'm sorry I had to do this," and turned around and marched back up.

I stood there a minute and thought about what she had said. I felt sorry for her and for all the soldiers. They didn't want to be in this position but they had orders they had to fulfill. I looked up the mountain and saw some soldiers dragging a young man about thirty years old. They looked tired and miserable. Then I knew what I would do. I pulled my small water bottle out of my pouch and went up to the soldiers. "Would you like a drink?" I asked them.

They looked at me, surprised a little, but then one of them said, "Yes, thank you," He took the bottle out of my hand and drank about half of the water and then passed it to his friend, who finished it off. They smiled at me, and then continued to carry the man down the mountain. I felt good. After all, we weren't fighting them. It wasn't their fault.

By now the sun was blazing with all its might and it was very hot. I went back up the mountain. I saw men soldiers carrying men and women soldiers carrying women. People were crying and yelling. I sat down in the tent again, and this time when a woman soldier came up to me she didn't ask me to leave. She just dragged me. I tried to resist, but she was strong and looked very strict. After about twenty feet, she pulled me to my feet and told another woman soldier to take me down. She took me all the way to the bottom this time. I saw a lot of police vans and policemen shoving men and a few women into them, probably to arrest them.

That's how it went for the rest of the day—until about four p.m. Then Pinchas Wallerstein told us to go down ourselves and not create any more problems and that he would be in negotiations with the government.

That's how it went on for a few weeks. We went up, they took us down, and we still didn't get approval from the government to build on the Artis. Then, because the government wouldn't let us build houses, we brought up two caravans and set them up as a temporary synagogue. There were prayer books and holy books in it and a couple scrolls of the Holy Torah taken from the main synagogue.

Then one day in the middle of August something terrible happened. Apparently the whole business with the mountain didn't annoy just the government. It also annoyed our

Arab neighbors in Dura el-Kara, and they decided to do something about it.

They gathered a few journalists and cameramen from the world media and took them to the mountain. At the time there was only a mother and her three kids on the mountain. The Arabs climbed up the mountain from the east side yelling *Itbach el yahud!* (Slaughter the Jews) and all sorts of horrible curses against Israel, the government, and the settlers. There were about a hundred of them—men, women, and children. The Jewish mother and her three children were taken by surprise and ran to call the settlement's security officer.

The Arabs broke into the synagogue. There was a gas-powered generator there which they smashed and took the gasoline. They doused the prayer books, holy texts, and the Torah scrolls with the gasoline and burnt them. Then they burnt the generator and the Israeli flag.

In a few minutes four men arrived on the mountain in the settlement's security vehicle. They fired warning shots into the air and the Arabs started running. Two men kept firing while the other two tried to put out the fire burning the holy books.

Then one of our men shot a bullet unintentionally into the neck of an Arab. The other Arabs started screaming and quickly carried the man away. Our men put out the fire and took away the burnt and damaged books.

News about what had happened traveled fast, but it wasn't until that night that I saw the pictures on the news. It was terrible. I saw the Arabs marching up, then screaming as they set the entire mountain on fire. All you could see was a mountain with an orange top and a big cloud of smoke over it. Then I saw the men shooting in the air and taking out the Torah scroll that looked more like charcoal and ashes than our holiest book.

I couldn't stand it anymore. How much longer could the Arabs humiliate us? I broke down and cried. I was shaking all over. My father came over and hugged me. I felt angry and humiliated. It was our land, our state. Why did they think they could do anything they wanted to harm us? Why did the government let them get away with it and not care about the humiliation of the Holy Bible and G-d's name and the holy land?

The government didn't care a bit that all this happened—that the Arabs attacked a settlement. Instead they got angry that the Arab was shot, even though it was accidentally and in the defense of life. And that wasn't the worst of it. The police arrested a suspect—Mr. Ze'ev Oz, the chairman of the Beit-El governing council—and charged him with murder. The man has a wife and a family with a daughter my age. I knew hard days were coming for me and the settlement.

That night I had another dream. My friends and I and all the people of the settlement were building new houses on the Artis. Then, like Noah, I sent away a white dove with a message in her mouth to all the land that they should come to the dedication of the new synagogue on the Artis where all the burnt Torah scrolls and holy books were restored. I waited for the dove's return, hoping it would return with an olive branch. But the dove returned with nothing. And I wondered if there would ever be peace.

∞

The Power of Life

*I*t was the seventh night of Chanukah. Outside it was stormy and windy and the moon was covered with a thick blanket of clouds. I was putting eight candles in my Chanukah lamp, one for each night and one for the "Shamash," the candle in the middle for lighting the other candles. I heard the door open and then slam shut from the wind. My father had come home from Maariv, the evening prayers, at the synagogue.

"Racheli, Miriam, Rikki, I'm home. It's time to light the candles," he called to us.

My two sisters, both younger than me, came running down the stairs. My father set up his Chanukah lamp and lit the candles. He recited the benedictions over the candles and then we sang "Maoz Tzur," a traditional Chanukah song. After that my father read us kids a story of Isaac Bashevis Singer from his book of Chanukah stories, *The Power of Light*.

I sat by my mother and stared at the Chanukah candles that were reflecting light on the windowpane. It is a religious obligation to put the Chanukah lamp near the window so the passing people will see the light and remember the great miracle that God gave us on Chanukah.

The candles had gone out and my father went upstairs to work in his office. Miriam and I had settled down on the couch to watch a movie on TV, and my mother and Rikki were preparing dinner. A few minutes after the movie started the phone rang.

"I'll get it," I shouted and picked it up lazily. "Hello, the Tal residence," I answered.

"Racheli? Hi! What are you doing?" It was Naamah, my best friend. She sounded pretty hysterical and I knew she had something to tell me. I also knew it wasn't wise to pressure her. She would tell me when she was ready.

"I'm fine," I said. "I'm watching a movie. *Beethoven.* Do you want to come over?"

She completely ignored me and rushed on. "Racheli, you don't know what happened tonight."

"You're right. I don't. And I don't want to play guessing games." I had seen the movie *Beethoven* before, but I wanted to see it again, and with Naamah on the other end of the line it was hard to concentrate.

"Racheli, there has been a terror attack tonight. Here, on the street close to Beit-El."

In an instant I wasn't paying attention to the movie anymore. "What!?" I shouted into the receiver. "Was it a family from Beit-El? How many were wounded?" I didn't dare ask if there were any killed.

"It was the Tzur family."

"Which one?" I asked hysterically. We have three Tzur families on our settlement.

"It was Etta and Yoel Tzur. Four are slightly wounded, one seriously, and one was killed.

"Etta and Yoel!? Who was killed?"

"I don't know," she said, and then I heard her cover the mouthpiece with her hand. I could hear her talking to someone in a muffled voice. After a few seconds she took her hand off. I could hear she was crying.

"Racheli, Ephraim is dead," she said.

I was shocked. Completely shocked. Ephraim? Dead? He was such a cute boy. It couldn't be!

"Racheli? Are you still there?" Naamah asked, still in tears.

"Yes, I'm still here. When did it happen?"

"About an hour ago—about 5:30. Listen, Racheli, I've got to go. I'll call you later. Bye." And she hung up.

I sat there for a few seconds with the receiver in my hand before I hung up. By that time my whole family had come into the den to hear what had happened.

"There was a terror attack on the street near Beit-El. It was on the Tzur family, Yoel and Etta. Ephraim was killed." My voice started to quiver. I couldn't continue anymore.

"Oh, no!" my father said and smacked his forehead. I thought he was going to cry. "Really? Ephraim was killed? Who was wounded?"

I said I didn't know who was wounded, just that one was serious and four light. Now my father started to cry. My mother and Miriam looked pretty shocked, and Rikki didn't exactly understand what was going on.

"Who's Ephraim?" my mother asked. "Is he the one with the braces?"

"No, that's Tzvi. Ephraim is the one who's Miriam's age." I started to cry.

It was the first time I really felt it hard that someone was killed. Other people from our settlement have been killed in terror attacks but I felt very close to the Tzurs. They were the first family to have us for a meal when we moved to Beit-El.

The oldest daughter, Shlomit, is in the eleventh grade and is the counselor of Miriam's youth group, Ariel. Avital, the youngest daughter, is Rikki's age and they are friends. Tamar, the daughter in the eighth grade, is Rikki's class counselor in school and Rikki is very close to her. Tzvi is my age.

The Tzur family was one of the first to establish the settlement and all of their kids were born here. Yoel is one of the head managers of Arutz 7, the "pirate" radio station of the settlement and religious Zionism movements. He is also one of the head managers of the Beit-El Yeshiva for religious boys who have finished high school. Etta was a housewife and a very nice woman who was organizing and taking charge of things that were happening on the settlement.

Why should such a disaster happen to them? I couldn't help asking myself. Why should it ever be this way? I was both sad and angry; sad about Ephraim and angry at the Arabs. But more than anything, I didn't want to believe it. It was just too terrible to be real.

My mother saw me crying and sat down by me. She tried to comfort me even though she was on the verge of tears too. Miriam went to call her friend in Jerusalem to tell her about what had happened because her friend had lived in Beit-El next to the Tzurs. My father went back to his office. The house was quiet.

After half an hour my mother and I heard a knock at the door. It was a neighbor and she had come to tell us to say psalms for the health of Etta because she was in critical condition and was being operated on in the hospital. My mother went to finish preparing dinner and Rikki and I sat down to pray for Etta. When I read Psalm 13 I thought it very relevant to what had happened:

> *How long must I set schemes in my spirit; melancholy in my heart even by day? How long will my enemy triumph over me?*

When I read it I started crying again. I hoped God was hearing my prayers.

At eight o'clock my family sat down to watch the news. The terror attack was in the headlines. It was a drive-by shooting attack. The Tzurs were on their way back from a day in Tel Aviv via the Dolev road. The road is windy and surrounded by Arab villages and is dangerous after dark, but it cuts about one-third of the traveling time to Tel Aviv. When their car was about one kilometer from Beit-El they were attacked from an Arab car. Like sharks in a feeding pattern, the Arabs had come from Ramallah looking for Jews to kill.

The actual shooting lasted between ten to twenty seconds; about thirty bullets smashed into the Tzurs' car. Then the terrorists fled back into Ramallah, one of the safe havens we created as part of the "peace process."

Yoel assessed the situation and saw that Ephraim was killed immediately and that Shlomit, Tamar, Shoshana, and Avital appeared to be lightly injured. He could not estimate Etta's condition although it looked serious. The other kids—Menachem, Tzvi, and Raaya—had stayed home. He tried to call Moked Binyamin, the region's emergency team set up for these situations, but his two-way radio was not working. He got out of the car and flagged down an Arab driver who drove him to Beit-El. When he got to the gas station at the entrance to the settlement he told the station attendants what had happened and they called the police, the army, and the ambulances.

When an ambulance arrived from Beit-El, Yoel rode back to his car in it with the doctor from the clinic, Dr. Matti Erhlichman. Matti gave the injured first-aid and then they were taken to the hospital. The news reported that Etta, Tamar, and Shoshana had been put into surgery and that Etta was in critical condition with three bullet wounds in her side. But before the news was over they reported that Etta had died of her wounds.

I felt like I couldn't cry anymore but my heart hurt. Now, out of a family of eight kids and two parents, only a father and seven kids were left. How would they manage? I knew Yoel was a strong person but what about the kids, especially Avital and Shoshana? Did they even know what happened? I later learned that Yoel did not tell them about their mother until they were in better condition.

That night I barely slept. I woke up every hour thinking about the kids in the hospital and how they were. One time I woke up from a terrible dream I had. In my dream my family and I were in a blue car like the Tzurs', driving through Ramallah. Suddenly our car broke down and we couldn't move another inch. Then all the Arabs from the nearby houses came out with guns and ambushed our car. I could see the evil gleam in their eyes. They broke the windows and started shooting at us. I woke up dripping with cold sweat. It was so real and scary. I could almost feel what it must have been like for the Tzurs.

The next day was the funeral. Etta and Ephraim were going to be buried in the Beit-El cemetery where now there are eight bodies, most victims of Arab terror. I didn't go to the funeral because my father had to take me to a doctor in Jerusalem.

Immediately when I got home I called Naamah to hear what the funeral was like. She said she didn't go but she heard all the funeral orations on Arutz 7 and the nicest ones were the ones of Rabbi Mordechai Eliyahu, former Chief Rabbi of Israel, and Yoel. After Rabbi Eliyahu said all the usual things about people who were killed, he started to cry and shouted out, "Etta, the daughter of Malka, and Ephraim, son of Etta! When you get to heaven and come before God's throne, ask for his mercy on his children! We can not continue this way any longer!" Then the Rabbi broke down and dissolved into tears. Naamah said his tears were heart-breaking.

Then it was Yoel's turn to speak. He talked in simple words about what Etta and Ephraim were for him and for the family. He didn't cry much but everyone around him was crying. Those simple words, the simple way he put things, touched everyone's hearts, including people who hadn't known Etta or Ephraim. At the end of his speech Yoel said the suitable Zionistic answer to Arab terror is to build a new neighborhood of one thousand homes on the Artis mountain, and he challenged the prime minister to do just that. Naamah said the idea was accepted with great enthusiasm and Yoel and the Beit-El Council vowed to press the government for results.

That night was the eighth night of Chanukah. Like the night before we lit our Chanukah lamps, this night with nine candles, one for each of the eight days of Chanukah and one for the Shamash. My father recited the benedictions and again we sang "Maoz Tzur." But things were not like the previous nights. My father was looking gloomy and my mother was very serious. When we got to the last verse of the song my father sang with all his might. The song has six verses and is about the various triumphs of God and the Jews over the gentiles in all the generations. The last verse is about the future and final victory of God and the Jews over the gentiles and the construction of the third temple. This last verse talks about when the messiah will come and the dead will rise from their graves and god will be victorious over the gentiles and the Jews will have their revenge on their enemies. I knew my father was thinking about Etta and Ephraim who would return to life, and the revenge we'd have with the Arabs when God would rule the Land of Israel and the whole world.

When we finished singing my father didn't start reading the last story of the book immediately. Instead he cleared his throat and said, "Kids, I want to teach you an important lesson about life. You should always know never to take anything for granted. We should always remember that God gives and God takes away, and we should thank Him for everything and thank Him every morning for allowing us to wake up another day. Look at the Tzur family. Did they ever imagine that they wouldn't celebrate the last night of Chanukah all together? You see how fast God took away both the mother and a son. Always pray that God will never put us through that kind of trial, but, if He wills it to be, that we will have the strength of Yoel Tzur to handle it."

With that my father finished. He wiped a tear out of the corner of his eye and then started reading us the last story. It was a story about a Jewish boy in Tzarist Russia who was kidnapped by soldiers at the age of eight on the third night of Chanukah. He was given to Russian peasants to raise him to be a Cossack, but he remained strong in his faith and in the end returns to his parents after many years.

I know the story well because I've heard it every Chanukah for the past several years, so I was barely listening. I was thinking about what my father had said and the way he almost started to cry when he sang "Maoz Tzur." Then I started thinking about the words of the song. "Maoz" is Hebrew for strength. "Tzur" is another name for God and also means a hard rock. Then I thought of the Tzur family.

The song was so relevant to their situation. "Maoz Tzur"—the Tzur family would have to be strong at a time like this. Etta and Ephraim were dead but they left a lot of memories behind them. Etta—a lovely woman who always put herself out to help others. And Ephraim—a good boy who loved animals and had a cute smile. And that is the way people would always remember them. Yoel and the kids would continue to live and remember Etta and Ephraim for who they were when they were alive. So would everyone else. I knew that in the battle between the Tzur family and the terrorists the Tzurs had won. They won because they wouldn't let the deaths of Ephraim and Etta break their spirits. They won because they have the power of life.

Epilogue: The Tzur family is continuing to live their lives in Beit-El as normally as possible in the circumstances. Because of pressure from America, the U.N., and Europe, Prime Minister Netanyahu has not given permission to build those one thousand homes on the Artis. The first baby born after the attack was named Yehuda Ephraim.

LIRAN ZVIBEL

Seventeen-year-old Liran Zvibel lives with his family in Tel Aviv, where he attends Tel Aviv University. In this story about his reactions to terrorist bombings on Purim, 1996, he says that although the inability to celebrate the holiday would be sad for many Jews, the loss of the holiday to terrorism evokes a different set of emotions—particularly for the young, for whom Purim has traditionally been a lighthearted celebration.

At the same time, Zvibel is careful to say that explosions aren't always on his mind and that Israel is a wonderful place to live.

(See photo insert.)

Two Awful Weeks in March

*M*y name is Liran Zvibel. I'm sixteen years old and I live in Tel Aviv. Usually I live an ordinary life like most students my age in the world. I watch TV, study, play with my friends, talk on the phone, surf the net, etc.

Several times every year, however, our life in Israel changes. This year [1996], for example, we had several bus explosions. On the third month of the year, week after week our "neighbors" made sure that our lives wouldn't be as easy and peaceful as they should be.

When the first explosion happened in Jerusalem all the students and teachers of my grade gathered together into one very big room and discussed the situation—how everyone was afraid and that our country isn't safe anymore. All who had something to say were free to say it and everybody supported them. Later we sang some sad songs and showed the pictures of the innocent dead people.

Two or three days later another explosion happened in Jerusalem and we did the same things. We all were even more upset and most of us cried. I especially remember something one of the students said. In Israel every person who dies is pictured on the cover of the morning papers. The students pointed out that after every explosion the pictures of the dead become smaller since there are more dead and the paper doesn't get any bigger. The wounded's pictures don't even make it to the front page. At a time like that, nobody smiled.

In days like these it is very hard for the students to learn and even harder for the teachers to teach. A teaching job in Israel is much harder than in a normal country since the teachers have to deal with some very serious problems. An example was when the third explosion happened during Chag Purim, a week after the first one. "Chag" in Hebrew means a special holiday. All the kids (and some of the adults too) dress up like funny things. Some people work months on their costumes, and every year there is a great festival. Since people worked for months we decided to go ahead and have the festival at school but not to make it too noisy and happy.

On the morning of the school celebration of Chag Purim I turned on the radio to hear the morning news, and I heard that there was another explosion. I was already dressed up —like a woman, actually. If I hadn't had the hair on my legs, I could have been a very convincing woman. I didn't know what to do. I didn't know whether to go dressed as I was or to change to regular clothes, and my parents didn't know what to tell me either. I called my teacher. I didn't wake her up because another student had already done it. After a little conversation she told me to bring my costume in a plastic bag and to see what the other students did.

I missed my bus because of having to undress and my father drove me to school. In the car I thought it over and came to the conclusion that teachers in Israel have a very hard job —they have to make too difficult decisions.

We were listening to the car radio and the reporter repeated the news from earlier, but this time he said, "For those who just woke up —this isn't a tape. There was another bus explosion THIS MORNING." This was a horrible line.

When I got to school there were some students who came dressed up. One said she didn't want to take her clothes off since it took her a lot of time to put them on and that if she had taken her clothes off she would probably have been late for school. The others didn't hear the bad news and felt bad about being dressed up. The festival, as you might have guessed, didn't take place. Every year the tenth graders are the ones who are in charge of the festival. They worked on it for more than four months and now they couldn't show what they had prepared. We couldn't concentrate on our lessons and so we just talked with each other and with our teachers.

We supported each other and were supported by the teachers. These kinds of tragic situations help to make the relationship between the students and the teachers much closer— even intimate sometimes.

Later that day there was an explosion by Disingof Center—a huge mall in Disingof Street. It was close to 4:00 P.M. and there were a lot of people there. The upper floors are offices and my father works in one of those offices. The explosion was under my father's office. Disingof Center, like most malls, has a lot of glass in it and the explosion destroyed most of it, so there were many wounded and dead. Our luck was that my father called us and told us about the explosion before it was on the radio or on the TV so that we wouldn't be worried. The only problem was that my father couldn't get home since the main road was destroyed by the bomb and the other roads were closed by the police.

About a year before there had been another explosion in Disingof. This explosion is known as "the bus number 5 explosion." My math teacher came and told us that something terrible happened in Disingof Street but tried to keep on teaching. Both of my parents work on Disingof Street and I didn't have any information about the situation. I had no way to contact my parents. When I got home I was so relieved to find them both at home.

In this story I told you about a very little part of my life as a teenager growing up in Israel. You might think that we don't live a regular life and are afraid all the time. Well, this is not true! I don't feel fear at all—at least not about explosions. Like most of the teenagers in the world I live my life in peace and don't even think of explosions. Israel is a great place to live in. We have a great climate, gorgeous people, and beautiful beaches. I remember walking in Washington D.C. after dark, and I think that then I was afraid! I saw all the poor homeless who were asking for money, and I ran to my hotel! In this aspect Israel is much safer than the United States.

The only problem is that we have some enemies around us and unless we have peace with them we won't be able to live in true peace with ourselves. I don't say that because I belong to the left wing. As a matter of fact, I belong to the right wing.

I don't know how well you get the whole picture. Wherever you live, I just want you to know that there is NOBODY in Israel who doesn't want peace. The problem is that many of us have different ideas for how this peace should be gotten and how much we should sacrifice for it.

JEFFREY KLEIN

Nineteen-year-old Jeffrey Klein, of Ardsley, New York, is currently a student at Wesleyan University in Middletown, Connecticut. While he was studying in Jerusalem, in the spring of 1996, two buses were bombed, killing twenty-two people and injuring many more. Despite the magnitude of this tragedy and the horror and pain it aroused in him, Klein says that he hopes to live in Israel permanently one day, as it is where he feels he belongs.

Not Again!

Anyone who has heard a sonic boom at close proximity can testify it is not a subdued thing. The unexpected crash, a year ago, a lifetime ago, only served to enhance the vulnerability and meekness both Aviva and I were feeling. We looked at each other with pleading eyes, asking for some reassurance it was not another one, not so soon. Neither had any reassurance to offer.

"Surely," my soul screamed, "if the House of Heaven had managed to slumber through the others, this must certainly have served as a wake-up call!"

But thankfully such musings finally proved unnecessary. We were never given proof that God had awakened though, we only knew that no households had been broken by the crash. It had only broken the sound barrier.

It had begun as such a pleasant afternoon in early March—as pleasant as any such afternoon could be. The air up on the roof was refreshing. The sun seemed friendly as it benevolently bestowed its warmth upon us. Although we were still technically within the walls of the Hebrew Union College —Jewish Institute of Religion, where our dormitories and classes were, and where we had been confined for our "safety" amid the recent string of terrorist attacks, this provided a much-needed respite. And the light breeze all but carried away the heavy burden of knowing only a few blocks away sat the skeleton of a bus whose passengers—all but one —had reached Heaven's gate and achieved unwanted martyrdom only the day before.

Aviva sat a yard or so away, striving vainly to find meaning in the sine curve. I was writing a letter, earnestly trying to repair a broken friendship in Connecticut. It is so incredibly hard when good, close friendships meet obstacles; it is even harder when brothers become mortal enemies.

Deborah and Leah, the secretary in the office and one of our counselors, came walking up the steps which led back into the Jerusalem stone courtyards of our little fortress.

"Hello. How are you?" Pleasantries were offered them. They declined.

"There was just another bomb, this time in Tel-Aviv. It was right outside Dizengoff Center."

Again. And again. And again. Why can't they leave us alone? Why aren't we allowed to just live in our homeland in peace? Are you there, God? Or do you sleep peacefully with dreams of the Messiah? Perhaps our walls could keep out the bombs, but not even lead could have kept out the pain.

The pain did not break my heart, though I did not fall apart. Nor did I clench my jaw and fists, determined to fight for my right to exist in my homeland. No. I could not. For I was numb. Shockingly, frighteningly numb to it all. It was like being at a shooting range for the first time, and being scared by the first shot that goes off. And then, ten or so minutes later, realizing the sounds of war no longer hold their capacity to frighten. And this is the scariest feeling of them all.

That first Sunday morning, back in February, had come as such a shock, and so it had hurt, a lot. And then a week later it happened again. This time, too, it had hurt, for yet again we had been caught off guard. The unexpected, yet indescribably welcome, silence of that third Sunday morning had come as such a relief to us all. And now there was this, and this was novocaine.

Deborah and Leah walked on, searching for more people to receive these evil tidings. A bus drove by on the street before us. Sonic boom. God's alarm clock? I wonder what the pilot of that plane's name was, what he looked like. I wonder if he knew the fright he gave us. I wonder if he knew anybody who'd been in Dizengoff Center ten short minutes earlier. I wonder if he had heard yet what had happened. I wonder . . .

Naturally, as after all such incidents, we had a meeting. Crammed inside the program office, eyes glued to the tiny television screen in the corner, we sat. We thought. We cried.

All of us— over fifty bodies all told—were cramped into

that little space, waiting. Now what would happen? What's next? What now?

We knew the routine by now: There would be more parents and friends on the other side of the ocean urging us to come "home," pleading with us not to be stupid and put ourselves in unnecessary danger. They just didn't realize we were home. They had no way of understanding that the only white flag going up would bear two blue horizontal stripes flanking a Magen David, forming Israel's banner.

The next evening was Purim. For months, I had been anticipating this. I had heard all the stories—Purim in Israel was a party in the streets, an Israeli version of Mardi Gras, with the added theme of Jewish strength and persistence. And now it had come, but without the celebrations. Dr. Seuss wrote *How the Grinch Stole Christmas*. This was How the Hamas Stole Purim. That was really how I thought of it.

National celebrations of the holiday were called off. The Israeli government canceled Purim! For how can one truly celebrate if it means dancing on streets stained with his comrades' blood? "*Ayn Li Eretz Ach Eret*—I Have No Other Country" and "*Livchot L'cha*—To Cry For You" ruled the nation's radio stations. The country was in mourning on this most joyous of holidays. Haman, the villain of the Purim story, was leading us to the gallows, and the lovely heroine, Queen Esther, was yet to muster up the courage to face the king and save her people.

Religious celebrations were still on, though, and the whole group of us went to a local synagogue to hear the *Megillat Esther* read. It was festive, as befits Purim, but a definite cloud hung over it all. Afterwards, we walked back to our dorms. We stopped at an intersection, waiting for it to clear so we could cross. Two from our group, in bored anticipation of the changing light, began to dance. There wasn't any music—there was no particular reason to dance—they just felt like dancing. And so they did. On the opposite corner, there stood an elderly Israeli man. He began to scream: "You're dancing?! You're dancing?! Jews are being killed—your people are dying—and you dance?!"

I kept silent, but my mind screamed, "Yes, they're dead—our brothers and sisters have been slaughtered. But we're alive! We live! It's Purim, and we're alive! *Am Yisrael chai!* The people of Israel live!"

Friday morning, a week and a half ago, it happened again in a cafe in Tel Aviv. I was there all over again. Skeletons of busses in the streets, the mourning songs on the radio, the dark cloud hanging over everything. All I could think was, "Not again! Not again! They can't steal Purim away again!"

And they didn't. I was so thrilled, as much as possible considering the circumstances, when Leah, my counselor from last year, told me that they had decided not to cancel national celebrations again. There is a life to be lived, so the memories of the slaughtered may live on. The Star of David, that ancient king's shield, yet guards the white flag. The state of Israel's motto rings true: *Sheinit Matzada lo Tipol*— Massada shall not fall again.

Bibliography

Chacour, Elias. *Blood Brothers*. Grand Rapids: Chosen Books, 1984.

Cohen, Guela. *Woman of Violence: Memoirs of a Young Terrorist 1943–1948*. New York: Holt, Rinehart & Winston, 1966.

Davis, Uri. *Crossing the Border: An Autobiography of an Anti-Zionist Palestinian Jew*. London: Books & Books, Ltd., 1995.

Diqs, Isaak. *A Bedouin Boyhood*. New York: Praeger, 1967.

Jabra, Jabra Ibrahim. *The First Well: A Bethlehem Boyhood*. Translated by Issa J. Boullata. Fayetteville: The University of Arkansas Press, 1995.

Khaled, Leila. *My People Shall Live: The Autobiography of a Revolutionary*. Edited by George Hajjar. London: Hodder and Stoughton, 1973.

Lyons Bar-David, Molly. *My Promised Land*. New York: G. P. Putnam's Sons, 1953.

Mansour, Atallah. *Waiting for the Dawn: An Autobiography*. London: Secker & Warburg, 1975.

Mozeson, I. E., and Lois Stavsky. *Young Voices from the Holy City*. New York: Four Winds Press, Macmillan, 1994.

Save the Children Fund. *Growing Up with Conflict: Children and Development in the Occupied Territories*. London: The Save the Children Fund, 1992.

Senesh, Hannah. *Hannah Senesh: Her Life and Diary*. New York: Schocken Books, 1972.

Sichrovsky, Peter. *Abraham's Children: Israel's Young Generation*. Translated from German by Jean Steinberg. New York: Pantheon Books, 1991.

Spielmann, Miriam. *If Peace Comes—: The Future Expectations of Jewish and Arab Israeli Children and Youth*. Stockholm: Almqvist & Wiksell International, 1984.

Bibliography

Tawil, Raymonda Hawa. *My Home, My Prison*. New York: Holt, Rinehart & Winston, 1980.

Tuqan, Fadwa. *A Mountainous Journey: An Autobiography*. Edited by Salma Khadra Jayyusi. Translated by Olive Kenny. St. Paul, Minn.: Graywolf Press, 1990.

Turki, Fawaz. *The Disinherited: Journal of a Palestinian Exile*. New York and London: Monthly Review Press, 1972.

Zak, Michal. *Walking the Tightrope: Encounters Between Jewish and Palestinian Youth in Israel*. Israel: The School for Peace : Neve Shalom/Wahat al-Salam, 1992.

Zim, Jacob, ed. *My Shalom, My Peace: Paintings and Poems by Jewish and Arab Children*. New York: McGraw-Hill, 1975.

Credits

"Tracings," © Basim Abdoraad (pseud.), East Jerusalem, Israel, 1998.

"Healing the Wounds of Childhood," © Ammar Z. Abu Zayyad, Bethany, Jerusalem, Palestine, via Israel, 1998.

"Early Lessons of Separation," © Anan Ameri, Detroit, Michigan, U.S.A., 1998.

"Hopes Are Hopes," © Leah Ayalon, Jerusalem, Israel, 1998.

"Marked For Destruction," © Ibtisam Barakat, Columbia, Missouri, U.S.A., 1998.

"My Mother Palestine," © Ramzy Baroud, Seattle, Washington, U.S.A., 1998.

"Yehezkel," © Yitzhak Bar-Yossef, Ra-anana, Israel, 1998. (Excerpted from *A Token of Love,* with permission of translator S. Shabtai. Tel Aviv: Am Oved Publishing House, 1995.)

"One More River to Cross," © Nahla Mary Beier, Natchitoches, Louisiana, U.S.A., 1998.

"Thumbprint," © Ehud Ben-Ezer, Tel Aviv, Israel, 1998. (Published with permission of translator Jeffrey M. Green.)

"Going to Jerusalem," © Gunter David, Ft. Washington, Pennsylvania, U.S.A., 1998.

"In the Courtyard of the Children's House of the Kibbutz," © Shuli Dichter, Kibbutz Ma'anit, D. N. Menashe, Israel, 1998.

"Marked by the Teeth," © Moshe Dor, Tel Aviv, Israel, 1998.

"Shards," © Tanya Gardiner-Scott, Somerville, Massachusetts, U.S.A., 1998.

"A Look into Memory," © Ghareeb (pseud.), Ramallah, West Bank, via Israel, 1998.

"Ten Centimeters of Dust," © by Shammai Golan. First published in

Credits

Escape for Short Distances in Hebrew, Tel Aviv: Massada, 1975. translated by Richard Flantz.

"The Arak of Abu-Anton," © Yehudit Hendel, Tel Aviv, Israel, 1998.

"I Survived the War," © Musa Jamil Jaffer (pseud.), Stamford, Connecticut, U.S.A., 1998.

"Alti Zachen," © Victoria Kay-Feinerman, Petach Tikva, Israel, 1998.

"Not Again!" © Jeffrey Klein, Ardsley, New York, U.S.A., 1998.

"Childhood/Manhood," © Omar Mahdawi, New York, New York, U.S.A., 1998.

"Borderland," © Mohammad Masad, St. Louis, Missouri, U.S.A., 1998.

"Paradise on the Border," © Yael Medini, Ramat Gan, Israel, 1998.

"The Dark Villages," © Reuven Miran, Binyamina, Israel, 1996. (Published with permission of the author and the translator, Elizabeth Maor.)

"Tzipori," by Reuven Miran, © The Institute for the Translation of Hebrew Literature, translated by Dalya Bilu, reprinted by permission of the author.

"Children of a Tenth-Class God?" © Nihaya Qawasmi, Jerusalem, Palestine, 1998.

"Face of Peace," © Redrose (pseud.), Rishon Le Tzion, Israel, 1998.

"Born in Bethlehem," © Marina Riadi, Atlanta, Georgia, U.S.A., 1998.

"Caught in Conflict," © Rivka Rosen (pseud.), Pittsburgh, Pennsylvania, U.S.A., 1998.

"A Christian Palestinian's Story," © Wadad Saba, Seattle, Washington, U.S.A., 1998.

"No Other Storm," © Moshe Shamir. (Excerpted from *My Life with Ishmael*. London: Valentine, Mitchell, 1970, by permission of the author.)

"My Life on the Firing Line," © Racheli Tal, Beit-El, Israel, 1998.

"The Power of Life," © Racheli Tal, Beit-El, Israel, 1998.

"A Child in Rafah Camp," © Ahmed Younis, Jerusalem, Israel, 1998.

"A Child's Misgivings About the War," © Mohammad Zahaykeh, Jerusalem, Israel, 1998.

"Two Awful Weeks in March," © Liran Zvibel, Tel Aviv, Israel, 1998.

Photo Credits

Photo of Victoria Kay-Feinerman © Jonathan Feinerman, Petach Tikva, Israel, 1998.
Photo of Ramzy Baroud © Mohamed Baroud, Gaza Strip, Palestine, 1998.
Photo of "Redrose" © Sigalit Asolin, Tel Aviv, Israel, 1998.
Photo of Racheli Tal © Michael Lixenberg, Beit-El, Israel, 1998.
Photo of Liran Zvibel © Moshe Zvibel, Tel Aviv, Israel, 1998.

The photographers of uncredited photographs are either unknown or the author has been unable to locate them. If you took a photograph in this book and your work was not credited, please contact the publisher so that credit can be arranged for future editions.

Chronology of the Israeli-Palestinian Conflict

The following chronology has been assembled from numerous historical works and newspaper accounts. Since sometimes there is a disagreement among sources, dates and figures should be understood as approximate.

1517–1917 Palestine was ruled by the Ottoman Turks.

1878 Petach Tikva, the first Jewish settlement in Palestine, was founded.

1882 Zionist immigration to Palestine began.

1891 Arabs in Jerusalem petitioned the Ottoman Empire to prohibit Jewish immigration and land purchases.

1896 Theodor Herzl, known as the father of modern Zionism, published *The Jewish State*, calling for "the restoration of the Jewish state."

1897 The first World Zionist Congress met in Basel, Switzerland, and declared Palestine the Jewish homeland. A structure of government was decided upon for Palestine as well as the means of purchasing land, the Jewish National Fund.

1900 There were twenty-two Jewish colonies in Palestine.

1908 Palestinian deputies served in the Ottoman parliament.

1914 Publication of first Arabic newspapers, *Al-Quds* in Jerusalem and *Al-Asma'i* in Jaffa. Both reflected the Arabic opposition to Jewish immigration and land purchases. There were about 535,00 Muslims, 70,000 Christians, and 85,000 Jews in Palestine at this time.

1915–1917 In exchange for support in World War I, Britain promised to create an Arab kingdom. After major battles, Jerusalem was captured by British and Allied forces under the direction of General Allenby.

1917 The Balfour Declaration promised the Jews a homeland in Israel with the understanding that "nothing shall be done which may prejudice the civil and religious rights of existing non-Jewish communities in Palestine. . . ."

1918 There were forty-seven Jewish colonies in Palestine.

1920 In April, at the Conference of San Remo, the Allies divided up the former territories of the defeated Ottoman Empire. Britain was given a League of Nations mandate to rule Palestine, Jordan, and Iraq, while France was given control of Syria and Lebanon. Haganah, the Jewish self-defense force, was begun. The Balfour Declaration allowed 16,500 Jews to immigrate this year.

1921 Anti-Zionist Arab groups opposed to Jewish immigration rioted throughout the country, killing forty-six Jews. The British made an official inquiry, the result of which was a reiteration of the Balfour principle that while the Jews might have a homeland in Palestine, Palestine as a whole was not to be a Jewish homeland.

1929–1933 Arabs in Palestine became increasingly disenchanted with Jewish immigration. Battles erupted throughout Palestine that amounted to a civil war. One hundred thirty-three Jews were killed and 116 Arabs. In 1930, to appease the Arabs, the British issued a major policy statement proposing a limitation on annual Jewish immigration, saying, "The Arabs have come to see in Jewish immigration not only a menace to their livelihood but a possible overlord of the future." Under pressure from Zionists, they rescinded it a year later. Arabs in Palestine became convinced that the British would maintain their colonialist power over them until the Jews had attained a majority and could declare Palestine an independent Jewish state.

1936–1939 The Arabs of Palestine rose up against Britain and declared a general strike, which lasted six months. Aided by volunteers from neighboring Arab countries, rural Arabs began a widespread armed revolt. In 1937 an official British inquiry into the revolt under the auspices of Lord Peel led to Britain's proposing the partition of Palestine and expulsion of 250,000 Palestinian Arabs from what would be a Jewish state. The Arabs were appalled by the idea of dividing their country and dislocating 250,000 Arab people, and the revolt intensified.

1939–1945 In response to the intensified Arab revolt, the British issued a White Paper in 1939 severely limiting Jewish immigration and land purchase but at the same time continuing Britain's mandate to rule Palestine. The Jews were outraged and the Arabs, although appreciative of immigration and land purchase limitations, did not agree with the continued British mandate, meaning that Britain became the enemy of both. World War II and the Holocaust killed nearly six million Jews. Palestine was seen as a refuge by many survivors. Arab Palestinians demanded an absolute end to Jewish immigration and what they viewed as a takeover of their land. Approximately two hundred rural Jewish colonies existed in Palestine at this time, although the majority of the Jewish population lived in the cities.

1944–1947 Jewish/British conflict. Haganah tried to expel Britain from Palestine. Two secret paramilitary groups (Irgun Zvai Leumi, led by Menachem Begin, and the Stern Gang, led by Yitzhak Shamir) used terrorist tactics of assassinations and bombings against both British soldiers and Arab civilians. The highly organized Jewish underground finally went so far as to blow up the part of the King David Hotel in Jerusalem which was used by the British government and military command; ninety-one people were killed.

1947 Despairing of ever resolving the Arab/Jewish conflict, Britain handed the Palestine problem over to the United Nations. U.N. Resolution 181 partitioned Palestine into Jewish and Palestinian states and designated Jerusalem and Bethlehem as shared, jointly ruled territory. The majority of Jews accepted the plan because it recognized a Jewish state and they were given 55 percent of Palestine. Arab leaders in Palestine rejected the plan, insisting on a united Palestine. Major fighting erupted between Jews and Palestinians; many Jews and Palestinians were killed and a great number of Palestinians became refugees.

1948 On May 14, Jewish leaders including David Ben-Gurion proclaimed the State of Israel, and the British mandate to govern Palestine was terminated. Arab army units from Egypt, Jordan, Syria, Iraq, and Lebanon tried to prevent the formation of the Jewish State and expansion into formerly Palestinian areas. This Arab-Israeli war is called the War of Independence by the Israelis, a war which they clearly won. The Palestinian Arabs called it *al-Nakba*—"the Disaster."

One of the Jewish victories (which is viewed by Palestinians as one of the greatest tragedies of all time and ample reason to flee Palestine) occurred in the village of Deir Yassin, near Jerusalem, in April 1948. Zionist paramilitaries killed 254 men, women, and children. This massacre of Palestinian villagers was led by Menachem Begin, who would later be twice elected as Premier of Israel .

The area that the U.N. had designated as the Arab state was provisionally split up into three parts: land taken over by Israelis and incorporated into their new state; the Gaza Strip, which was held by Egypt; and the West Bank, which was held by Jordan. The U.N. stipulated that this provisional division allowing Jews to take over Palestinian land must be accompanied by the right of Palestinians to return to their homes or to be fully compensated for their loss. Neither the right of return nor the right of compensation would be honored by the new State of Israel. By the time the war was over, Israel had taken over nearly three-fourths of Palestine.

1948–1952 After the creation of the Jewish State, more than 700,000 Arab Palestinians were driven out of their homes or fled in fear for their lives and were forced to take refuge in neighboring Arab countries. Only 160,000 remained in Israel. Very few of those who fled were allowed by the Israeli government to return to their homes. By 1950, over one million Palestinians lived in refugee camps in Gaza, the West Bank, Lebanon, and Jordan, and two-thirds of the people living in Jordan were Palestinian. They were given citizenship in 1949, but those Palestinians living in other Arab countries were viewed as cheap labor and afforded few civil rights. Palestinians living in refugee camps in the West Bank and Gaza suffered tremendous deprivation and many remained in the camps for the rest of their lives. Palestinians who stayed in what had become the State of Israel were granted citizenship but did not enjoy the same rights as Jewish Israeli citizens.

1949 Armistice agreements were signed with Egypt, Lebanon, Jordan, and Syria. Chaim Weizmann was elected the first president of Israel and David Ben-Gurion became its first prime minister.

1950 Israel passed a law confirming the right of every Jew in the world to settle in Israel.

1951 Yasser Arafat began organizing Palestinian activists in Cairo who later would be leaders of the Palestine Liberation Organization (PLO).

1952–1956 Israel was plagued by numerous raids from adjoining Arab states. To Israel, the Arabs were terrorists invading their country; to the Palestinians, the raiders were freedom fighters intent on the return of their land.

1956 The Suez War. Israel, France, and Britain attacked Egypt. Egypt's army was no match for vastly superior forces and armaments, and the war was over in a few days. Concurrently, approximately 35,000 Arabs living in Israel—who were Israeli citizens—were expelled from the country. Israel captured the Sinai from Egypt and took over the Gaza Strip.

1964 The Palestine Liberation Organization was formed under Egyptian direction. Its charter called for a united Palestine and the expulsion of Jews who moved to Palestine after 1946.

1967 The June War takes place from June 5 to 10 (the Six-Day War). Claiming that Egypt was amassing such forces in the Sinai peninsula that an Arab attack and "genocide" were imminent, Israel made a pre-emptive strike against Egypt. The Israeli Army defeated the combined forces of Egypt, Syria, Jordan, and Iraq. In addition, Israel captured the Sinai Peninsula and Gaza Strip from Egypt and the Golan Heights from Syria, thereby increasing the size of the land it occupied from approximately 8,000 to 30,000 square miles. Sources vary, but an estimated 250,000 to 500,000 more Palestinian refugees were forced to flee their homes in what the Israeli Army called "land clearing operations." Those who did not flee found themselves under Israeli occupation.

1969 Yasser Arafat became head of the PLO and claimed to speak for all Palestinians.

1969–1970 What the Israelis called the War of Attrition occurred, with Egypt and Syria making numerous attacks along the Suez Canal and the Golan Heights. Israel's heavy retaliation brought the war to an end.

1973 The Ramadan or Yom Kippur War, in which Egypt and Syria attempted to regain territory captured and occupied by Israel in 1967. The U.S. airlift of massive amounts of arms to Israel brought the war to an end and Israel, Syria, and Egypt signed disengagement agreements.

1974 Yitzhak Rabin became prime minister. Yasser Arafat, speaking at the United Nations, called for a united Palestine where Christians, Jews, and Muslims might live together peacefully. Israel refused to recognize the PLO.

1971–1975 The PLO was expelled from Jordan and relocated in Lebanon. It ultimately became part of the civil war in Lebanon, which resulted in tremendous destruction and loss of life.

1975–1978 Palestinians continued raids into Israel, and Palestinians living under Israeli rule began to be less acquiescent to Jewish power. On March 30, 1976, they began what would become an annual "Day of the Land" to protest Zionist appropriation of land within Israel and in the Occupied Territories.

1977 Menachem Begin became prime minister of Israel. Anwar Sadat reached out to Israel to discuss a peace agreement. President Jimmy Carter called for the participation of the Palestinians in the Mideast peace process and spoke of the need for a Palestinian homeland.

1978 The Camp David Accords were signed by Israel and Egypt. Israel invaded Lebanon and seized what it called "a security zone."

1979 The Israel-Egypt Peace Treaty was signed in Washington, D.C. Israel agreed to withdraw from the Sinai Peninsula.

1981 Israel and the PLO signed a truce.

1982 Israel began its "Operation Peace for Galilee," allegedly to eliminate PLO bases in Lebanon. Eventually, Israel forcefully occupied most of Lebanon from Beirut south. The United States intervened and constructed an agreement based on the PLO moving to Tunis, but Israel's bombing of Beirut quickly sabotaged all peace efforts. Despite President Reagan's expressed disapproval, the Israelis continued to bomb Beirut. In the first three months of Israel's invasion of Lebanon it is estimated that over nineteen thousand Lebanese and Palestinians were killed. The vast majority of the dead and injured were civilians, many of them children.

1983 Menachem Begin resigned and Yitzhak Shamir became prime minister of the State of Israel.

1984 Shimon Peres became prime minister. A bomb killed 241 marines, and U.S. troops pulled out of Lebanon.

1987 In December the Palestinian Intifada (uprising) began in response to four Palestinians being killed by an Israeli Army jeep in the Gaza Strip. The Palestinian revolt quickly spread to the West Bank, where protesters were met with gunfire. The United Nations Security Council (with the United States abstaining from the vote) approved a resolution that strongly deplored Israel's treatment of the Palestinian protesters. Many were killed, many more wounded, and some were tortured.

1988 Because of intense international criticism of their handling of the Palestinian protesters, Israel refused to allow journalists into the Occupied Territories. President Reagan opened talks with the PLO after it recognized Israel's right to exist and renounced terrorism.

1990 Iraq's Saddam Hussein invaded Kuwait. Yitzhak Shamir once again headed the Israeli government. In October an Arab-Israeli peace conference took place in Madrid. President Bush ended the dialogue with the PLO after a terrorrist faction of the PLO attacked Israel.

1991 The Gulf War, during which the United States rescued Kuwait and Iraq fired Scud missiles into Israel. The Madrid Peace Conference brought together Israel, Jordan, Lebanon, Syria, and the Palestinians. Official bilateral talks were continued in Washington, D.C.

1992 Yitzhak Rabin became prime minister of Israel. Secret informal talks between Israel and the PLO began after official talks failed.

1993 Informal talks continued in Oslo, Norway. In August, Israel and the PLO came to an agreement on Palestinian self-rule. President Clinton invited Yitzhak Rabin and Yasser Arafat to sign the Declaration of Principles at the White House, which they did in September. Two of the goals set out in the Declaration of Principles were the complete withdrawal of Israeli troops from the Gaza Strip and the West Bank, and the Palestinians' right to self-rule in those territories.

1994 In February Jewish settler Baruch Goldstein murdered twenty-nine Arabs praying in a mosque in Hebron in the West Bank. The survivors beat him to death. On April 6 a suicide bomber, a member of the radical Palestinian organization Hamas, blew up a bus, killing himself and eight Israelis. On April 13 a Hamas bomber killed himself and five Israelis. In October Hamas blew up a city bus, killing twenty-two Israelis in Tel Aviv. On November 11 a Palestinian suicide bomber on a bicycle killed three Israeli soldiers in the Gaza Strip.

1995 On January 22 two Palestinians blew themselves up in central Israel, killing twenty-one Israelis. On April 2 an explosion in Gaza City killed several Palestinians including Hamas leader Kamal Kheil and one of his assistants. Hamas vowed revenge. A week later two Palestinians blew themselves up near Israeli settlements in the Gaza Strip. The blast killed several Israeli soldiers and an American. On July 24 a Palestinian suicide bomber blew up a bus in Tel Aviv. Hamas claimed responsibility for six Israeli deaths. On August 21 a Palestinian suicide bomber blew up a bus in Jerusalem, killing one American and four Israelis and wounding over 100 people. On November 4 Yitzhak Rabin was murdered by a Jewish assassin.

1996 In February and March there were four Islamic militant suicide bombings in Jerusalem, Tel Aviv, and Ashkelon that killed 63 people. In April Israel attacked southern Lebanon, killing 165 people including 91 Lebanese refugees at a United Nations base. On May 31 Benjamin Netanyahu was declared prime minister of Israel after winning a narrow victory over peace advocate Shimon Peres. In late September, Palestinians protested the opening of a tunnel near a Muslim holy site. More than seventy people were killed. The Palestinians established their own police force and elected a parliament with Yasser Arafat as their first president.

1997   On January 1 an Israeli soldier in Hebron opened fire on Palestinians, injuring seven. On January 14 Israelis and Palestinians signed an accord for the withdrawal of Israeli troops from the disputed city of Hebron and other portions of the West Bank. On March 13 a Jordanian soldier murdered seven schoolgirls on a field trip to a border observation post. On March 17 Israel began construction of a Jewish housing development at Har Homa in East Jerusalem, regarded by Palestinians as part of their future capital. On March 21 a suicide bomber blew himself up in a crowded Tel Aviv outdoor cafe, killing three Israeli women and wounding dozens of others during the celebration of Purim. On July 30 two suicide bombers killed thirteen people and wounded 150 in a Jerusalem market. Hamas claimed responsibility. On August 3 a Palestinian was shot to death near a Jewish settlement on the West Bank. Settlers were thought to have killed him. In early August the Israeli government confiscated money it owed to the Palestinian Authority that comprised two-thirds of its annual revenue. On September 4 three suicide bombers killed four Israelis in Jerusalem. On September 5 twelve Israeli naval commandos on a raid in Lebanon were ambushed and killed. On September 25 Israeli operatives tried to assassinate a Hamas leader, Khaled Meshal, by posing as Canadian tourists. In the failed attempt, the Israeli spies used a powerful opiate administered transdermally. This attack with a biological weapon so angered King Hussein of Jordan that he forced Israeli Prime Minister Netanyahu to release as many as seventy Hamas prisoners and to publicly apologize for the covert actions sanctioned by the Israeli government.